Automated Accounting
FOR THE MICROCOMPUTER
3RD EDITION

WARREN W. ALLEN, M.A.
DALE H. KLOOSTER, ED.D.

BA22CB
PUBLISHED BY
SOUTH-WESTERN PUBLISHING CO.
CINCINNATI, OH   DALLAS, TX   LIVERMORE, CA

ISBN: 0-538-60729-7

Library of Congress Catalog Card Number: 90-63568

1 2 3 4 5 6 7 8 9 10 DH 0 9 8 7 6 5 4 3 2 1

Printed in the United States of America

Production Editor: *Anne Noschang*

Associate Editor/Production: *Mary Todd*

Designer: *J. E. Lagenaur*

Marketing Manager: *Gregory Getter*

PREFACE

Today, the power of microcomputer technology is increasing rapidly while the cost of that technology is on a downward spiral. Now, for the first time, nearly any school can provide computerized accounting instruction for students using a hands-on approach. The programs provided on the disk(s) which accompanies *Automated Accounting for the Microcomputer* remove the technical barriers of using a computer for the student. Therefore, the major objectives of this book and the accompanying software are (1) to present and integrate automated accounting principles in such a way that no prior knowledge of computers or computerized accounting is required, and (2) to provide a hands-on approach for learning how automated accounting systems function.

The contents of this book and the accompanying software are intended for use by students who desire a knowledge of computerized accounting principles. Flexibility has been designed into the software to permit it to be used in conjunction with most traditional accounting textbooks. This has been accomplished in such a way that nearly all manual accounting problems may be solved using this text-workbook and computer program.

The *Automated Accounting for the Microcomputer* package, consisting of a text-workbook and a disk(s), provides a realistic approach to automated accounting principles. It consists of four major accounting systems commonly found in computerized accounting environments: the general ledger, accounts payable, accounts receivable, and payroll.

The general ledger, accounts payable, and accounts receivable systems are totally integrated in such a way that transactions need be key-entered only once; data is then transferred automatically from one system to another. In other words, if a transaction is entered into one system, the other systems affected by that transaction are automatically updated. For example, a cash receipt entered into the Accounts Receivable System automatically (1) updates the accounts receivable open-item data in the accounts receivable data file (this file is similar to an accounts receivable subsidiary ledger in a manual system) and (2) updates the accounts receivable control account and cash account in the general ledger.

This package has been modularly designed so that the material and the computer exercises presented in the text can be introduced gradually. In this way, experience can be gained with each of the individual system components prior to working with the entire system as a whole. Problems and student exercises have been placed at the end of each chapter of the text to ensure comprehension of the subject matter. This approach permits the students to work independently at their own rates.

Chapter 1 provides an overview of the impact of the computer on society and identifies some of the major differences between manual and computerized accounting systems. This chapter also defines the standards, capabilities, limitations, and flexibility of the software supplied on the accompanying diskette(s). Basic start-up procedures for the brand of microcomputer being used are provided to get the student using the computer as soon as possible.

The remaining chapters guide the student through the accounting cycle on the computer using sample screen displays, transaction input forms, sample problems, student exercises, computer-generated output, transaction problems, and descriptive step-by-step instructions for operating each major computerized system. These chapters define what each system does and explain how each system integrates with other systems. In addition, fundamental data processing terms are defined in the context in which they are used throughout the entire text.

Appendix A contains a numerical list of error messages arranged by major accounting system with a description of what causes each error message and what operator action should be taken to correct the error.

The General Ledger System is introduced first, followed by the Accounts Payable System, the Accounts Receivable System, and finally the Payroll System. The systems are designed so that the computer-generated output, the integration processes, and the accounting procedures are very similar to those currently used in business and industry on large-scale computer systems and small microcomputers. The significant difference is the simplicity of operation, or "user friendliness," of *Automated Accounting for the Microcomputer*.

When a business or industry uses a computerized system to control such valuable assets as cash and accounts receivable, very tight controls are maintained on security, data entry, and audit-trail procedures. These controls complicate the operation of a computerized system. Some of these restrictions have been intentionally omitted from this package in the interest of simplifying the operations, thus making it a more usable educational tool for the high school classroom.

The *Automated Accounting for the Microcomputer* package is available for the Apple® IIGS®, Apple IIe, Apple IIc,[1] IBM® Personal System/2®, IBM PC,[2] and Tandy®[3] 1000 microcomputers. The software requires each student to record his or her data onto a formatted/initialized data diskette. The minimum configuration to run the *Automated Accounting for the Microcomputer* software for each computer supported is as follows:

1. Apple IIe (with an 80-column card installed), Apple IIc, or Apple IIGS with minimum 128K memory, one monitor, and one disk drive. Access to an 80-column, continuous-feed printer is optional but recommended.
2. IBM PC with 256K memory using DOS 2.0 or above, one monitor,

---

[1]ProDOS, Apple, and IIGS are registered trademarks of Apple Computer, Inc.

[2]IBM and Personal System/2 are registered trademarks of International Business Machines Corporation.

[3]Tandy is a registered trademark of Tandy Corporation.

and one dual-sided disk drive. Access to an 80-column, continuous-feed printer is optional but recommended.

3. IBM Personal System/2 with 256K memory using DOS 3.3 or above, one monitor, and one disk drive. Access to an 80-column, continuous-feed printer is optional but recommended.

4. Tandy 1000 with 256K memory, one monitor, one disk drive, and an 80-column card installed. Access to an 80-column, continuous-feed printer is optional but recommended.

CONTENTS

CHAPTER 3   GENERAL LEDGER ACCOUNTING CYCLE (SERVICE BUSINESS)   59

CHAPTER 4   GENERAL LEDGER FOR A MERCHANDISING BUSINESS   101

PART 2   ACCOUNTS PAYABLE   131

CHAPTER 5   ACCOUNTS PAYABLE SETUP   132

CHAPTER 6   ACCOUNTS PAYABLE TRANSACTIONS AND REPORTS   159

PART 5   PAYROLL   309

CHAPTER 10   PAYROLL SETUP   310

CHAPTER 11   PAYROLL TRANSACTIONS AND REPORTS   335

APPENDIX A   ERROR CODES, MESSAGES, AND OPERATOR ACTION

Part 1

INTRODUCTION AND GENERAL LEDGER

1 INTRODUCTION TO AUTOMATED ACCOUNTING

Upon completion of this chapter, you will be able to:

1. Identify and define the key terms associated with automated accounting systems.
2. Describe how hardware and software must work together in order for the computer to perform given tasks.
3. Describe the differences between manual and computerized accounting methods.
4. Respond to computer messages using the proper keyboard keys, system rules, and standards.
5. Describe accounting system integration.
6. Recognize and respond to error conditions.
7. Perform start-up procedures.
8. Perform accounting system setup.
9. Select and load data from disk.
10. Provide company information for processing.
11. Save work in progress data to disk.
12. Perform system shut-down procedures.

INTRODUCTION

Computers can be found everywhere. For example, they can be found in research laboratories, airplanes, ships, cars, hospitals, space vehicles, government agencies, grocery stores, businesses, factories, schools, traffic lights, calculators, watches, and throughout our homes. Their existence and use have made an impact on how our society functions, as well as how we function at work and during leisure time in our everyday lives. A growing widespread use of computers has been nourished by an ever-changing, expanding, global technological growth. As technology continues to find more efficient ways of building more powerful computers, the users of these computers continue to find more ways to utilize the computer's capabilities.

In general, a **computer** can be defined as an electronic device which accepts data and automatically processes it into meaningful information in a form useful to humans. Computers are complex, powerful tools that enable us to perform many different tasks. Most of the tasks computers perform can be accomplished in a fraction of the time it would take a human being, and some tasks a human could not possibly perform at all. However, as with any tool, the degree of its usefulness is determined by its user. In other words, a computer's usefulness is often limited only by the imagination and abilities of the humans who use it. As complex and powerful as it is, a computer can do only what it is told to do by humans.

COMPUTER SYSTEMS
A **computer system** can be defined as a combination of related elements working together as a whole to achieve a common goal. These related elements which must work together in order to comprise a computer system are called hardware and software. **Hardware** is the tangible, physical equipment that can be seen and touched. **Software** is the intangible set of instructions that tell the computer what to do. When both the hardware and software work together to accomplish a common goal, they make up a computer system.

Hardware devices come in various sizes and shapes, and perform a variety of different functions. It is the hardware devices that enable the computer to accept (input) data, process it into meaningful information, store it, and report (output) it in a form humans can understand. For example, a common hardware device that enables the computer to input data for processing is a keyboard. The hardware device which processes inputted data into meaningful information is the computer's **central processing unit**. A hardware device which permits storage of data is a disk drive. Two common hardware devices that are used to output processed information in a form we can understand are the display screen (monitor) and printer.

A computer system is also composed of software, called programs, that control the hardware devices, and in turn tell the computer what to do. A **program** is a series of detailed, step-by-step instructions that tell the computer precisely what actions to perform. Just as each of the computer's hardware devices must work together, there are several software programs which must also work together as one system. A program called a **system program** (also commonly referred to as the operating system) controls the computer's circuitry and hardware devices. Another program, called an **application program**, instructs the computer to perform specific, user-defined tasks — such as posting journal entries and generating financial reports.

When the input, processing, storage, and output hardware devices work together with system and application software programs toward the completion of a common goal or task, they comprise a computer system. In turn, when a computer system is used to process data for the purpose of generating useful information (i.e., accounting reports and financial records), it is called an **information processing system**.

There is little disagreement that we are living in a complex society which requires complex information processing systems. Many businesses (including small businesses) have been forced to turn to the computer as a means to help process accounting records, control costs, and manage financial resources. Information processing systems can be a significant aid to management in decision making and as a tool to facilitate efficient and profitable operation of the company. Today, professional business managers and accountants need to know how to use the computer as a tool for accounting applications and for making sound management decisions. Thus, as a student who may well enter a business profession, you can expect to work with a computer and automated accounting information processing systems.

***AUTOMATED
ACCOUNTING
INFORMATION
PROCESSING
SYSTEMS***

In a manual accounting system, all accounting records must be prepared by hand, perhaps with the help of a calculator. Business transactions, such as sales and purchases, are recorded in journals. The transactions are then posted manually from the journals to the general ledger accounts and various subsidiary ledgers. At the end of each accounting cycle, a worksheet is prepared, and adjusting entries are journalized and posted. Financial statements and various other accounting reports are then prepared from the worksheet, general ledger, and subsidiary ledger data.

A computerized accounting system is divided into various components based on function. The number of components depends on the sophistication of the accounting system, the type of business (manufacturing, retail, wholesale, etc.), and the size of the business. The components of the computerized accounting system utilized in this text are as follows:

1. General ledger
2. Accounts payable
3. Accounts receivable
4. Payroll

All but one of these components (payroll) are integrated. **Integration** means that when a transaction is entered into one component of the system, the computer will generate the related data (or entries) required by the other components. The effect of this integration is that a transaction need be entered into the system only once. In a manual accounting system, it is often necessary to record figures from the same transaction numerous times. For example, a single sale requires that the invoice amount be recorded in a journal, posted to the general ledger, posted to a subsidiary ledger, and listed on the monthly customer statement as a record of activity in that account. In a computerized accounting system, only one entry must be entered to record the sale. The computer then performs the required integration so that no further recording of the transaction is necessary.

Some of the advantages of a computerized accounting system over a manual accounting system are:

1. The computer can immediately post transaction data so the balances of the accounts are always current.
2. The computer can perform calculations at fantastic speeds. The computer rarely makes mistakes, and it is programmed to catch many errors at the time transactions are entered.
3. The computer can prepare the financial statements immediately at the close of the accounting period, or at any other time desired, because the balances in the accounts are always current.
4. The computer can arrange accounts in different sequences, and it can compute and print subtotals and totals.
5. The computer can rapidly and neatly display or print accounting reports on an attached display screen or printer.

A computer accepts data, processes it, and provides informational results. A computer can do none of this without specific instructions contained in application programs. The automated accounting application programs that will be used with this text consist of many detailed instructions that tell the computer how to accept data, recognize various types of errors, process data from each transaction, prepare reports, and communicate with the operator.

Just as in a manual accounting system, each transaction in a computerized accounting system must be analyzed for errors and completeness. It is necessary to identify and correct as many errors as possible before computer processing to prevent creating incorrect accounting reports. Therefore, to take full advantage of the capabilities of the computer system, it is important that you be as careful as possible in providing the computer with correct data for processing.

DISK MEDIUM   *Automated Accounting for the Microcomputer* requires a microcomputer with at least one disk drive. The disk drive is either connected to or built into the computer. The **disk drive** is a device which permits the computer to read programs and data electronically into its memory. In addition, data can be written to a disk (or diskette) in the disk drive so that computer programs and data can be stored. The **disk(s)** accompanying this text is the medium on which the programs and/or data are stored. Without these programs and accompanying data, the computer cannot perform its automated accounting tasks. Therefore, proper care and handling of the disk(s) and disk drive(s) will prevent the loss of programs or data. If you are using 5 1/4-inch floppy diskettes, please refer to the protective disk envelope for helpful diskette care and handling information.

Program Disk   The program disk (Apple 5 1/4-inch floppy diskette users will use two disks) which accompanies this text-workbook contains the computer programs that direct the computer to perform its automated accounting tasks. The programs stored on the program disk(s) permit the software to operate on computers with one or two 5 1/4- or 3 1/2-inch disk drives, or hard disk drive systems. The program disk(s) also contains all the beginning data and opening balances for the problems in this text-workbook.

Data Disk   The automated accounting software stored on the program disk(s) permits the storage of data on a data disk. This feature enables you to save data entered into the computer and all processing performed by the computer, for future reference or completion. Your instructor will provide you a separate disk that must be formatted/initialized before it can be used as your data disk. For information on formatting/initializing a disk, refer to your computer system's operations manual. (Apple users should initialize the data disk with the path name **\DATA** unless the instructor has provided a different name.)

Template Disk   The *Automated Accounting for the Microcomputer* software can be utilized to solve problems and practice set simulations that accompany *Century 21 Accounting: First Year Course* for both the fourth and fifth editions. Disks, called template disks, are available that contain beginning data and opening balances for selected problems and practice set simulations. The template disk is unprotected and can be copied. Your instructor will provide you a copy of any template disk you are to use.

Beginning data for a problem can then be loaded directly into the computer from this disk. This same disk can also be used as a data disk to store your data. Using a template disk in this manner provides for data storage and eliminates the time-consuming work of key-entering account titles and beginning balances for every problem.

KEYBOARD OPERATION

The keyboard of your microcomputer is similar to that of a typewriter. There are, however, a few keys which are different and which, when pressed, direct the computer to perform certain control functions. These special keys are described in the following sections. Some keyboards may vary slightly from the following information.

Cursor

Even though the cursor is not a key on the keyboard, it is controlled through keyboard operation. A **cursor** is a character used on the screen display to indicate where data is displayed as it is entered. This character also indicates that the computer is ready to accept data from the keyboard. Different computers have different cursor symbols. In this text, a square (■) is used to indicate the cursor.

ENTER/RETURN

Different computer manufacturers use different names for this key. For example, one system may use a key labeled ENTER, while the same function is accomplished on another system with the RETURN key. The **ENTER/RETURN key** is used in this text for two purposes:

1. The ENTER/RETURN key is used to advance the cursor down to the first position in the next field of data.
2. When the cursor is positioned in the last data field, the ENTER/ RETURN key tells the computer that data entry is complete. Subsequently, the computer will request the user to indicate whether he/she wishes to make changes to the data as it appears on the display screen or accept it for processing or storage.

Throughout this text-workbook, the term **key-enter** is used to indicate that you should key the correct information and then press ENTER/RETURN.

Escape Key

When pressed, this key (usually labeled the **Esc key**) tells the computer to exit (or escape) from where it is or what it is doing. For example, it is a convenient way to interrupt lengthy displays or printouts to save time or paper.

Left Arrow Key

The **left arrow key** (←) is used to position the cursor in the proper location for error correction and data entry purposes. Each time this key is pressed, the cursor moves back one space. If the cursor is at the first position of the first data field and this key is pressed, the cursor wraps around to the first position of the last data field.

Right Arrow Key

The **Right Arrow key** (→) is also used to position the cursor in its proper location for error correction and data entry purposes. Each time this key is pressed, the cursor moves forward one space. If the cursor is at the last position of the last data field and this key is pressed, the cursor wraps around to the first position of the first data field.

Up Arrow Key   The **Up Arrow key** (↑) is also used to position the cursor in its proper location for error correction and data entry purposes. Each time the Up Arrow key is pressed, the cursor moves up to the first position of the data field directly above the current data field. If the cursor is located in the first data field and this key is pressed, the cursor wraps around to the first position of the last data field. This wraparound feature is a convenient shortcut to get to the last data field.

Down Arrow Key   The **Down Arrow key** (↓) is also used to position the cursor in its proper location for error correction and data entry purposes. Each time the Down Arrow key is pressed, the cursor moves down to the first position of the data field directly below the current data field. If the cursor is in the last data field and the Down Arrow key is pressed, the cursor wraps around to the first position of the first data field.

Page Up Key   The Page Up key (on some IBM and Tandy computers, this key may be labeled PgUp; on the Apple, the Open Apple/Up Arrow keys are used) is used to scroll data in display windows. Pressing the Page Up key will display the data in the previous window.

Page Down Key   The Page Down key (on some IBM and Tandy computers, this key may be labeled PgDn; on the Apple, the Open Apple/Up Arrow keys are used) is used to scroll data in display windows. Pressing the Page Down key will display the data in the next window.

Backspace/Delete Key   The **Backspace key** on the IBM and Tandy personal computers and the **Delete key** on the Apple microcomputer provides destructive backspace as opposed to the Left Arrow key which is a nondestructive backspace. That is, each time the Backspace key is pressed, the cusor moves left one space after any character which may occupy that space is erased.

Home Key   The **Home key** (if using an Apple microcomputer, press the Open Apple and Left Arrow keys) will move the cursor to the first position of the first data field within any of the data entry screens.

End Key   The **End key** (if using an Apple microcomputer, press the Open Apple and the Right Arrow keys) will move the cursor to the first position of the last data field within any of the data entry screens.

Function Keys   The **function keys** are keys that control the window displays which appear on your screen. On the IBM and Tandy 1000 personal computers, the F1 key is Function 1, the F2 key is Function 2, and the F3 key is Function 3. On the Apple microcomputer, use the Open Apple key along with the number 1, 2, and 3 keys respectively. The purpose of these **window displays** is to provide information you may need in order to complete certain data entry tasks and to obtain informational displays which pertain to your input. Figure 1.1 shows the window display from the General Ledger Enter/Correct Journal Entries screen that appears when the Function 1 key is struck.

Function keys can be used only when a prompt message appears at the bottom of the screen to indicate that they are active. These prompt

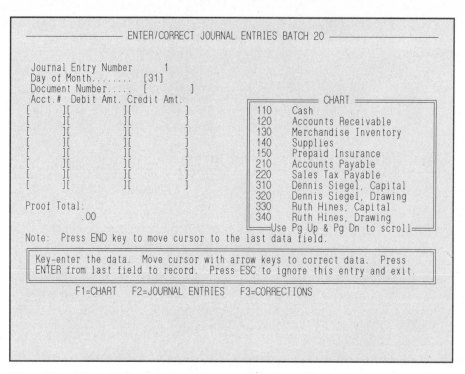

Figure 1.1   Journal Entry Screen Showing Function 1 Window Display

messages also indicate which of the function keys are active and the specific window displays or other special functions that will be activated if they are used.

Zero   The numeric character zero (0), located on the top row of keys, appears similar to the alphabetic character "O" on the keyboard. Therefore, be careful to use the appropriate key when key-entering your data.

Ten-Key Pad   Numeric data may be key-entered more quickly on the IBM, Tandy, and Apple IIGS using the computer's ten-key pad. When the ten-key numeric pad is used on the IBM PC, the Num Lock key must be depressed. This activates the numeric key pad but deactivates the Up, Down, Left, and Right Arrow cursor control keys on the numeric key pad. The Num Lock key is a toggle switch. It toggles the numeric key pad and directional cursor control keys on and off each time it is pressed. To permit cursor movement while the numeric key pad is activated, the two-directional Tab key (⇆), located below the Esc key, is programmed to operate identical to the Right Arrow directional key as discussed above. Pressing the Tab key while holding down the Shift key causes cursor movement identical to the the Left Arrow directional key as discussed above.

STANDARDIZED DISPLAY SCREEN FORMAT   Data entry and processing options are accessed or performed through the accounting system menus. The standardized screen format shows information such as the processing options permitted, prompting messages, and the format of the data which may be keyed. Each screen display has been designed in a standardized format to aid the user in screen-to-screen transition. Figure 1.2 illustrates the standardized display screen format used throughout this system.

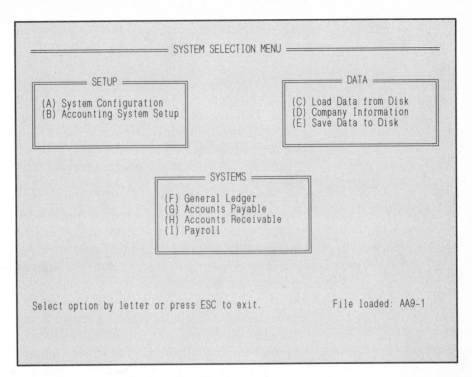

Figure 1.2   Standardized Display Screen Format

The first horizontal line on the screen is called a **screen title**. This is the line used to identify the screen being displayed. The large central area, or body, of the screen which follows is called the **menu option and data entry display**. This is the area where menu processing options and data entry activities are displayed. The area located at the bottom of the screen (usually depicted as a rectangular shaped box) is the **message display**. The message display is reserved for prompt messages, informational messages, and error messages. There are three general types of messages that may be displayed:

1. A **prompt message** indicates what kind of operator action is required. Its purpose is to guide you in giving the proper response on the screen displayed. The prompt message indicates the valid response(s) available. You are required to choose one of these responses in order to continue.
2. An **informational message** is a brief description of the specific activity the computer is performing or what it has done. Informational messages do not require any operator action.
3. An **error message** describes errors detected by the computer. A typical error message contains a three-digit error number, a description of what caused the error, and operator action required to correct the problem. Error numbers, arranged in numeric sequence with detailed descriptions and operator action, are provided in Appendix A. You may refer to this appendix whenever additional information regarding the error condition is required.

The area immediately beneath the message display area (last line on the screen) is reserved for **window and special function prompt option(s)**. This line displays the names of windows and other special functions which are active and available for use at various times throughout processing. A **window** is a special screen display containing helpful information which may be brought up on the display screen during processing. For example, windows may contain lists such as a chart of accounts, a list of vendors or customers, or the status of transactions previously key-entered into the computer. Windows normally do not take up the entire display screen area. Therefore, it is possible to display any number of windows containing helpful information while performing data entry activities. Other special function options which appear in this area of the display screen will be discussed later in this text.

ENTRY MODES

Data is keyed into the computer from the computer's keyboard and displayed on the monitor as it is keyed. This activity is called **data entry** and is defined as the process of keying numbers, alphabetic characters, and special characters into the computer's memory.

There are three modes in which data can be entered: menu mode, decision mode, and data entry mode. In the **menu mode**, you must make a selection from a menu. A **menu** is a list of options from which you must make a choice. Menu mode responses are identified by the name of the menu in the screen title area at the top of the screen, by the menu itself in the middle of the screen, and by an action message displayed in the message area at the bottom of the screen with a cursor blinking next to the message. Figure 1.3 depicts an example of a menu mode in which the computer is waiting for a selection. The selection that is entered appears at the cursor position, and the computer reacts appropriately to reflect the action chosen.

The second mode of entry, **decision mode**, is a mode of entry which requires you to make a choice or decision from the items displayed in

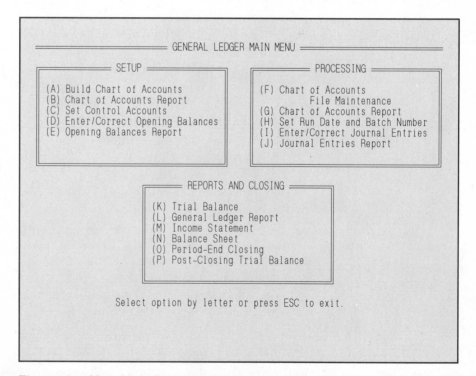

Figure 1.3   Menu Mode Screen

the message area of the screen. Figure 1.4 illustrates a screen display in the decision mode. Note the decision prompt message which appears within the rectangular shaped area at the bottom of the display in which you are asked to choose one of two options (or press the Esc key to exit).

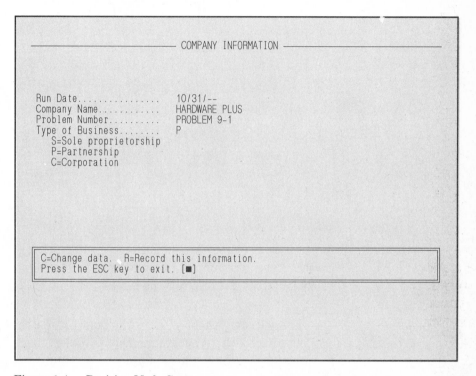

```
──────────────────────── COMPANY INFORMATION ────────────────────────



    Run Date...............    10/31/--
    Company Name...........    HARDWARE PLUS
    Problem Number.........    PROBLEM 9-1
    Type of Business.......    P
       S=Sole proprietorship
       P=Partnership
       C=Corporation





    ┌────────────────────────────────────────────────────────────────┐
    │ C=Change data.  R=Record this information.                       │
    │ Press the ESC key to exit. [■]                                   │
    └────────────────────────────────────────────────────────────────┘
```

Figure 1.4   Decision Mode Screen

The third and final mode of entry, **data entry mode**, is used most frequently. The data entry mode can be identified by a set of brackets [ ] with the cursor positioned at the first position of the first data field. Figure 1.5 shows a screen in data entry mode.

As each character is keyed, it occupies one of the spaces within the brackets. The number of spaces which appear inside the brackets indicates the size of the field and the maximum number of characters that may be keyed. You are not always required to enter as many characters as there are spaces available. The data keyed is not actually read by the computer until you finish keying all the data required, correct any errors, and inform the computer to record your input. When in doubt, always refer to the prompt message at the bottom of the screen.

Most keys on the keyboard can be used for data entry. You are most likely to use letters, numbers, and punctuation symbols for entering data. When keying numeric data, only the digits 0 through 9, the decimal point, and the space bar can be used. Blank or unused spaces that precede or follow numeric data have no effect on the value of the data. The computer will ignore the extra spaces in the field and read the correct value. Even dollar amounts can be keyed without the zeros representing decimal digits. The computer automatically adds the zeros for cents (.00).

Changes can be made to data which has already been keyed by using the directional arrow keys to position the cursor over the data to be

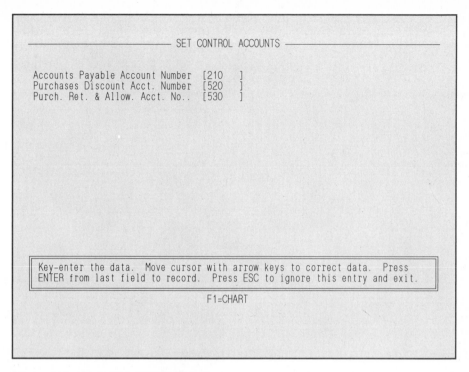

Figure 1.5   Data Entry Mode Screen

changed and then keying the correct data. Be sure to "zero out" numeric data by pressing the zero key and "blank out" unused or unwanted alphanumeric data by pressing the space bar.

PROCESSING METHODOLOGY

The *Automated Accounting for the Microcomputer* programs were written so that when you choose a system (i.e., general ledger system), the chosen program is loaded into the computer's memory where it resides with its data (i.e., journal entries, chart of accounts). The computer is not required to search through the disk to read or record data each time it performs processing functions during system execution. Because all the information the computer requires is in its processor memory, the computer's response time is very short. This increases the amount of work that can be accomplished in a very short period of time.

INTERRUPTIONS AND SHUT-DOWN PROCEDURES

If you must interrupt your computer work session at any time prior to completing your work, or wish to save the data of a completed problem prior to computer shut-down, return to the System Selection Menu and choose Option E, *Save Data to Disk*. After selecting this option, the computer will record all the work (which is stored in its memory) you have done during the current work session onto your own data disk. This will enable you to continue an unfinished problem from the point of interruption, or retrieve data of a previously completed problem. When you return to finish your problem, or retrieve a previously completed problem, select the *Load Data from Disk* option from the System Selection Menu. *If you fail to save data to disk prior to exiting the Automated Accounting system, all data keyed during your work session will be lost.*

START-UP   Each time the *Automated Accounting for the Microcomputer* software is started, four opening copyright screens and a System Configuration data entry screen will appear. The start-up procedure and data which must be provided in the System Configuration data entry screen are provided below. Since the IBM and Tandy personal computer start-up procedures and system configuration data differs from the Apple microcomputer, be sure to refer to the appropriate section which follows.

IBM and Tandy 1000 Start-Up Procedures   The start-up procedures for the IBM PC, IBM Personal System/2, and Tandy 1000 computers are as follows:

Step   1   Open the door to Disk Drive A and carefully insert your DOS disk (If you are using a hard disk system, do not insert a DOS disk; instead skip to Step 3.):

a. IBM PC - DOS 2.0, 2.1, 3.0, 3.1, 3.2.
b. IBM Personal System/2 - DOS 3.3 or above.
c. Tandy 1000 - DOS 2.11.

Step   2   Close the door to the disk drive.

Step   3   If the computer is off, turn on all power switches. If the computer is already on, hold down the Ctrl, Alt, and Del keys at the same time. This will boot (start) the system, and the computer will be ready for use.

Step   4   The computer will prompt you to enter the date and time. Key-enter the date (in the MM/DD/YY format). You may key-enter the time (in the HH:MM:SS format), or simply press the ENTER key to bypass this entry. The next line on the screen will then display *A>*. (If you are using a hard disk drive system, a *C>* will be displayed.)

Step   5   Remove your DOS disk from Disk Drive A (not necessary if booting from a hard disk in Drive C), carefully insert your *Automated Accounting for the Microcomputer* disk in Disk Drive A, and close the door. If you are using a hard disk system, key-enter *A:*.

Step   6   Key-enter *CONTROL*.

Step   7   After a short pause, four screens displaying copyright information will appear. Press ENTER four times to move through these displays, or press Esc to bypass these four displays. The System Configuration data entry screen shown in Figure 1.6 will appear.

Step   8   Key-enter your Student ID Code, and the cursor will then move to the *Data drive designation* field. You may enter any three-character code (consisting of letters and/or numbers) as your student identification code. Unless your instructor has provided you an ID code, use your initials. Always enter the same code whenever you start up the system because the software uses this information to uniquely identify your data files when they are saved to disk and subsequently loaded from disk. (You will be shown how to load and save data files later in this chapter.)

Step   9   Key-enter the letter identifying the disk drive that will be used to store your data files.

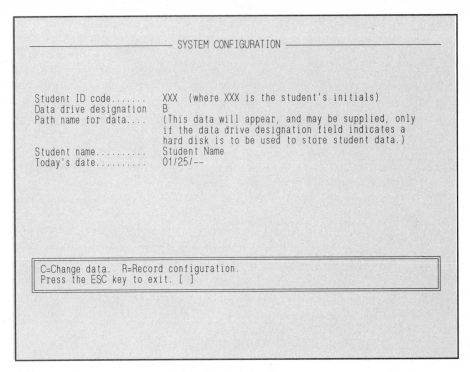

Figure 1.6   System Configuration Data Entry Screen

Note: The data disk must first be formatted before it can be used for storage. (For information on formatting your disk, refer to your DOS operations manual.)

Step 10   If the drive designation that you entered in Step 9 above specifies a hard disk, you will be prompted to enter a path name. If you do not enter a path name, the computer will search the current directory in an effort to locate your data files. If your data files are stored in a subdirectory on the hard disk, you should enter the path name (from the current directory) of your subdirectory. Ask your instructor to provide the path name you should enter.

Note: Once the system configuration information is entered, the computer will automatically check (1) that the specified data drive exists; (2) that the specified data drive indeed has a data disk in it (if not, you will be prompted to insert the data disk); (3) if a hard disk is specified, that the subdirectory exists; and (4) if the Student ID has been entered before in a previous computer session, it will display the student's name.

Step 11   Key-enter your name.

Step 12   Key-enter today's date (if it is different than the date shown) in the format MM/DD/YY. If the correct date is shown on the screen, press ENTER.

Step 13   When the decision prompt message *C = Change data. R = Record configuration.* appears, verify the accuracy of your input. If errors are detected, strike the **C** key to inform the computer that you wish to make changes. Use the directional Arrow keys to position the cursor on the field to be changed, then key-enter the correct data. If no errors are detected, strike the **R** key to tell the computer to record your input and continue processing.

Step 14   After a short pause, the System Selection Menu screen display will appear. You are now ready to use the *Automated Accounting for the Microcomputer* software.

Apple Start-Up Procedures   The start-up procedures for the Apple IIe, Apple IIc, and Apple IIGS microcomputers are as follows:

Step 1   Open the door to Disk Drive 1 and carefully insert Disk 1 (insert Disk 1, ProDOS, Payroll, and Opening Balances if you are using the 5 1/4-inch Apple disks) of your *Automated Accounting for the Microcomputer* software.

Step 2   Close the door to the disk drive.

Step 3   If the computer is off, turn on all power switches. If the computer is already on, hold down the Control, Open Apple, and Reset keys at the same time. This will boot (start) the system, and the computer will be ready for use.

Step 4   After a short pause, four screens displaying copyright information will appear. Press RETURN four times to move through these displays, or press Esc to bypass these four displays. The System Configuration data entry screen shown in Figure 1.7 will appear.

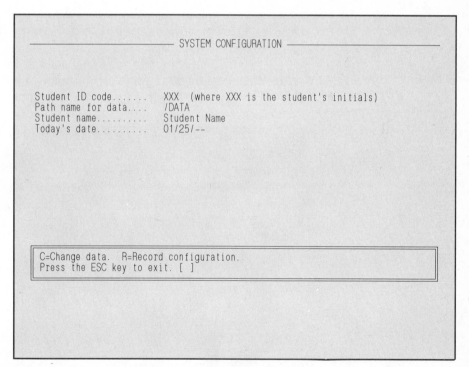

Figure 1.7   System Configuration Data Entry Screen

Step 5   Key-enter your Student ID Code, then press RETURN to move the cursor to the *Path name for data* field. You may enter any three-character code (consisting of letters and/or numbers) as your student identification code. Unless your instructor has provided you an ID code, use your initials. Always enter the same code whenever you start up the system because the software uses this information to uniquely identify your data files when they are saved to disk and subsequently loaded from disk. (You will be shown how to load and save data files later in this chapter.)

Step 6   Key-enter a valid path name. Unless your instructor has provided you a path name, use *DATA*. Your data disk must be formatted under ProDOS with the path name you enter in this step. (For information on formatting your disk, refer to the Apple ProDos operations manual.)

Note: Once the system configuration information is entered, the computer will automatically verify that the path name specified exists on the data disk. It will also check the Student ID. If the Student ID has been entered before in a previous computer session, it will display the student's name.

Step 7   Key-enter your name.

Step 8   Key-enter today's date in the format MM/DD/YY.

Step 9   Verify the accuracy of your input when you see the decision prompt message *C = Change data. R = Record configuration.*   If errors are detected, strike the **C** key to inform the computer that you wish to make changes. Use the directional Arrow keys to position the cursor on the field to be changed, then key-enter the correct data. If no errors are detected, strike the **R** key to tell the computer to record your input and continue processing.

Step 10   After a short pause, the System Selection Menu screen display will appear. You are now ready to use the *Automated Accounting for the Microcomputer* software.

SYSTEM SELECTION MENU   After the system configuration data has been entered, the System Selection Menu shown in Figure 1.8 will appear.

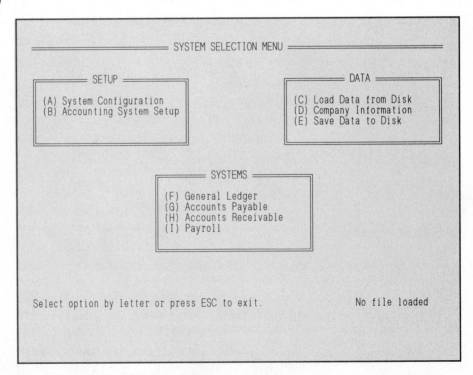

Figure 1.8   System Selection Menu

From the System Selection Menu, you may select the option or the system you wish to use. Simply enter the letter of the menu option you wish to select. Once you have made your selection, the computer will take the appropriate action as a result of your selection. Always return to this menu and select Option E, *Save Data to Disk*, when you have finished your work, to save your data prior to shutting down the computer. If you press the Esc key to exit without first saving your data to disk, a decision prompt message will appear providing one last chance to save your data prior to exiting the automated accounting software.

The System Selection Menu is made up of three boxes which consist of three different types of functions from which you may choose. The box labeled **Setup** contains two options (Options A and B) that provide the software initial start-up data it needs to perform its processing activities. The box labeled **Data** contains three options (Options C, D, and E) that perform data handling tasks. The box labeled **Systems** contains the names of the four major accounting systems (*General Ledger*—Option F, *Accounts Payable*—Option G, *Accounts Receivable*—Option H, and *Payroll*—Option I) that perform the processing activities provided by the automated accounting software.

System Configuration Option A

When the *System Configuration* option of the System Selection Menu is selected, the data entry screen shown earlier in Figure 1.7 will appear. The data you entered onto this screen during initial start-up will also display. The purpose of this option is to provide a way to change the data previously entered during start-up. Use the directional Arrow keys to move the cursor to the field(s) to be changed and key-enter the change(s). Move the cursor to the last data field (if it is not already there), and press the ENTER/RETURN key. When the decision prompt message *C = Change data. R = Record configuration.* appears, verify the accuracy of your input. If errors are detected, strike the **C** key to inform the computer that you wish to make additional changes. If no errors are detected, strike the **R** key to tell the computer to record your input and continue processing.

Accounting System Setup Option B

The *Accounting System Setup* option of the System Selection Menu enables you to tailor the *Automated Accounting for the Microcomputer* software to the level of presentation desired and the specific printing features available for your use. To select the *Accounting System Setup* option, strike the **B** key. The screen illustrated in Figure 1.9 is displayed and you are permitted to tailor your use of the software at this time by following the screen prompts.

The Accounting System Setup menu has six different fields of information which are stored in memory. All of this information is then available for reference to each of the four major software systems during program execution. The procedure to change and record the existing default values, or values already assigned to these fields, is the same as that followed when changing the system configuration data explained above. Key-enter a valid entry as explained in the following description of each field.

Simplified/Expanded General Ledger (S/E). In this field, you may strike **S** for *Simplified* or **E** for *Expanded*. The purpose of this option

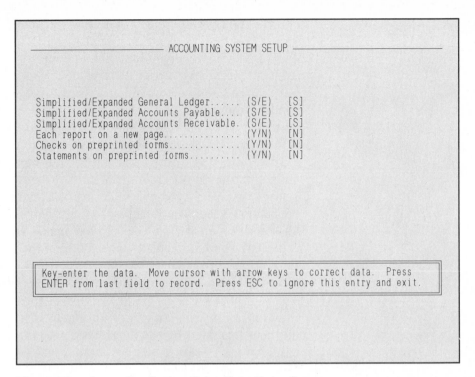

Figure 1.9   Accounting System Setup Data Entry Screen

is to tailor the software for a service or merchandising business. General ledger merchandising applications are not discussed until later in most traditional accounting textbooks. Therefore, you should strike **S** for *Simplified* in this option to set the software for a service business. This inhibits the software from displaying and reporting general ledger account data relative to a merchandising business. Later, as subjects regarding general ledger merchandising applications are presented and discussed in class, this option can be changed to **E** for *Expanded*. This sets the software to display and report general ledger account data for a merchandising business.

Simplified/Expanded Accounts Payable (S/E). In this field, you may also strike **S** for *Simplified* or **E** for *Expanded*. The purpose of this option is to tailor the level of presentation of the accounts payable software. For example, accounts payable cash discounts and debit memos are more advanced concepts which are usually discussed in later chapters of traditional accounting textbooks. Striking **S** for *Simplified* in this option inhibits the software from displaying or reporting accounts payable cash discounts and debit memos. This allows the software to be more closely coordinated with the sequence of presentation in accounting texts. Later, as cash discounts and debit memos are presented and discussed in class, this option can be changed to **E** for *Expanded* in order to utilize these features in the automated accounting software.

Simplified/Expanded Accounts Receivable (S/E). In this field, you may also strike **S** for *Simplified* or **E** for *Expanded*. The purpose of this option, similar to the *Accounts Payable* option, is to tailor the level of presentation of the accounts receivable software. For example, accounts receivable cash discounts and credit memos are more advanced concepts which are usually discussed in later chapters of traditional accounting textbooks. Striking **S** for *Simplified* in this option inhibits the software from displaying or reporting accounts receivable cash discounts and credit memos. This allows the software to be more closely coordinated with the sequence of presentation in accounting texts. Later, as cash discounts and credit memos are presented and discussed in class, this option can be changed to **E** for *Expanded* in order to utilize these features in the automated accounting software.

Each Report on New Page (Y/N). In this field, you may strike **Y** for *Yes* or **N** for *No*. If you strike **Y**, each printed report generated by the computer begins on a new page with page overflow based on 8 1/2-by-11-inch paper. In order for this feature to work properly, the printer must be positioned to begin printing at the top of a page when it is turned on. A **Y** response to this option causes the computer to consume much more paper than the **N** response, which merely leaves a few blank lines between each printed report.

Checks on Preprinted Forms (Y/N). In this field, you may strike **Y** for *Yes* or **N** for *No*. If you strike **Y**, each time the computer is asked to print accounts payable checks and payroll checks, you must insert and align a preprinted check form in the printer. Be sure you have such a form available before setting this option to **Y**, because printer spacing and alignment depends on the use of this form. Set this option to **N** for *No* unless your instructor has specifically indicated that this form is available. Striking **N** directs the automated accounting software to print and format its own checks on standard, 8 1/2-by-11-inch continuous-form paper.

Statements on Preprinted Forms (Y/N). In this field, you may also strike **Y** for *Yes* or **N** for *No*. If you strike **Y**, each time the computer is asked to print customer statements, you must insert and align a preprinted form in the printer. Be sure you have such a form available before setting this option to **Y** because printer spacing and alignment depend on the use of this form. Set this option to **N** for *No* unless your instructor has specifically indicated that this form is available. Striking **N** directs the automated accounting software to print and format its own statements on standard, 8 1/2-by-11-inch continuous-form paper.

Load Data from Disk Option C

The *Load Data from Disk* option of the System Selection Menu enables you to load data from a disk or create your own data files. To select this option, strike the letter **C**. The Load Data from Disk menu shown in Figure 1.10 will appear.

This option consists of four different data handling features. You may load opening balances from the program disk, load opening balances from a template disk, load work in progress data from your student data disk, or create empty files prior to entering your own accounting data. Once the desired selection is made, the information loaded (or empty data fields that are created) is available for reference to each of the four major software systems during execution. Select the desired option as explained in the following descriptions.

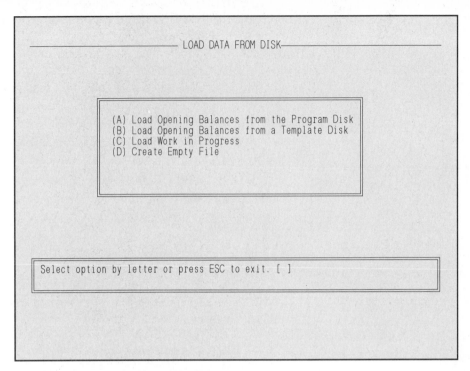

Figure 1.10   Load Data from Disk Menu

Load Opening Balances from the Program Disk—Option A. The data files on the *Automated Accounting for the Microcomputer* program disk contain all the opening balances that are used to complete the problems in this text-workbook only. If you are using an Apple microcomputer with 5 1/4-inch disks, these opening balances are all in the data files located on Program Disk 1. Select the *Load Opening Balances from the Program Disk* option only when you begin to work one of the problems in this text-workbook. When you strike the letter **A**, a directory of file names identifying the opening balance data files (shown in Figure 1.11) will appear.

In addition, a prompt message will appear at the bottom of the display requesting you to key-enter the file name (from the directory listing above) of the desired file. Simply key-enter the name of the file you wish to work with (you will be told which file name to enter in the step-by-step instructions for each problem). The computer will then load the appropriate data into its memory from the program disk. If you are using a hard disk system, the appropriate data file will be loaded from the directory containing the automated accounting programs.

If the computer detects data already in its memory, a decision prompt message will appear asking if you want to replace this data with the selected data. This decision prompt message is provided in the event you forgot to save your data from a previous problem prior to loading new data.

After the desired opening balances from the program disk are loaded into memory, the System Selection Menu will be displayed. The name of the file whose data has been loaded into your computer's memory

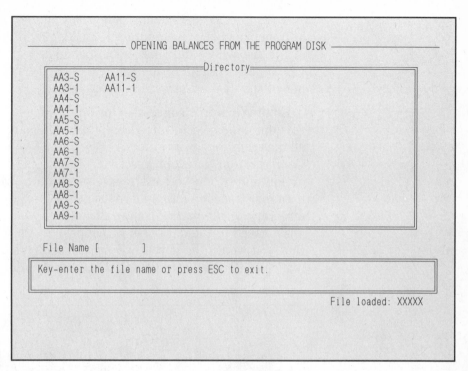

Figure 1.11   Load Opening Balances from the Program Disk Menu

will appear in the *File loaded* field located in the lower right-hand corner of the display screen.

Load Opening Balances from a Template Disk—Option B. Opening balances may also be loaded into your computer's memory from the copy of another disk called a template disk. This copied template disk contains account titles and numbers, opening balances, and other general information which have already been set up for you. Use this option only when directed to by the text or your instructor. To select this option, strike the letter **B.** The computer will search the disk in the disk drive specified in the System Configuration data entry screen for template files. If you are using a hard disk system, the computer will search the subdirectory specified in the System Configuration data entry screen. If the directory name is left blank, the current directory will be searched. If necessary, disk-handling messages may appear at the bottom of the display screen prompting you to insert the template disk in the specified disk drive, and to press the Space Bar to continue. When the computer finishes searching for template data files, it will display a list of the template file names (in a directory similar to that shown in Figure 1.11 above). Simply key-enter the file name (as it appears in the directory list) of the data file you wish to work with. If further disk handling is required, follow the prompt messages provided.

If the computer detects data already in its memory, a decision prompt message will appear asking if you want to replace this data with the selected template file data. This decision prompt message is provided in the event you forgot to save your data from a previous problem prior to loading new data.

After the desired opening balances from the template disk are loaded into memory, the System Selection Menu will be displayed. The name of the file whose data has been loaded into your computer's memory will appear in the *File loaded* field located in the lower right-hand corner of the display screen.

Load Work in Progress—Option C. When the *Load Work in Progress* option is selected, the computer will search the data disk and list all files containing the student ID code that you specified in the System Configuration data entry screen. Select the *Load Work in Progress* option only when you wish to retrieve data previously saved to your data disk for completion or reference. When you strike the letter **C**, a directory of file names representing each work in progress file previously saved to the data disk will appear. Figure 1.12 shows the display that you would see if you had previously saved two files using the file names of PROB1-1 and PROB1-2, respectively.

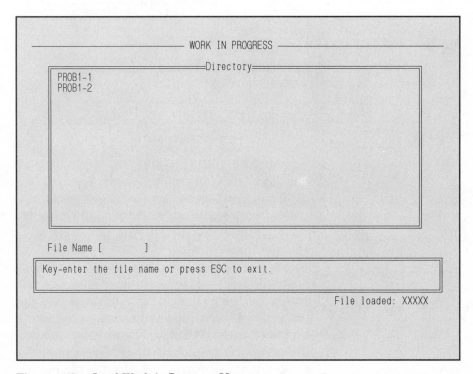

Figure 1.12   Load Work in Progress Menu

After you select the *Load Work in Progress* option, a prompt message will appear at the bottom of the display requesting you to key-enter the file name (as it appears in the directory listing) of the desired file. Simply key-enter the name of the file you wish to load. The computer will then load the appropriate data into its memory from the data disk. If you are using a hard disk system, the appropriate data file will be loaded from the subdirectory specified in the System Configuration data entry screen. If the computer detects data already in its memory, a decision prompt message will appear asking if you want to replace this data with the selected data. This decision prompt message is provided in the event you forgot to save your data from a previous problem prior to loading new data.

After the desired work in progress data are loaded into memory, the System Selection Menu will be displayed. The name of the file whose data has been loaded into your computer's memory will appear in the *File loaded* field located in the lower right-hand corner of the display screen.

Create Empty File—Option D. The purpose of this option is to erase any existing data in memory and establish empty accounting system files. Because of the serious consequences of this option, the computer will ask a second time (via a warning decision message) if you indeed want to perform this task. Enter **Y** (for *Yes*) to erase all previous accounting data and proceed. Select **N** (for *No*) or press Esc if you wish to leave the existing data intact and return to the System Selection Menu. If you select *Yes*, all of the data for all of the accounting systems that may currently be in your computer's memory will be erased so that a new accounting system may be established. *(Note: this option will not erase any data stored on disk.)* Once the empty accounting system has been established, an informational message will appear to confirm this action, and the System Selection Menu will be displayed. The term *Work File* (since the data file is unnamed until it is saved) will appear in the *File loaded* field located in the lower right-hand corner of the display screen.

Company Information Option D

The Company Information menu has four fields of information which are used by each of the four major systems for reference while problems are being executed or run. To select the *Company Information* option, strike the letter **D**. The screen display illustrated in Figure 1.13 is then displayed. You may then enter the data by following the screen prompt messages.

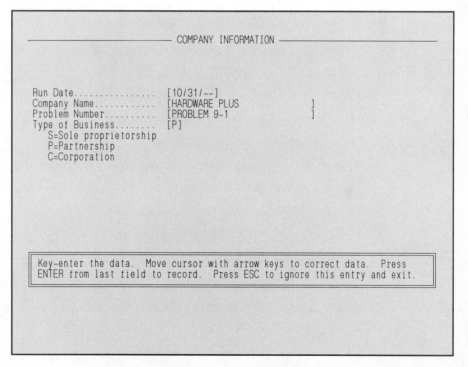

Figure 1.13   Company Information Data Entry Screen

You are required to supply the run date, company name, problem number, and type of business. The run date, company name, and problem number are printed on each of your computer-generated reports. The type of business code is needed by the computer since some of the processing varies depending on the type of business. This information is stored in your computer's memory and remains there until changed or another problem is loaded. Therefore, any necessary changes must be made immediately after loading data from disk, prior to starting a problem, and as often as needed thereafter. You may strike the **C** key to make changes, the **R** key to record your changes, or you may press the Esc key to exit (do nothing) and return to the System Selection Menu.

If you load opening balances from the program disk, opening balances from a template disk, or work in progress data, this information will automatically be provided. However, you may be required to change the run date or other information as specified in the step-by-step instructions for solving the problems.

Run Date. The run date to be used on reports must be key-entered in the format MM/DD/YY (where MM is a two-digit month, DD is a two-digit day, and YY is the year). Notice that the slashes (/) which separate the month, day, and year have been provided and need not be key-entered.

Company Name. The name of the company you want to appear on each computer-generated report must be key-entered in this field. The company name may be no longer than 27 characters.

Problem Number. The problem number must be key-entered in this field. Although this field is labeled as a number field, alphabetic characters may also be entered to further identify the problem on which you are working. The problem number may be no longer than 27 characters.

Type of Business. The type of business you are working with must be key-entered in this field. Key-enter **S** for a *sole proprietorship*, **P** for a *partnership*, and **C** for a *corporation*. After all this information has been key-entered, strike the **R** (Record) key to inform the computer to record your data.

Save Data to Disk Option E

The *Save Data to Disk* option enables you to save your work in progress to disk so that you can continue a problem in a later session. When you select this option, a screen display listing a directory of the data files for your student ID code will appear. You will then be asked to key-enter the name under which you would like to store your accounting data. You may enter a file name with a maximum of eight characters. You may use the same file name as that used to identify the opening balances. If you choose a name already shown in the directory list, the computer will replace the data stored in the selected file with the current accounting data. You will not replace the opening balances data, however, even if you use the same file name. The opening balances are stored on the program disk or separate template disk, and you must store your data on a separate disk. If you are using a hard disk system, your work in progress data will be stored in the subdirectory specified in the System Configuration data entry screen. If you key-enter a file name not listed in the directory, the current accounting data will be stored under this new name. For example, after using the *Create Empty File* option and entering the data to create your own data files, you will want to save your data under a name not already listed in the directory.

The *Save Data to Disk* option is very useful for making a **backup**, which is simply a copy of a database file stored on your data disk. The copy is made so that the data will still exist if the data disk is damaged or destroyed. This option may be run at any time, and as many backup copies may be made as desired. For example, you may want to make a backup copy of your data onto your data disk or another disk before performing period-end closing or before processing payroll for a new pay period, quarter, or year. To make a backup, simply load the data from disk that you wish to back up into your computer's memory, then use the *Save Data to Disk* option to save it (under a different name) as a work in progress backup file.

The Work in Progress Save Data to Disk screen is illustrated in Figure 1.14. The screen in Figure 1.14 contains three work in progress files named AA1-1, AA1-2, and AA2-S respectively.

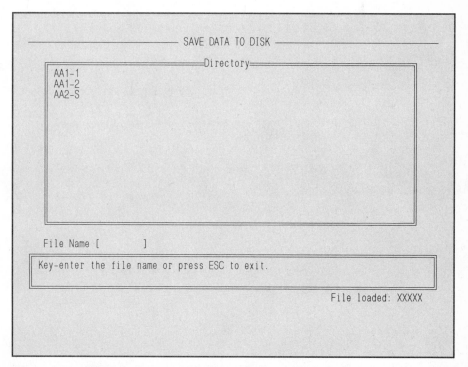

Figure 1.14   Work in Progress Directory Display

After your data is saved on your data disk (or on your hard disk), you will be able to retrieve it using the *Load Data from Disk* option, and then the *Load Work in Progress* option. In order to retrieve the data, you must use the same student ID code that you used to save the data.

Options F, G, H, and I   After the start-up procedure and loading data from disk activities are completed, the accounting system you wish to work with may be selected. Simply strike the letter (**F** through **I**) of the system you wish to select (General Ledger, Accounts Payable, Accounts Receivable, or Payroll Systems). The appropriate program will be loaded into memory and you will be ready to proceed with automated accounting processing.

Now complete the student exercise and computer problems which follow.

Name _____

Class _____ Date _____

CHAPTER 1
STUDENT EXERCISE

I. Matching   For each of the following definitions, write the letter of the term which best fits that definition in the space provided.

a. System
b. Program
c. Menu
d. Disk
e. Cursor
f. ENTER/RETURN
g. Integration
h. Window display
i. Computer
j. Down Arrow key

k. Data entry
l. Prompt message
m. Informational message
n. Error message
o. Load data from disk
p. Disk drive
q. Hardware
r. Software
s. Key-enter
t. Backup

1. _____ A character used on the screen display to indicate where data will be displayed as it is entered and that the computer is ready to accept data from the keyboard. (Objs. 1, 4)

2. _____ A screen display which indicates what kind of operator action is required. (Objs. 1, 4)

3. _____ An electronic device which accepts data and processes it into meaningful information in a form useful to humans. (Obj. 1)

4. _____ A screen display which describes errors detected by the computer. (Objs. 1, 4)

5. _____ A combination of related elements working together as a whole to achieve a common goal. (Obj. 1)

6. _____ A series of detailed instructions which tell the computer precisely what actions to perform. (Obj. 1)

7. _____ A screen display which shows a brief description of the specific activity the computer is performing or what it has done. (Objs. 1, 4)

8. _____ The medium on which data or programs are stored. (Obj. 1)

9. _____ The process of keying numbers, alphabetic characters, and special characters into the computer's memory. (Objs. 1, 4)

10. _____ A screen display which shows a list of options from which you must make a selection. (Objs. 1, 4)

11. _____ Tangible, physical equipment that can be seen and touched. (Objs. 1, 2)

12. _____ Intangible instructions that tell the computer what to do. (Objs. 1, 2)

13. _____ The key that advances the cursor to the first position of the next field of data and also, when pressed while in the last data field, indicates to the computer that data entry is complete. (Objs. 1, 4)

14. _____ The condition which occurs when a transaction is entered into one component of the system and the computer generates the related data or entries required by the other components. (Obj. 5)

15. _____ A key which can be used to position the cursor in the proper location for error correction and data entry purposes. (Objs. 1, 4)

16. _____ An option on the System Selection Menu which enables you to load data from the program disk, load a template disk, load work in progress, or create empty files. (Obj. 9)

17. _____ A device which is either connected to or built into the computer and reads programs and data electronically and then writes them on a diskette for storage. (Objs. 1, 9, 11)

18. _____ A special screen display containing helpful information which may be brought up on the display screen during processing. (Objs. 1, 4)

19. _____ A copy of a database file stored on your data disk. (Obj. 11)

20. _____ A term used in this text-workbook to indicate that you should key the correct information and then press ENTER/ RETURN. (Obj. 1)

II. Short Answer

1. Name the four components of the computerized accounting system presented in this text. (Obj. 1)

_____

_____

_____

_____

2. Briefly describe two advantages of a computerized accounting system. (Obj. 3)

_____

_____

3. Explain the purpose of function keys. (Objs. 1, 4)

_____

_____

Name _____

Class _____ Date _____

4. What is a system program? (Obj. 1)

   _____

   _____

5. What is an application program? (Obj. 1)

   _____

   _____

   _____

6. What is an information processing system? (Obj. 1)

   _____

   _____

7. Explain why you must always choose the option to *Save Data to Disk* before shutting down the computer. (Obj. 11, 12)

   _____

   _____

   _____

8. Write the letter corresponding to the correct answer in the appropriate place on the screen shown on the following page. (Objs. 1, 6)

   a. Message display

   b. Cursor

   c. Menu option and data entry display

   d. Screen title

   e. Window and special function prompt options

Illustration of System Selection Menu with Blanks for Answers

PROBLEM 1-1

The following computer exercise will enable you to practice what you have learned in this chapter. *Note: Make sure you have a properly formatted data disk (or hard disk subdirectory) for saving your data prior to starting this problem.* (Objs. 4, 5, 7-12)

Instructions

Step 1   Start-up the *Automated Accounting for the Microcomputer* software for the type of computer you are using according to the startup instructions presented in this chapter. When the System Configuration data entry screen appears, key-enter the appropriate data, including the disk drive designation (and/or path name) which informs the computer where your data is to be saved. If you are uncertain, ask your instructor.

Step 2   Select Option B, *Accounting System Setup*, from the System Selection Menu by striking the letter B. You do not need to press ENTER/RETURN. Tailor the software to the level of presentation desired and the printer-generated output specifications desired. Be sure to strike **R** (for Record) after you have key-entered the last entry. This will record your choices and return you to the System Selection Menu.

Step 3   Select Option C, *Load Data from Disk*.

Step 4   Select Option A, *Load Opening Balances from the Program Disk*.

Note: If you are using an Apple microcomputer with 5 1/4-inch disks, all opening balances are on Program Disk 1.

Step 5   When the Opening Balances from the Program Disk directory (shown in Figure 1.11) appears, key-enter the file name **AA3-S**.

Step 6   The computer will then ask for an affirmation response because all data in memory will be lost when the new data is loaded. Key-enter **Y** for Yes. The computer will load the opening balances for file *AA3-S* from the disk into your computer's memory, then return to the System Selection Menu.

Step 7   Select Option D, *Company Information*, from the System Selection Menu.

Step 8   When the Company Information data entry screen appears, change and record the data that was loaded from file AA3-S as follows:

Run Date   (Last day of current month)
Company Name   (Advertising Specialists Co.)
Problem Number   (Problem 1-1)
Type of Business   (P - for partnership)

Step 9   Select Option E, *Save Data to Disk*.

Step 10   When the Save Data to Disk blank directory screen appears, key-enter **AA3-S**. The computer will save your data as a work in progress file to your own data disk (or directory, if using a hard disk system) under the file name **AA3-S**.

Step 11   From the System Selection Menu, press Esc to exit the automated accounting system. You have now completed Problem 1-1.

PROBLEM 1-2

The following computer exercise will demonstrate how to load the work in progress file you saved to disk in Problem 1-1. You must complete Problem 1-1 before attempting this problem. (Objs. 4, 6, 7, 8, 9, 10, 11, 12)

Instructions

Step 1   Perform start-up (same as Step 1 in Problem 1-1).

Step 2   When the System Selection Menu appears, select *Load Data from Disk*.

Step 3   Select Option C, *Load Work in Progress*.

Step 4   When the Work in Progress directory appears (the directory should contain the file name of the data saved in the previous probelm), key-enter the file name **AA3-S**.

Step 5   Key-enter **Y** for Yes. The computer will load this work in progress data from your data disk (or directory, if you are using a hard disk system) into your computer's memory, then return to the System Selection Menu.

Step 6   Select the *Company Information* option. Verify that the Company Information you key-entered in Problem 1-1 has been loaded, then press Esc to exit back to the System Selection Menu.

Step 7   From the System Selection Menu, press Esc to exit the automated accounting system. A decision prompt message will appear asking if you wish to save your data before exiting the system. Since you have not made any changes, enter N (for No). You have now completed Problem 1-2. Hand in your completed student exercise sheets.

2 GENERAL LEDGER SETUP

LEARNING OBJECTIVES

Upon completion of this chapter, you will be able to:

1. Describe the differences between manual and computerized general ledger methods.
2. Build a chart of accounts.
3. Display or print a chart of accounts.
4. Set control accounts.
5. Enter/correct opening balances.
6. Display or print opening balances.
7. Save data to disk.
8. Identify the components and procedures for general ledger setup.

INTRODUCTION

In a manual accounting system, business transactions are first recorded on some sort of business paper called a **source document**. Check stubs and invoices prepared at the time the transaction takes place are examples of source documents. These transactions are later recorded in a journal. A **journal** is a form on which accounting information is recorded in chronological order. Each item or transaction recorded in a journal is called an **entry**. An accounting form used to sort and summarize changes in a particular item is called an **account**. A group of accounts is called a **ledger**. Periodically, the transactions which have been entered in a journal are posted to the proper accounts, which are contained in ledgers. **Posting** is the process of transferring or copying information from a journal to a ledger account. In a manual accounting system, the term **general ledger** refers to that group of accounts used to prepare the income statement and balance sheet.

In a computerized accounting system the term **general ledger** has a much broader definition. A **computerized general ledger system** is a computer program or collection of programs which direct the computer to perform the accounting cycle functions of building and maintaining the chart of accounts, recording and posting journal entries, and preparing financial statements. The computerized general ledger system is most often integrated. This means that it must be able to accept journal entries created by other computerized accounting systems such as accounts payable or accounts receivable.

A computerized accounting system follows most of the same principles of accounting as a manual system. One difference is the way in which the records are stored. In a manual accounting system, records are recorded chronologically in journals and then posted to ledger accounts. In a computerized system, records are stored on auxiliary storage devices such as magnetic tape or, as in this system, a magnetic disk. An **auxiliary storage device** is a hardware device that is under direct control of the computer and is capable of storing data. Most routine accounting tasks, such as posting, determining account balances, preparing financial statements, and making closing entries, are performed by the computer. Another difference in computerized accounting systems is the way in which debits and credits are indicated. In a manual system, debits are recorded in the Debit column of a journal or ledger account, and credits are recorded in the Credit column. In a computerized accounting system, debits and credits are recorded in separate data fields on each data entry screen rather than in Debit and Credit columns.

The computerized General Ledger System is the basis for the automated accounting system and contains all data related to the general ledger. Each unique item of data, such as the debit or credit amount, account number, account title, and account balance, is referred to as a **field** (also commonly known as a data element). All related fields of data which are treated together as a unit are called a **record**. The fields which define the record for one account include the account number, account title, and account balance. A collection of related records treated as a unit is termed a **data file**. All of the general ledger account records for a company form the general ledger data file. The general ledger data file is also a part of a larger group of data files called a database. A **database** is a collection of interrelated data files linked together in such a manner as to provide efficient access to data stored on an auxiliary storage device. Later, you will see how the data fields and records from the other major accounting systems (accounts payable, accounts receivable, and payroll) also form data files, and in turn, make up the automated accounting database.

The general ledger setup procedure is a set of steps which: (1) builds the chart of accounts, (2) informs the computer of special account numbers it needs in order to perform such tasks as period-end closing, and (3) enters account opening balances. Screen display and print options are provided for the chart of accounts and the opening balances to assist you in verifying the accuracy of your work. In addition, corrections to opening balances may also be made in the event errors are detected. In order to build the chart of accounts, all of the account titles and account numbers must first be recorded on a General Ledger File Maintenance input form. This data must then be key-entered into the computer and stored in computer memory. Each chart of accounts entry consists of an account number and title. As each account is key-entered into the computer, it is immediately stored in computer memory and space is allocated for the account balances. Next, the opening account balances must be recorded on the General Ledger input form and then key-entered into the computer and stored in computer memory. General ledger setup activities are required only when establishing a new company. The data that is key-entered during this process can be saved as a work in progress file on a data disk. Therefore, this activity will not be required again until another new company is to be created.

To establish the chart of accounts, each account in the chart of accounts used by the company must be assigned a number from one to six digits in length. The first digit in the account number identifies the account classification. The account classifications for a service business are shown in Figure 2.1.

1 = Asset
2 = Liability
3 = Capital
4 = Revenue
5 = Expense

Figure 2.1   Account Classifications

Chart of account entries are key-entered into the computer from the input form and stored in the database. As a new chart of accounts entry is created by the computer, the account balance is set to zero.

Account numbers that require special handling by the computer, called **control accounts**, must be set during the general ledger setup process. The account numbers that are required depend on the account numbers built into the chart of accounts and the type of business entered in the *Company Information* option of the System Selection Menu (recall Figure 1.13). The control accounts that the computer requires depend on whether the business is a sole proprietorship, a partnership, or a corporation.

In this chapter, you will set up the General Ledger System for Advertising Specialists, a sole proprietorship service business. The capital account number is needed by the computer to prepare financial statements and to complete the period-end closing process. The computer will bring forward the income or loss from the previous period to this account. The drawing account number and the income summary account number are needed in order for the computer to close these accounts to the capital account during the period-end closing process.

COMPLETING THE INPUT FORMS

Each of the forms used with this text-workbook contains a form number in the upper right-hand corner. The data required to perform general ledger setup is recorded on two different forms: the General Ledger File Maintenance input form (Form Number GL-1) and the General Ledger input form (Form Number GL-2). In this chapter, you will learn how each of these forms is used to record the data required by the computer to set up the chart of accounts and establish account opening balances.

General Ledger File Maintenance Input Form (Form GL-1)

The General Ledger File Maintenance input form serves two separate functions. First, it is used to record the accounts to be established in the general ledger data file during general ledger setup. Second, it is used to record additions, changes, and deletions to the chart of accounts after general ledger setup has been completed and during the ongoing processing of the accounting cycle. The second use of this form will be discussed in Chapter 3.

The General Ledger File Maintenance input form shown in Figure 2.2 illustrates how the account numbers and corresponding account titles are recorded in order to set up the chart of accounts for Advertising Specialists.

The run date recorded in the upper left corner of the form, 10/01/--, is the first day of the month or the start of the accounting cycle. The

	GENERAL LEDGER FILE MAINTENANCE — Input Form		
RUN DATE 10 , 01 , -- (MM DD YY)		Problem No. *Sample* — FORM GL-1	

	ACCOUNT NUMBER	ACCOUNT TITLE	
1	1110	Cash	1
2	1120	Office Supplies	2
3	1130	Prepaid Insurance	3
4	1140	Office Equipment	4
5	2110	Winton Office Supply	5
6	2120	A-Z Office Supply	6
7	2130	Larson Office Equipment	7
8	3110	Sandra Coleman, Capital	8
9	3120	Sandra Coleman, Drawing	9
10	3130	Income Summary	10
11	4110	Fees	11
12	5110	Insurance Expense	12
13	5120	Miscellaneous Expense	13
14	5130	Rent Expense	14
15	5140	Office Supplies Expense	15
16	5150	Utilities Expense	16
17			17
18			18
19			19
20			20
21			21
22			22
23			23
24			24
25			25

Figure 2.2   General Ledger File Maintenance Input Form (Form GL-1)

body of the form contains the account numbers and account titles which are to be used to set up the chart of accounts data. Notice how the first digit of each account number identifies the account classification (asset, liability, capital, revenue, or expense).

General Ledger Input Form (Form GL-2)

The General Ledger input form also serves two separate functions. First, it is used to record opening balances which are to be key-entered into the computer during general ledger setup. Second, it is used to record journal entries. The second use of this form will be discussed further in Chapter 3. After the chart of accounts has been built and the control accounts are set, the opening balances must be established for each account with a beginning balance. These opening balances update the chart of accounts as they are entered. Each of these entries is stored in the database. The database is used to store journal entry transactions (including opening balances) for one fiscal period. A General Ledger input form should be completed and used as the source document from which these opening balances are key-entered. The General Ledger input form shown in Figure 2.3 illustrates how to record the opening account balances for Advertising Specialists.

	DAY	DOC. NO.	ACCOUNT NUMBER	DEBIT AMOUNT	CREDIT AMOUNT	
	1	2	3	4	5	
1	01	BALANCE	1110	1023 55		1
2			1120	451 13		2
3			1130	440 00		3
4			1140	11110 00		4
5			2120		495 00	5
6			2130		55 00	6
7			3110		12474 68	7
8						8
9						9
10						10
11						11
12						12
13						13
14						14
15						15
16						16
17						17
18						18
19						19
20						20
21						21
22						22
23						23
24						24
25						25
			BATCH TOTALS	13024 68	13024 68	

RUN DATE 10/01/-- (MM DD YY) BATCH NO. 1

GENERAL LEDGER Input Form

Problem No. Sample   FORM GL-2

Figure 2.3   General Ledger Input Form (Form GL-2)

The run date (10/01/--), located in the upper left corner of the form, is usually the first day of the month or the start of an accounting cycle. A batch number is located beneath the run date in the upper left corner of the form. The **batch number** is a one- or two-digit number consecutively assigned to a group of journal entries for the purpose of identification. The batch number shown here is Batch No. 1, which is the batch number specifically reserved for all opening balances. The computer will automatically assign Batch No. 1 to the opening balances as they are key-entered into the computer. By using Batch No. 1 to identify all the opening balances, it will later be possible to distinguish opening balance entries from other key-entered transactions. Each line on the body of the form represents the data required to establish the opening balances. Recorded in the Day column is the day of the month that the opening balances are established, usually the first day of the month. The Document Number column contains the word *BALANCE* to indicate that each entry is an opening balance amount. Although the name of this column is Document Number, alphabetic characters and special symbols may also be recorded in this field. Its purpose is to provide descriptive information about the source document which identifies each entry. The Account Number column represents the account number from the chart of accounts. The amount that is to be entered as a debit or credit to the account specified in the Account Number column is entered in one of the last two columns, Debit Amount or Credit Amount.

GENERAL LEDGER SETUP OPERATIONAL PROCEDURES

There are four steps that must be followed before the general ledger setup activities can be performed. These steps need to be followed only when setting up (creating) a new data file or when specifically called for in the text. First (after start-up procedures are completed), Option B, *Accounting System Setup*, must be selected from the System Selection Menu. This option allows simplified and expanded levels of the accounting systems and certain printing options to be selected. Second, Option C, *Load Data from Disk*, must be selected. When the Load Data from Disk menu appears, Option D, *Create Empty File* must be chosen to inform the computer that you will be creating a new general ledger data file. Third, Option D, *Company Information*, must be selected from the System Selection Menu. This option allows data fields for run date, company name, problem number, and type of business to be established. Fourth, Option F, *General Ledger*, must be selected. Once the General Ledger System is selected, it will be loaded from the program disk into computer memory. The General Ledger Main Menu (shown in Figure 2.4) will then appear on your screen. When the General Ledger System has been loaded into computer memory and the input forms containing the account titles, account numbers, and opening balances are completed, the data contained on these input forms must be key-entered into the computer and various reports may be displayed or printed.

Any option may be selected from the General Ledger Main Menu by simply keying the appropriate letter. Subsequently, a new data entry display will appear on the screen that will allow you to enter the appropriate data or choose a course of action (in the decision mode). The following sections explain Options A through E (the setup options) of the General Ledger Main Menu. These menu options will be used to create a new general ledger data file containing a chart of accounts and their opening balances. Each option should be performed in sequence, A through E, in order to complete the setup process.

Build Chart of Accounts Option A

When you select Option A, *Build Chart of Accounts*, from the General Ledger Main Menu, the Build Chart of Accounts data entry screen shown in Figure 2.5 will appear.

Notice the Chart window displays **EMPTY** to indicate that there are

```
GENERAL LEDGER MAIN MENU

SETUP
(A) Build Chart of Accounts
(B) Chart of Accounts Report
(C) Set Control Accounts
(D) Enter/Correct Opening Balances
(E) Opening Balances Report

PROCESSING
(F) Chart of Accounts
        File Maintenance
(G) Chart of Accounts Report
(H) Set Run Date and Batch Number
(I) Enter/Correct Journal Entries
(J) Journal Entries Report

REPORTS AND CLOSING
(K) Trial Balance
(L) General Ledger Report
(M) Income Statement
(N) Balance Sheet
(O) Period-End Closing
(P) Post-Closing Trial Balance

Select option by letter or press ESC to exit.
```

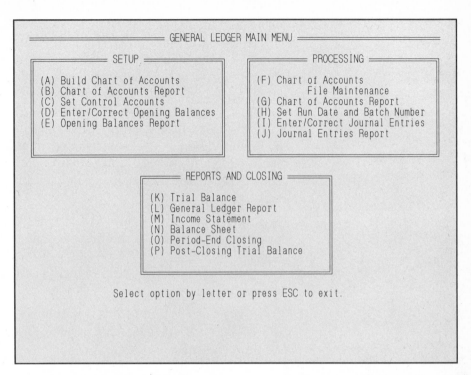

Figure 2.4 General Ledger Main Menu

```
BUILD CHART OF ACCOUNTS

Account Number.. [      ]

Title..........

CHART

EMPTY

Key-enter the account number or press ESC to exit.
```

Figure 2.5 Build Chart of Accounts Data Entry Screen

no accounts currently in computer memory. However, if the computer detects accounts currently stored in the computer's memory, a decision prompt message will appear and you will be asked to strike the **Y** key (for *Yes*) or **N** key (for *No*) to erase the chart of accounts data currently in memory. Also, because of the serious consequences of selecting this option, a warning decision prompt message is displayed on the screen when the option is selected. The **N** option should be selected if you were unable to key-enter all of your chart of accounts data during a previous work session. When you are ready to complete the chart of accounts, you may select the *Build Chart of Accounts* option, choose the **N** option, and key-enter the remaining chart of accounts data. Strike the **Y** key to erase all previous data and proceed.

The General Ledger File Maintenance input form is to be used as the source document from which the account numbers and titles are keyed. In order to key-enter the account numbers and titles, complete the following steps:

1. Key-enter an account number from one to six digits in length. The cursor will then move to the first position of the corresponding title field.
2. Key-enter the account title which corresponds to the account number just keyed.

   Note: After the account title is key-entered, the account number and title will appear in the Chart window indicating that the account has been created.

3. Continue key-entering account numbers and titles until all the accounts have been entered.

If you detect an error or wish to delete a previously entered account, simply key-enter the account number of the account to be changed or deleted. The computer will check to see if the account number is already in the chart of accounts. If the account number already exists, the computer will display the account title and number and assume that you wish to either change the account title or delete the account. In this case, a decision prompt will ask you to strike **C** if you want to change the account title, **R** to record the title as it appears on the screen, or **D** to delete this account. If the account already exists, and you wish to change the account title, strike **C** for change, key-enter the correct account title, and then strike **R** to record the account data. If the account already exists and you wish to delete it, strike **D**, and the account will be deleted. An account cannot be deleted if it has a balance. You may press Esc to exit and not make any changes.

Chart of Accounts Report Option B

When you select Option B, *Chart of Accounts Report*, from the General Ledger Main Menu, you will be able to get a printout or screen display of the chart of accounts. When this option is chosen, a decision prompt will appear which consists of three choices: (1) strike **D** to display the Chart of Accounts report on the screen, (2) strike **P** to print the Chart of Accounts report on an attached printer, or (3) press Esc if you wish to exit this option (do nothing) and return to the General Ledger Main Menu. To display the chart of accounts on the screen, strike **D**. In order to print the Chart of Accounts report on an attached printer, check to see that the printer is properly connected to the computer. Turn on the printer power switch, align the paper if necessary, and strike **P**. If you want to interrupt the printer and return to the General

Ledger Main Menu during printing, press the Esc key. Figure 2.6 illustrates both a displayed and a printed Chart of Accounts report for Advertising Specialists.

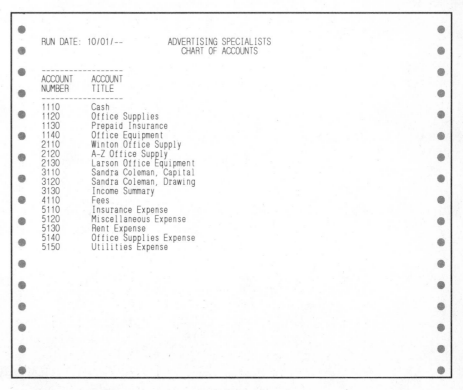

```
RUN DATE: 10/01/--          ADVERTISING SPECIALISTS        CHART OF ACCOUNTS
ACCOUNT    ACCOUNT
NUMBER     TITLE
------------------
1110       Cash
1120       Office Supplies
1130       Prepaid Insurance
1140       Office Equipment
2110       Winton Office Supply
2120       A-Z Office Supply
2130       Larson Office Equipment
3110       Sandra Coleman, Capital
3120       Sandra Coleman, Drawing
3130       Income Summary
4110       Fees
5110       Insurance Expense
5120       Miscellaneous Expense
5130       Rent Expense
5140       Office Supplies Expense
5150       Utilities Expense


                    Press SPACE BAR to continue.
```

```
   RUN DATE: 10/01/--          ADVERTISING SPECIALISTS
                                 CHART OF ACCOUNTS

       ------------------
       ACCOUNT    ACCOUNT
       NUMBER     TITLE
       ------------------
       1110       Cash
       1120       Office Supplies
       1130       Prepaid Insurance
       1140       Office Equipment
       2110       Winton Office Supply
       2120       A-Z Office Supply
       2130       Larson Office Equipment
       3110       Sandra Coleman, Capital
       3120       Sandra Coleman, Drawing
       3130       Income Summary
       4110       Fees
       5110       Insurance Expense
       5120       Miscellaneous Expense
       5130       Rent Expense
       5140       Office Supplies Expense
       5150       Utilities Expense
```

Figure 2.6   Displayed and Printed Chart of Accounts Report

Set Control Accounts Option C

There are certain account numbers that require special identification and handling by the computer. These account numbers must be established, or *set up*, through Option C, *Set Control Accounts*, of the General Ledger Main Menu. This setup should be performed immediately after the chart of accounts is built and displayed or printed. These control accounts may also be changed at any time.

When the *Set Control Accounts* option is selected, the Set Control Accounts data entry screen shown in Figure 2.7 will appear. The account titles displayed for which numbers must be set can vary. The account titles displayed depend on the type of business you selected in the Company Information data entry screen (Option D of the System Selection Menu). The account titles shown in Figure 2.7 are for a sole proprietorship. If the company is set up as a corporation, a different set of account titles will appear.

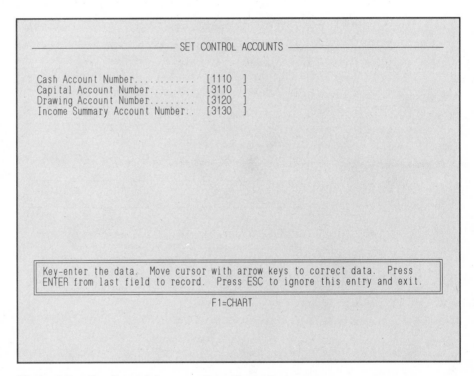

Figure 2.7   Set Control Accounts Data Entry Screen

To set the control accounts or to change current values, complete the following steps. (Note that pressing the Function 1 key opens a window on the screen which enables you to view your chart of accounts if you wish to verify an account number.)

1. Key-enter the appropriate account number for each of the control account titles displayed.
2. After all control accounts have been keyed, verify the accuracy of your keying. If you detect an error, move the cursor to the error and make the correction. When finished, move the cursor to the last field and press the ENTER/RETURN key to indicate that you want the computer to accept your data.
3. At this time, the computer will match the account numbers you have key-entered to the chart of accounts to verify that they exist.

If an account number cannot be found, an error message is displayed, and you will be permitted to make a correction. If all the account numbers match, the computer will display them along with their assigned titles. In addition, a decision prompt will appear at the bottom of the screen. Strike **C** to change the data, **R** to record the account numbers, or press Esc to ignore the data and exit to the General Ledger Main Menu.

Enter/Correct Figure 2.8 illustrates the data entry screen which is used to enter, and
Opening Balances make corrections to, the opening balances.
Option D

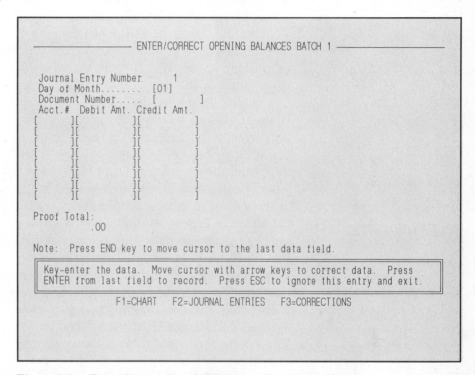

```
┌─────────────────────────────────────────────────────────────────────┐
│                                                                      │
│  ──────────────── ENTER/CORRECT OPENING BALANCES BATCH 1 ─────────── │
│                                                                      │
│     Journal Entry Number      1                                      │
│     Day of Month........  [01]                                       │
│     Document Number.....  [        ]                                 │
│     Acct.#  Debit Amt. Credit Amt.                                   │
│     [     ][          ][          ]                                  │
│     [     ][          ][          ]                                  │
│     [     ][          ][          ]                                  │
│     [     ][          ][          ]                                  │
│     [     ][          ][          ]                                  │
│     [     ][          ][          ]                                  │
│     [     ][          ][          ]                                  │
│     [     ][          ][          ]                                  │
│                                                                      │
│  Proof Total:                                                        │
│             .00                                                      │
│                                                                      │
│  Note:  Press END key to move cursor to the last data field.         │
│  ┌────────────────────────────────────────────────────────────────┐ │
│  │ Key-enter the data.  Move cursor with arrow keys to correct data.  Press │ │
│  │ ENTER from last field to record.  Press ESC to ignore this entry and exit. │ │
│  └────────────────────────────────────────────────────────────────┘ │
│             F1=CHART    F2=JOURNAL ENTRIES    F3=CORRECTIONS          │
│                                                                      │
└─────────────────────────────────────────────────────────────────────┘
```

Figure 2.8   Enter/Correct Opening Balances Data Entry Screen

The Enter/Correct Opening Balances data entry screen allows you to key opening account balances from the General Ledger input form. You may open a window to view the chart of accounts by pressing the Function 1 key. You may open another window to view any of the opening balances previously entered by pressing the Function 2 key. You may also inform the computer that you wish to make corrections by pressing the Function 3 key.

Note that during computer processing, all the opening balances entered on each Enter/Correct Opening Balances data entry screen is automatically assigned a number called a **journal entry number**. This number will be used by the computer to locate opening balances. These journal entry numbers appear on the Opening Balances report and are used when making corrections. To establish the opening account balances, complete the following steps:

1. Key-enter the day of the month.
2. Key-enter **BALANCE** in the *Document Number* field. The cursor will move automatically to the first position in the *Acct.#* field.

3. Key-enter the account number.
4. Key-enter the debit amount, or move the cursor to the *Credit Amt.* field and key-enter the credit amount, depending on whether the opening balance is a debit or credit.
5. Continue key-entering account numbers and corresponding opening balance amounts until all have been entered or until the screen is filled.
6. Move the cursor to the last data field (Credit Amt.), if it is not already there, by pressing the End key, and press ENTER/RETURN to indicate that you want the computer to accept your data. At this time, the computer will check to see if each of the account numbers entered are in the chart of accounts. If not, a decision prompt message will appear asking if you wish to set up the missing account. If you respond *Yes*, the Build Chart of Accounts data entry screen will appear, and you will be permitted to set up the account in the chart of accounts. After the account has been set up and recorded in the computer's memory, the Enter/Correct Opening Balances data entry screen will again appear, and you will be permitted to continue. If the account number is in the chart of accounts (or has been added), the account titles and complete edited date (month/day/year) will appear beside the corresponding fields. Also, the proof total will be displayed on the screen. The **proof total** is the sum and balance of all entries made to this point. A decision prompt will appear asking if you wish to make a change, post the entries, or ignore data (do nothing) and return a blank Enter/Correct Opening Balances data entry screen.
7. When you are certain that all data is correct, strike **P** to post the entries. A new Enter/Correct Opening Balances data entry screen will appear and the *Journal Entry Number* field will be increased by one. The Day of Month value remains from the previous screen. The reason for this is to save data entry keying time. If the Day of Month number is the same for the next opening balance transactions, press ENTER/RETURN to move the cursor past the field and leave the data intact. If the value changes, rekey the changed data. Continue key-entering the remaining opening balances.
8. After all opening balances have been key-entered and posted, press the Esc key to exit this data entry screen and return to the General Ledger Main Menu.

To make corrections to opening balances, simply press the Function 3 key. When this function key is pressed, the Enter/Correct Opening Balances data entry screen shown in Figure 2.8 will again appear. This time, instead of the cursor positioned in the *Day of Month* field, it will be positioned in the *Journal Entry Number* field. Remember that when entering opening balances, each entry is automatically assigned a journal entry number in order for the computer to locate a specific opening balance. These journal entry numbers appear as the first column on the opening balance display or printout and must be used when making corrections. The journal entry numbers may also be obtained by pressing the Function 2 key, which in turn displays a Journal

Entries window. Complete the following steps when making corrections to opening balances:

1. Key-enter the journal entry number for the opening balance you wish to correct or delete, then press the ENTER/RETURN key. The computer will check to see if the journal entry number exists. If the journal entry number exists, all the current data associated with it will be displayed. If the journal entry number does not exist, an error code and message will be displayed and you will be asked to reference your opening balance display, printout, or Journal Entries window to obtain a valid journal entry number.

2. After the computer verifies the journal entry number, finds the corresponding opening balances, and displays the opening balance entries, a prompt will appear telling you to strike **C** to change any of the data fields, strike **P** to post the changed data, or strike **D** to delete all the opening balance data that appears on the screen. To make a change, strike **C**, move the cursor to the appropriate field, and key-enter the change. Continue this procedure until all corrections have been made.

3. Press the Esc key to exit this data entry screen and return to a blank Enter/Correct Opening Balances data entry screen to continue making corrections or additional entries.

It is a good idea to display or print another Opening Balances report after making corrections. This will prove that all corrections have been recorded properly, verify that you are in balance, and provide an audit trail (if printed) for future reference. An **audit trail** is a computer-generated printout of accounting data that may be referred to at a later date if necessary.

Opening Balances Report Option E

By selecting Option E, *Opening Balances Report*, from the General Ledger Main Menu, you may obtain a printout or screen display of the Opening Balances report. This report consists of the journal entry number and date, followed by the account number, account title, debit or credit amounts, and document number for each journal entry number. An example of a displayed Opening Balances report for Advertising Specialists is shown in Figure 2.9.

When this option is chosen, a decision prompt similar to that discussed in "Chart of Accounts Report" will appear. Strike **D** to display the Opening Balances report on the screen, strike **P** to print the Opening Balances report on an attached printer, or press the Esc key if you wish to exit this option and return to the General Ledger Main Menu.

Save Data to Disk

After the general ledger setup has been completed (Options A through E), press Esc to return to System Selection Menu. Choose Option E, *Save Data to Disk*, and save your newly created data to disk as a work in progress file. This option *must* be the last option selected prior to ending the automated accounting session. If you fail to perform this procedure prior to computer shutdown, or before loading another problem or creating empty files, all data keyed and processed during the session will be lost.

```
RUN DATE: 10/01/--        ADVERTISING SPECIALISTS        OPENING BALANCES BATCH 1
JE#   DATE     ACCOUNT NUMBER & TITLE                 DEBIT AMOUNT  CREDIT AMOUNT
-----------------------------------------------------------------------------------
0001  10/01/-- 1110   Cash                               1023.55
               1120   Office Supplies                     451.13
               1130   Prepaid Insurance                   440.00
               1140   Office Equipment                  11110.00
               2120    A-Z Office Supply                                  495.00
               2130    Larson Office Equipment                             55.00
               3110    Sandra Coleman, Capital                          12474.68
                      DOCUMENT: Balance


               TOTALS                                 -------------  -------------
                                                       13024.68       13024.68
               IN BALANCE                             =============  =============



                       Press SPACE BAR to continue.
```

Figure 2.9   Displayed Opening Balances Report

GENERAL LEDGER SETUP (SAMPLE PROBLEM)

Setting up a business on a computerized accounting system involves several one-time activities to establish (set up) the general ledger data file. The step-by-step procedures for establishing a computerized general ledger system for Advertising Specialists are described in the following sections.

The chart of accounts data for Advertising Specialists has been recorded for you on the General Ledger File Maintenance input form (Form GL-1) shown in Figure 2.10. Each account has been assigned a number from one to six digits in length. Notice that the first digit in the account number is the account classification as specified in Figure 2.1. The account title is limited to 25 characters.

The opening balances have been recorded for you on the General Ledger input form (Form GL-2). The completed General Ledger input form showing Advertising Specialists's opening balances is shown in Figure 2.11 on page 48.

Instructions

Step 1 Perform the start-up procedures.

Step 2 When the System Selection Menu appears, select Option B, *Accounting System Setup*. Set each field as follows. You may wish to set *Each Report on New Page* to **N** (for *No*) if your instructor wishes. After you have key-entered all of the settings, strike **R** to record your data and return to the System Selection Menu.

	ACCOUNT NUMBER	ACCOUNT TITLE	
1	1110	Cash	1
2	1120	Office Supplies	2
3	1130	Prepaid Insurance	3
4	1140	Office Equipment	4
5	2110	Winton Office Supply	5
6	2120	A-Z Office Supply	6
7	2130	Larson Office Equipment	7
8	3110	Sandra Coleman, Capital	8
9	3120	Sandra Coleman, Drawing	9
10	3130	Income Summary	10
11	4110	Fees	11
12	5110	Insurance Expense	12
13	5120	Miscellaneous Expense	13
14	5130	Rent Expense	14
15	5140	Office Supplies Expense	15
16	5150	Utilities Expense	16
17			17
18			18
19			19
20			20
21			21
22			22
23			23
24			24
25			25

GENERAL LEDGER FILE MAINTENANCE Input Form

RUN DATE 10/01/-- (MM DD YY)

Problem No. 2-S

FORM GL-1

Figure 2.10   General Ledger File Maintenance Input Form Showing Chart of Accounts (Problem 2-S)

Simplified/Expanded General Ledger ....S
Simplified/Expanded Accounts Payable ....S
Simplified/Expanded Accounts Receivable .....S
Each Report on New Page .... Y
Checks on Preprinted Forms .... N
Statements on Preprinted Forms............ N

Step **3**   From the System Selection Menu, select Option C (*Load Data from Disk*). When the Load Data from Disk menu appears, select Option D, *Create Empty File.*

Step **4**   From the System Selection Menu, select Option D (*Company Information*). Set each field as follows, then strike **R** to record your data and return to the System Selection Menu:

Run Date ....10/01/-- (use the current year)
Company Name ....Advertising Specialists

RUN DATE _10 / 01 / --_ MM DD YY		GENERAL LEDGER Input Form			Problem No. _2-S_ FORM GL-2	
BATCH NO. [_1_]						

	1	2	3	4	5	
	DAY	DOC. NO.	ACCOUNT NUMBER	DEBIT AMOUNT	CREDIT AMOUNT	
1	01	BALANCE	1110	1023 55		1
2			1120	451 13		2
3			1130	440 00		3
4			1140	11110 00		4
5			2120		495 00	5
6			2130		55 00	6
7			3110		12474 68	7
8						8
9						9
10						10
11						11
12						12
13						13
14						14
15						15
16						16
17						17
18						18
19						19
20						20
21						21
22						22
23						23
24						24
25						25
			BATCH TOTALS	13024 68	13024 68	

Figure 2.11   General Ledger Input Form Showing Opening Balances (Problem 2-S)

Problem Number ....Problem 2-S
Type of Business ....S

Step **5**   From the System Selection Menu, select Option F, *General Ledger*.

Step **6**   When the General Ledger Main Menu appears, select Option A, *Build Chart of Accounts*.

Step **7**   When the Build Chart of Accounts data entry screen appears, key-enter the data from the General Ledger File Maintenance input form shown in Figure 2.10. When finished, press Esc, which will return you to the General Ledger Main Menu.

Step **8**   From the General Ledger Main Menu, select Option B, *Chart of Accounts Report*. Tell the computer whether you wish to print or display the report. The Chart of Accounts report for Advertising Specialists is shown in Figure 2.12. If you find errors on the Chart of Accounts report, return to the *Build Chart of Accounts* option and key-enter the missing or incorrect accounts.

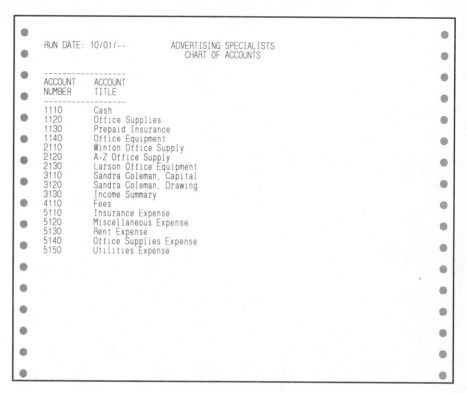

```
RUN DATE: 10/01/--          ADVERTISING SPECIALISTS
                               CHART OF ACCOUNTS

---------------------
ACCOUNT   ACCOUNT
NUMBER    TITLE
---------------------
1110      Cash
1120      Office Supplies
1130      Prepaid Insurance
1140      Office Equipment
2110      Winton Office Supply
2120      A-Z Office Supply
2130      Larson Office Equipment
3110      Sandra Coleman, Capital
3120      Sandra Coleman, Drawing
3130      Income Summary
4110      Fees
5110      Insurance Expense
5120      Miscellaneous Expense
5130      Rent Expense
5140      Office Supplies Expense
5150      Utilities Expense
```

Figure 2.12   Chart of Accounts Report (Problem 2-S)

Step 9 Select Option C, *Set Control Accounts*. Key-enter and record the following control accounts:

Account	Account No.
Cash	1110
Capital	3110
Drawing	3120
Income Summary	3130

Step 10 Select Option D, *Enter/Correct Opening Balances*. Key-enter and post the opening balances from the General Ledger input form shown in Figure 2.11.

Step 11 Return to the General Ledger Main Menu and select Option E, *Opening Balances Report*. Indicate whether you wish to display or print the report. The Opening Balances report for Advertising Specialists is shown in Figure 2.13.

Step 12 If your opening balances report is out of balance or if you have made an error, return to the *Enter/Correct Opening Balances* option and press Function 3, Corrections. Make the necessary corrections to the opening balances and display or print a new Opening Balance report.

Step 13 Press Esc to exit from the General Ledger Main Menu and return to the System Selection Menu.

Step 14 From the System Selection Menu, select Option E, *Save Data to Disk* and save your data as a work in progress file (recommend you use file name **AA2-S**).

Step 15 Press Esc to end your automated accounting session. Then complete the student exercise and transaction problem which follow.

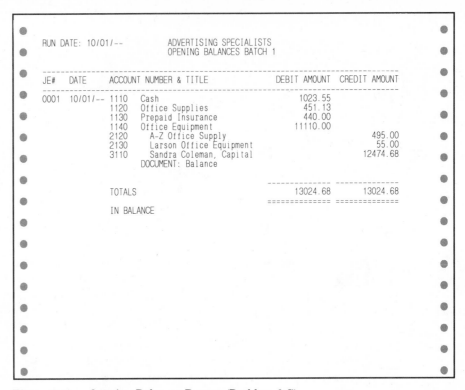

Figure 2.13   Opening Balances Report (Problem 2-S)

Name _____

Class _____ Date _____

CHAPTER 2
STUDENT EXERCISE

I. Matching   For each of the following definitions, write the letter of the term which best fits that definition in the space provided.

a. Computerized general ledger   e. Data file
   system   f. Data Base
b. Auxiliary storage device   g. Control accounts
c. Field   h. Journal entry number
d. Record   i. Batch number

1. _____ A hardware device capable of storing data, which is under direct control of the computer. (Obj. 1)

2. _____ Each unique item of data (also commonly known as a data element), such as the debit or credit amount, account number, account title, and account balance. (Obj. 1)

3. _____ A collection of interrelated data files linked together in such a manner as to provide efficient access to data stored on an auxiliary storage device. (Obj. 1)

4. _____ All related fields of data which are treated together as a unit (for example, a complete set of fields used to describe a particular account in a general ledger system). (Obj. 1)

5. _____ A number assigned by the computer to each opening balance for the purpose of identification. (Objs. 1,5)

6. _____ A collection of related records, or a complete set of account records. (Obj. 1)

7. _____ Account numbers that require special handling by the computer. (Obj. 1)

8. _____ A computer program or collection of programs which direct the computer to perform all the accounting cycle functions of building and maintaining the chart of accounts, making and posting journal entries, and preparing financial statements. (Obj. 1)

9. _____ A one- or two-digit number consecutively assigned to a group of journal entries for the purpose of identification. (Objs. 1,5)

II. Short Answer   1. The computer recognizes the first digit of the account number as the account classification. Identify these five classifications for a service business. (Obj. 2)

_____

_____

_____

_____

_____

2. What is the purpose of the Chart of Accounts report? (Obj. 3)

_____

_____

_____

_____

3. What is the purpose of the *Set Control Accounts* option? (Obj. 4)

_____

_____

_____

_____

4. Why should a second Opening Balances report be printed after making corrections to the opening balances? (Objs. 5, 6)

_____

_____

_____

5. What function does the *Save Data to Disk* option perform? (Obj. 7)

_____

_____

_____

GENERAL LEDGER TRANSACTION PROBLEM 2-1

As of October 1 of the current year, Steven Waldorf establishes a sole proprietorship called Waldorf Realty. He wants to use the following accounts and account opening balances: (Objs. 1-8)

Account Number	Account Title	Debit	Credit
110	Cash	1650.56	
120	Office Supplies	586.67	
130	Office Furniture	8970.00	
140	Office Equipment	7187.50	
210	Sara's Office Equip. Co.		2289.33
220	Bender Company		97.75
230	Blue Chip Printing Co.		
310	Steven Waldorf, Capital		16007.65
320	Steven Waldorf, Drawing		
330	Income Summary		
410	Fees		
510	Advertising Expense		
520	Miscellaneous Expense		
530	Office Supplies Expense		
540	Utilities Expense		

Instructions

Step 1 Remove the blank input forms and the Chapter 2 Audit Test at the end of this chapter. Fill in the answers to the audit test as you work through the following steps.

Step 2 Record the accounts on the General Ledger File Maintenance input form (Form GL-1).

Step 3 Record the account opening balances on the General Ledger input form (Form GL-2).

Step 4 Bring up the System Selection Menu according to the instructions for your microcomputer.

Step 5 From the System Selection Menu, select Option B, *Accounting System Setup*. Set each field as follows, then record your data and return to the System Selection Menu.

Simplified/Expanded General Ledger ....S
Simplified/Expanded Accounts Payable........S
Simplified/Expanded Accounts Receivable .....S
Each Report on New Page ....Y
Checks on Preprinted Forms ....N
Statements on Preprinted Forms ....N

Step 6 From the System Selection Menu, select Option C (*Load Data from Disk*). When the Load Data from Disk menu appears, select Option D, *Create Empty Files*.

Step 7 From the System Selection Menu, select Option D (*Company Informa-*

tion). Set each field as follows, then strike **R** to record your data and return to the System Selection Menu:

Run Date . . . . 10/01/-- (use the current year)
Company Name . . . . Waldorf Realty
Problem Number . . . . Problem 2-1
Type of Business . . . . S

Step   8   From the System Selection Menu, select Option F, *General Ledger*.

Step   9   When the General Ledger Main Menu appears, select Option A, *Build Chart of Accounts*.

Step 10   When the Build Chart of Accounts data entry screen appears, key-enter the data from the General Ledger File Maintenance input form prepared in Step 2. When finished, press Esc, which will return you to the General Ledger Main Menu.

Step 11   From the General Ledger Main Menu, select Option B, *Chart of Accounts Report*. Tell the computer whether you wish to print or display the report. If you find errors on the chart of accounts report, return to the *Build Chart of Accounts* option and key-enter the missing or incorrect accounts.

Step 12   Select Option C, *Set Control Accounts*. Key-enter and record the following control accounts:

Account	Account No.
Cash	110
Capital	310
Drawing	320
Income Summary	330

Step 13   Select Option D, *Enter/Correct Opening Balances*. Key-enter and post the opening balances from the General Ledger input form prepared in Step 3.

Step 14   Return to the General Ledger Main Menu and select Option E, *Opening Balances Report*. Indicate whether you wish to display or print the report.

Step 15   If your Opening Balances report is out of balance or if you have made an error, return to the *Enter/Correct Opening Balances* option and press Function 3, Corrections. Make the necessary corrections to the opening balances and display or print a new Opening Balances report.

Step 16   Press Esc to exit from the General Ledger Main Menu and return to the System Selection Menu.

Step 17   From the System Selection Menu, select Option E, *Save Data to Disk, and save your data as a work in progress file (recommend you use file name* **AA2-1**).

Step 18   Press Esc to end your automated accounting session.

Step 19   Hand in the completed student exercise sheets, input forms, the audit test, and any printouts to your instructor.

You have now completed the computer exercise for Chapter 2.

Name _____

Class _____ Date _____

	GENERAL LEDGER FILE MAINTENANCE Input Form	Problem No. _____

RUN DATE ___ / ___ / ___
                 MM   DD   YY

FORM GL-1

	ACCOUNT NUMBER	ACCOUNT TITLE	
1			1
2			2
3			3
4			4
5			5
6			6
7			7
8			8
9			9
10			10
11			11
12			12
13			13
14			14
15			15
16			16
17			17
18			18
19			19
20			20
21			21
22			22
23			23
24			24
25			25

RUN DATE ____/____/____
         MM   DD   YY

BATCH NO. [   ]

GENERAL LEDGER
Input Form

Problem No. _____

FORM GL-2

	DAY	DOC. NO.	ACCOUNT NUMBER	DEBIT AMOUNT	CREDIT AMOUNT	
1						1
2						2
3						3
4						4
5						5
6						6
7						7
8						8
9						9
10						10
11						11
12						12
13						13
14						14
15						15
16						16
17						17
18						18
19						19
20						20
21						21
22						22
23						23
24						24
25						25

BATCH TOTALS [|]

Name _____

Class _____ Date _____

CHAPTER 2
AUDIT TEST

1. What is the run date shown on the Chart of Accounts report?

   _____

2. What is the account number for Office Equipment?

   _____

3. What is the account title for Account No. 330?

   _____

4. How many liability accounts are listed on the chart of accounts?

   _____

5. How many expense accounts are listed on the chart of accounts?

   _____

6. What is the batch number shown on the Opening Balances report?

   _____

7. Is the opening balance entered for Steven Waldorf, Capital a debit or credit amount?

   _____

   What is the amount of the debit or credit balance?

   _____

8. The totals of the *Debit* and *Credit* columns for each batch of transactions should be equal. What are the totals for Batch No. 1?

   Total debits: _____

   Total credits: _____

9. How many liability accounts have balances?

   _____

10. How many capital accounts have balances?

    _____

3 GENERAL LEDGER ACCOUNTING CYCLE (SERVICE BUSINESS)

Upon completion of this chapter, you will be able to:

1. Perform chart of accounts file maintenance.
2. Display or print a Chart of Accounts report.
3. Set the run date and batch number.
4. Enter/Correct journal entry transactions.
5. Display or print a Journal Entries report.
6. Display or print a Trial Balance report.
7. Display or print a General Ledger report.
8. Display or print an income statement and a balance sheet.
9. Perform and describe the period-end closing process.
10. Display or print a post-closing trial balance.
11. Identify the components and procedures required to generate General Ledger reports.

INTRODUCTION

In Chapter 2, you learned how to set up the computerized general ledger accounts and opening balances. This chapter will cover the accounting cycle used in an automated accounting system. You will soon see that the activities performed in a computerized accounting system are very similar to those performed in a manual accounting system. The major difference is that in a computerized accounting system, much of the detail work, such as posting journal entries, analyzing and recording closing entries, and preparing financial reports and statements, is done by the computer. In both the manual and computerized systems, the accounting cycle is completed for each fiscal period. A **fiscal period** is a regular interval of time for which a business analyzes its financial information. This interval of time is also known as an accounting period. Typically, businesses choose the length of the fiscal period which best meets their needs. All accounting activities performed during the fiscal period make up what is referred to as the **accounting cycle** and are illustrated in Figure 3.1.

The accounting cycle consists of several general categories of steps. First, new accounts must occasionally be added to the chart of accounts, account titles must be changed, and inactive accounts must be deleted from the file. This process of adding, changing, and deleting records in the chart of accounts is called **file maintenance**. After the chart of accounts file maintenance is completed, a new chart of accounts should be displayed or printed. Second, journal transactions which occur during the fiscal period must be analyzed, recorded on an input document, key-entered into the computer, and posted in the chart of accounts. Each time journal entries are made, a Journal

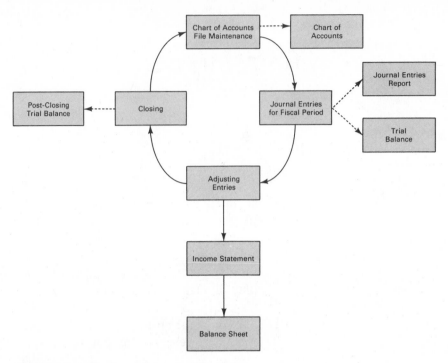

Figure 3.1   The Accounting Cycle

Entries report is displayed or printed. In addition, a trial balance of the chart of accounts is displayed or printed each time journal entries are made in order to verify that the general ledger is in balance. Third, at the end of the fiscal period, adjusting entries are key-entered into the computer and another Journal Entries report is displayed or printed to again verify that the general ledger is in balance. After adjusting entries have been verified, the financial statements (income statement and balance sheet) may be displayed or printed. Finally, the period-end closing process is performed which directs the computer to close all temporary income statement accounts (expense and revenue accounts), the income summary account, and the drawing account to the capital account. A post-closing trial balance is displayed or printed immediately after the period-end closing and serves as the basis for the start of the next fiscal period.

The sections which follow will take you through a typical automated accounting cycle using examples from the Advertising Specialists business we created in the previous chapter. For the purpose of the discussion which follows, Advertising Specialists' fiscal period will be a one-month period. You will first be shown how to use the input forms necessary to record all the monthly transactions. Then, the operating procedures which explain how to perform one complete monthly accounting cycle using the *Automated Accounting for the Microcomputer* software will be presented.

COMPLETING THE INPUT FORMS   General ledger input is recorded on two different input forms. These forms include the General Ledger File Maintenance input form (Form GL-1) and the General Ledger input form (Form GL-2). You have already worked with each of these forms in Chapter 2 to build the chart of accounts. In this chapter, you will learn how the General Ledger File Maintenance input form and the General Ledger input form are utilized to record the data the computer requires to process each accounting cycle.

General Ledger File Maintenance Input Form (Form GL-1)

Once the chart of accounts has initially been built, it must be maintained. Occasionally new accounts must be added to the chart of accounts, account titles must be changed, and inactive accounts must be deleted from the file. The chart of accounts for Advertising Specialists is illustrated in Figure 3.2.

1110	Cash
1120	Office Supplies
1130	Prepaid Insurance
1140	Office Equipment
2110	Winton Office Supply
2120	A-Z Office Supply
2130	Larson Office Equipment
3110	Sandra Coleman, Capital
3120	Sandra Coleman, Drawing
3130	Income Summary
4110	Fees
5110	Insurance Expense
5120	Miscellaneous Expense
5130	Rent Expense
5140	Office Supplies Expense
5150	Utilities Expense

Figure 3.2   Advertising Specialists Chart of Accounts

Let's suppose that during the course of the month, Account No. 5115, Legal Expenses, needs to be added; the title for Account No. 2120, A-Z Office Supply, needs to be changed to A-Z Supply, Inc.; and Account No. 2130, Larson Office Equipment, has become inactive and should be deleted. In order to record these changes and maintain an audit trail, a General Ledger File Maintenance input form (Form GL-1) should be completed as shown in Figure 3.3.

The first entry is an addition, and the second entry is a change. Note that in each case, you simply record the account number and the account title. The third entry is a deletion. To delete an account, record **D** (for delete) in the Account Title column. Only accounts with a zero balance can be deleted. Account No. 2130 has been inactive and has a zero balance. Therefore, the computer will allow it to be deleted from the chart of accounts.

General Ledger Input Form (Form GL-2)

In a manual accounting system, transactions are analyzed and recorded in a journal. Periodically, the transactions are posted from the journal to the general ledger. In a computerized accounting system, the procedures for analyzing, recording, and posting transactions are somewhat different. Although the computer does most of the detail work, the accounting principles used in a computerized system are the same as those in a manual system. In a computerized general ledger system, business transactions must be analyzed, recorded on a General Ledger input form, and key-entered into the computer. These business trans-

GENERAL LEDGER FILE MAINTENANCE Input Form			

RUN DATE 11 / 30 / --
MM DD YY

Problem No. *Sample*

FORM GL-1

	ACCOUNT NUMBER	ACCOUNT TITLE	
1	5115	Legal Expenses	1
2	2120	A-Z Supply, Inc.	2
3	2130	D	3
4			4
5			5
6			6
7			7
8			8
9			9
10			10
11			11
12			12
13			13
14			14
15			15
16			16
17			17
18			18
19			19
20			20
21			21
22			22
23			23
24			24
25			25

Figure 3.3   Completed General Ledger File Maintenance Input Form

actions, called journal entries, update the balances in the chart of accounts. Each of these entries (and the updated chart of accounts) is stored in the computer's memory and can be saved to disk in a work in progress file. This file is used to store transactions for one fiscal period and has a maximum capacity of 250 entries (150 entries for the Apple microcomputer). If this limit is exceeded, a *Journal File Full* message will occur. When this message appears, you will be asked to erase the journal file **Y** (Yes) or **N** (No) so that additional transactions can then be entered. If you select **Y**, the following action will occur: (1) all journal entries except for the current batch will be erased, and (2) all deleted journal entries will be erased. If there are no deleted entries and all of the entries in the journal are in the current batch, a message indicating that the journal file is full within the current batch and that the system is unable to add new entries will appear. At this point, you have reached the journal entry capacity of the automated accounting system. If you wish to purge the current batch, simply increase the batch number by one and again select the *Enter/Correct Journal Entries* option. When the *Journal File Full* message appears, select **Y** (for Yes) and purge the journal file. As you can see, the journal entry capacity is unlimited, provided that you do not exceed 250 (150 for the Apple) journal entries within any one batch. Since journal entries are automatically posted to account balances which reside in the chart of accounts, account balances will not be lost when this data is erased.

In this general ledger system, journal entries are recorded on the General Ledger input form (Form GL-2). This form is similar to the journal in a manual accounting system and can accommodate any type of general ledger transaction. Figure 3.4 illustrates a completed General Ledger input form.

The date, located in the upper left corner of the form, is entered as the **run date** and will appear as part of the heading on each report

	DAY	DOC. NO.	ACCOUNT NUMBER	DEBIT AMOUNT	CREDIT AMOUNT	
RUN DATE 11/30/--			GENERAL LEDGER		Problem No. Sample	
BATCH NO. 2			Input Form		FORM GL-2	
1	1	C436	1140	600 00		1
2			1110		600 00	2
3	2	R310	1110	875 00		3
4			4110		875 00	4
5	3	R311	1110	750 00		5
6			3110		750 00	6
7	4	C437	5150	57 50		7
8			1110		57 50	8
9	5	M715	1120	62 00		9
10			2110		62 00	10
11	10	C438	3120	280 00		11
12			1110		280 00	12
13						13
14						14
15						15
16						16
17						17
18						18
19						19
20						20
21						21
22						22
23						23
24						24
25						25
			BATCH TOTALS	2624 50	2624 50	

Figure 3.4   Completed General Ledger Input Form

which is printed by the computer. This date is usually the date transactions are key-entered and processed by the computer (for example, the end of the month). The **batch number**, located immediately below the run date, should contain a one- or two-digit number which identifies a specific group of journal entries. Remember that Batch No. 1 is reserved to identify the opening balances you worked with in Chapter 2 during the general ledger setup. In Figure 3.4, all journal entries to be key-entered into the computer for Advertising Specialists covering the first through the fifteenth of the month are identified as Batch No. 2. Succeeding batch numbers should be assigned to subsequent groups of journal entries. The use of batch numbers is helpful in finding and isolating errors by providing a convenient method of tracing an error back to its source.

Each line on the form represents one part of a transaction. The Day column is the day of the month that the transaction occurred. The rest of the date (month and year) will automatically be added by the computer from the run date provided earlier. Recorded in the Document Number column is a number which identifies the source document for the transaction. This is descriptive information that will provide an **audit trail** (a means by which the transaction may be traced to its original source document). Typical entries in this column include check numbers, sales invoice numbers, cash receipt numbers, or purchase invoice numbers. The day and document numbers are only recorded once for each journal entry. The Account Number column represents the number of the account from the chart of accounts to be debited or credited. The last two columns, labeled Debit Amount and Credit Amount, contain the amount that is to be debited or credited to the account specified in the Account Number column. Six different types of transactions are illustrated in Figure 3.4, the General Ledger input form for Advertising Specialists.

The first transaction (lines 1 and 2) is an example of buying an asset for cash.

November 1, 19--
Bought office equipment for cash, $600.00 (Check No. 436).

In order to record this transaction, Office Equipment is debited for $600.00 and Cash is credited for $600.00. The debit to Office Equipment (Account No. 1140) is shown on line 1. The credit to Cash (Account No. 1110) is shown on line 2. Note that the day and document number are recorded on the first line only of the journal entry.

The second transaction (lines 3 and 4) is an example of a cash sale.

November 2, 19--
Received cash from fees, $875.00 (Cash Receipt No. 310).

To record this transaction, Cash (Account No. 1110) is debited for $875.00 and Fees (Account No. 4110) is credited for $875.00.

The third transaction (lines 5 and 6) is an example of an additional investment made by the owner.

November 3, 19--
Received cash from the owner, Sandra Coleman, as an additional investment in the business, $750.00 (Cash Receipt No. 311).

To record this transaction, Cash (Account No. 1110, line 5) is debited for $750.00, and Sandra Coleman, Capital (Account No. 3110, line 6) is credited for $750.00.

The fourth transaction (lines 7 and 8) is an example of paying an expense with cash.

November 4, 19--
Paid cash for utilities expense, $57.50 (Check No. 437).

In order to record this transaction, Utilities Expense is debited for $57.50, and Cash is credited for $57.50. The debit to Utilities Expense (Account No. 5150) is shown on line 7. The credit to Cash (Account No. 1110) is shown on line 8.

The fifth transaction (lines 9 and 10) illustrates an example of buying supplies on account.

November 5, 19--
Bought supplies on account from Winton Office Supply, $62.00 (Memorandum No. 715).

To record this transaction, Office Supplies (Account No. 1120, line 9) is debited for $62.00, and Winton Office Supply (Account No. 2110, line 10) is credited for $62.00.

The sixth and final transaction (lines 11 and 12) is an example of a withdrawal by the owner.

November 10, 19--
Paid cash to Sandra Coleman for personal use, $280.00 (Check No. 438).

To record this transaction, the Sandra Coleman, Drawing account (Account No. 3120, line 11) is debited for $280.00, and the Cash account (Account No. 1110, line 12) is credited for $280.00.

The bottom of the form contains batch totals for the Debit Amount and Credit Amount columns. After all transactions have been recorded on the General Ledger input form, the sum of the Debit Amount and Credit Amount columns should be determined on a calculator and the totals entered in the appropriate boxes at the bottom of the form. These totals must be equal because they are used to prove the equality of debits and credits in each batch of entries.

Journal entries may be displayed or printed at any time. The displayed or printed list is called a **Journal Entries report** and serves two important functions: (1) it is useful in balancing and correcting errors (proving that the batch totals on the General Ledger input form match the batch totals of the computer-generated Journal Entries report), and (2) it becomes a permanent accounting document. When a Journal Entries report is requested, any batch may be printed at any time. Thus, the report serves a function similar to that of a handwritten journal in a manual system by providing an audit trail whereby transactions may be traced to their original source documents.

ADJUSTING ENTRIES   After all transactions for the accounting period have been recorded, key-entered into the computer, and posted, a Trial Balance or General Ledger report is displayed or printed. The account balances shown on these reports are needed for the period-end adjustments. Some of the account balances shown on the trial balance may not be correct. For example, during the fiscal period, supplies have been used. However, the Supplies account balance does not yet reflect the amount of supplies that have been used. Therefore, the balance of the account is incorrect at the end of the fiscal period and must be brought up to date. An entry which brings a ledger account balance up to date is known as an **adjusting entry**.

The amount of supplies used must be shown as an expense in the Supplies Expense account and a decrease in the asset account (Supplies). Merchandise Inventory and Prepaid Insurance are examples of other accounts which must be brought up to date with adjusting entries at the end of the fiscal period.

Any necessary adjustments are recorded on a General Ledger input form (Form GL-2) using the next batch number. These adjusting entries are then key-entered into the computer and posted. A new Journal Entries report for this batch is then displayed or printed to prove the equality of the debits and credits.

Advertising Specialists has two accounts that require adjustment: the Office Supplies account and the Prepaid Insurance account. Suppose that the Office Supplies account must be adjusted to $758.01 to reflect the current office supplies on hand and the amount of office supplies used during the month. Also, suppose that the Prepaid Insurance account must be adjusted to $650.00 to reflect the value of the prepaid insurance at the end of the month and the amount of insurance which expired during the month. The completed adjusting entries for these two accounts and the previous trial balance from which the amounts for the adjustments are determined are shown in Figure 3.5.

The first adjusting entry (lines 1 and 2) is for Office Supplies. Notice the Office Supplies account balance in the first Trial Balance report after the monthly transactions is $1120.74. The difference between this amount and the current supplies on hand ($758.01) is $362.73. This difference represents the amount of supplies consumed during the month. In order to record this adjustment, Account No. 5140, Office Supplies Expense, is debited for $362.73 (line 1); and Account No. 1120, Office Supplies, is credited for $362.73 (line 2). The words **ADJ ENTR** are entered in the Document Number column of the first part of the entry to explain that this is an adjusting entry.

The second adjusting entry (lines 3 and 4) is for Prepaid Insurance. Notice the Prepaid Insurance account balance in the Trial Balance report after the monthly transactions is $690.00. The difference between this amount and the current value of prepaid insurance ($650.00) is $40.00. This difference represents the amount of prepaid insurance which expired during the month. In order to record this adjustment, Account No. 5110, Insurance Expense, is debited for $40.00 (line 3); and Account No. 1130, Prepaid Insurance, is credited for $40.00 (line 4).

In a manual accounting system, a worksheet is used as a tool to analyze adjusting entries and prepare the financial statements. Since the computer generates the financial statements automatically from the general ledger data stored in its memory, a worksheet is not required for an automated accounting system. Therefore, once the adjusting

RUN DATE _11_ / _30_ / _--_
MM DD YY

GENERAL LEDGER
Input Form

Problem No. _Sample_

FORM GL-2

BATCH NO. __3__

	DAY	DOC. NO.	ACCOUNT NUMBER	DEBIT AMOUNT	CREDIT AMOUNT	
1	30	ADJ ENTR	5140	362 73		1
2			1120		362 73	2
3	30	ADJ ENTR	5110	40 00		3
4			1130		40 00	4
5						5

```
RUN DATE: 11/30/--          ADVERTISING SPECIALISTS
                                TRIAL BALANCE

ACCOUNT    ACCOUNT
NUMBER     TITLE                     DEBIT AMOUNT      CREDIT AMOUNT

1110       Cash                         1703.69
1120       Office Supplies              1120.74
1130       Prepaid Insurance             690.00
1140       Office Equipment            11615.00
2120       A-Z Office Supply                              141.87
2130       Larson Office Equipment                         55.00
3110       Sandra Coleman, Capital                      12474.68
3120       Sandra Coleman, Drawing       850.00
4110       Fees Revenue                                  4687.32
5105       Advertising Expense           410.00
5120       Miscellaneous Expense          45.50
5130       Rent Expense                  610.00
5150       Utilities Expense             313.94

           TOTALS                      17358.87         17358.87
                                     ============     ============
```

Figure 3.5   Adjusting Entries and Trial Balance

entries have been key-entered, posted, and verified for equality of debits and credits, the financial statements (income statement and balance sheet) may be displayed or printed.

GENERAL LEDGER OPERATIONAL PROCEDURES

Once the General Ledger File Maintenance input form(s) and the General Ledger input form(s) are completed, the data contained on them must be key-entered into the computer and various reports must be printed in order to complete the accounting cycle processing. As you saw in the previous chapter, the General Ledger Main Menu (illustrated in Figure 3.6) is divided into three menu sections. The Setup menu contains Options A through E, the Processing menu contains Options F through J, and the Reports and Closing menu contains Options K through P. The options which appear on this menu appear in the same sequence in which you must select them in order to complete the accounting cycle. The sections which follow explain how Options F through P are used to complete this task.

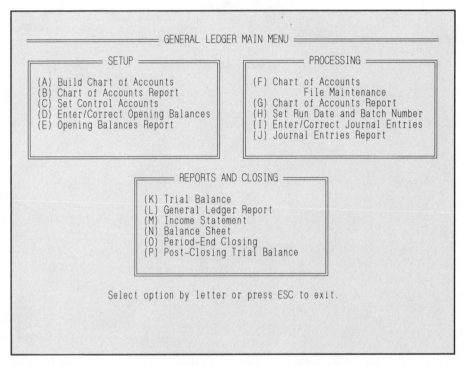

Figure 3.6   General Ledger Main Menu

Chart of Accounts File Maintenance Option F

Option F, *Chart of Accounts File Maintenance*, is similar to the *Build Chart of Accounts* option (Option A) you used during general ledger setup. This option permits you to make additions, changes, and deletions to an existing chart of accounts. When this option is selected, the Chart of Accounts File Maintenance data entry screen shown in Figure 3.7 will appear. Notice in Figure 3.7 the title for account number 4110, Fees, is being changed to Fees Revenue.

In order to add, change, or delete accounts, complete the following steps:

1. Select Option F, *Chart of Accounts File Maintenance*, from the General Ledger Main Menu.
2. Key-enter an account number. The computer will check to see if the account number is already on the chart of accounts. If it is not, the computer will assume that you wish to add a new account. If the account number already exists on the chart of accounts, the computer will display the account title and number and assume that you wish to either change the account title or delete the account. In this case, a decision prompt will ask you to strike **C** if you want to change the account title, **R** to record the title as it appears on the screen, or **D** to delete this account. An account cannot be deleted if it has a balance. You may press Esc to exit and not make any changes.
3. If you are adding a new account, key-enter the title of the account. A decison prompt will appear, and you will be asked to strike **C** to

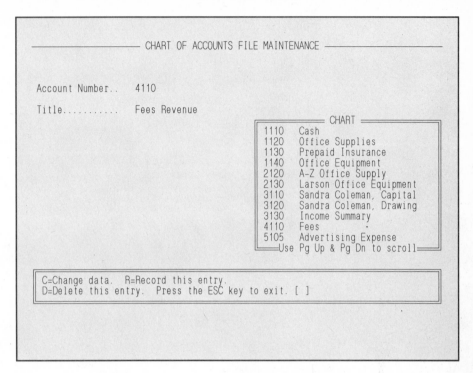

Figure 3.7   Chart of Accounts File Maintenance Data Entry Screen

correct the account title if entered incorrectly, **R** to record the account as keyed, or **D** to delete the entry. When the account title and number are correct, strike **R** to record the account.

4. If the account already exists and you wish to change the account title, strike **C** for change, key-enter the correct account title, and then strike **R** to record the account data.
5. If the account already exists and you wish to delete it, strike **D** and the account will be deleted.
6. Repeat this procedure until all additions, changes, and deletions have been key-entered from the General Ledger File Maintenance input form. After all the data has been keyed, press the Esc key without keying any data in the *Account Number* field to exit this menu and return to the General Ledger Main Menu.

Chart of Accounts Report Option G

This option is similar to the *Chart of Accounts Report* option (Option B) you used during general ledger setup. When this option is chosen, a decision prompt will appear which consists of three choices: (1) strike **D** to display the Chart of Accounts report on the screen, (2) strike **P** to print the Chart of Accounts report on an attached printer, or (3) press the Esc key if you wish to exit this option and return to the General Ledger Main Menu. In order to print the Chart of Accounts report (or any other report generated by the computer) on an attached printer, check to see that the printer is properly connected to the computer, turn on the printer power switch, align the paper if necessary, and strike **P**. If you want to interrupt the printer during printing and return to the General Ledger Main Menu, press the Esc key. Figure 3.8 illustrates a displayed Chart of Accounts report for Advertising Specialists.

```
RUN DATE: 11/30/--              ADVERTISING SPECIALISTS          CHART OF ACCOUNTS
ACCOUNT    ACCOUNT
NUMBER     TITLE
-------------------
1110       Cash
1120       Office Supplies
1130       Prepaid Insurance
1140       Office Equipment
2120       A-Z Office Supply
2130       Larson Office Equipment
3110       Sandra Coleman, Capital
3120       Sandra Coleman, Drawing
3130       Income Summary
4110       Fees Revenue
5105       Advertising Expense
5110       Insurance Expense
5120       Miscellaneous Expense
5130       Rent Expense
5140       Office Supplies Expense
5150       Utilities Expense




                        Press SPACE BAR to continue.
```

Figure 3.8   Displayed Chart of Accounts Report

Set Run Date and Batch Number Option H

The purpose of this option is to provide the computer with the run date to be printed on reports and a batch number that will identify a grouping of journal entries. The batch number, which is key-entered, is the number located on the upper left-hand corner (beneath the run date) of the General Ledger input form. Recall that Batch No. 1 is reserved to identify the opening balances you worked with in Chapter 2 during general ledger setup. Succeeding batch numbers (2, 3, etc.) should be assigned to subsequent groups of journal entries. For example, Batch No. 2 could be assigned to journal entries covering the first through the fifteenth of the month, and Batch No. 3 could be assigned to journal entries covering the sixteenth through the end of the month. The batch number will prove helpful in locating errors and providing an audit trail by which you will be able to trace a transaction to its source. The data entry screen display for the *Set Run Date and Batch Number* option is shown in Figure 3.9.

In order to key-enter the run date and batch number, complete the following steps:

1. From the General Ledger Main Menu, select Option H, *Set Run Date and Batch Number*. Check the run date and batch number displayed. If both data fields are correct as displayed, exit this menu and return to the General Ledger Main Menu by pressing the Esc key.

2. If either or both data fields require a change, position the cursor over the data field you wish to change and key-enter the correct data. Key-enter the run date in the MM/DD/YY format. Do not key the slashes. After the batch number has been key-entered (or the ENTER/RETURN key pressed while the cursor is in the *Batch*

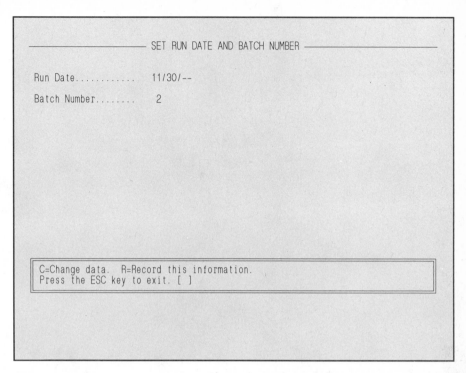

Figure 3.9   Set Run Date and Batch Number Data Entry Screen

Number field), a decision prompt will appear, and you will be asked to strike **C** if you want to change the data or **R** to record the date and batch number as they appear. You may press Esc to exit and not make any changes.

3. After the date and batch numbers have been changed and recorded or the Esc key pressed, the General Ledger Main Menu will be displayed.

Enter/Correct Journal Entries Option I   The procedure for key-entering the journal entry transactions from the General Ledger input form is identical to the procedure introduced in the previous chapter for key-entering the account opening balances during general ledger setup. The only difference is that you will enter one journal entry (with each of its parts as illustrated in Figure 3.10) for each Enter/Correct Journal Entries data entry screen.

If the last option selected was not the *Set Run Date and Batch Number* option, a window display will appear that allows you to verify the current settings of the run date and batch number. If these data fields are correct, press the Space Bar to continue. If these data fields are incorrect, press Esc to exit back to the General Ledger Main Menu, select the *Set Run Date and Batch Number* option, and enter the correct data.

A window may be opened by striking the Function 1 key to reference the chart of accounts if you need to verify whether a particular account exists in the chart of accounts. You may press the Function 2 key to open another window to view journal entries previously entered for the batch number specified in the Set Run Date and Batch Number data entry screen. You may also inform the computer that you wish to make corrections by pressing the Function 3 key.

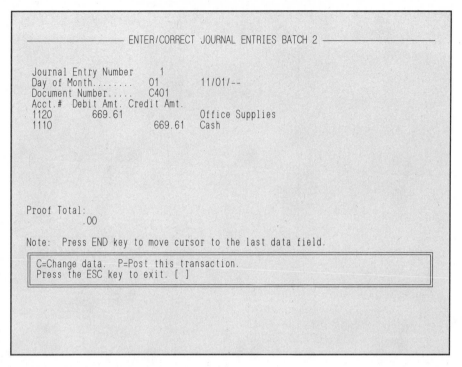

Figure 3.10   Example of Journal Entry Keyed in Enter/Correct Journal Entries
Data Entry Screen

The first field that appears on the Journal Entries data entry screen is referred to as the **journal entry number**. This number is used to identify each journal entry transaction. Each journal entry transaction is automatically assigned a new, unique journal entry number by the computer. The purpose of the journal entry number is to locate journal entry transactions that need to be changed or deleted.

When key-entering journal entries, complete the following steps:

1. From the General Ledger Main Menu, Select Option I, *Enter/Correct Journal Entries*. Be sure to verify that the batch number and run date are correct if they appear in a window display immediately after selecting this option.
2. Key-enter the two-digit day of the month.
3. Key-enter the document number. The cursor will automatically move to the first position of the first *Acct. #* field.
4. Key-enter the account number.
5. If this part of the transaction is a debit entry, key-enter the debit amount in the *Debit Amt.* field. If not, press ENTER/RETURN to move the cursor to the *Credit Amt.* field. If this part of the transaction is a credit entry, key-enter the credit amount in the *Credit Amt.* field.
6. Continue key-entering account numbers and corresponding debit/credit amounts until all the parts of the journal entry have been keyed.
7. Move the cursor to the last data field (*Credit Amt.*), if it is not already there, by pressing the End key, and press ENTER/RETURN to indicate that you want the computer to accept your data. At this time, the computer will check to see if each of the

account numbers entered are in the chart of accounts. If not, a decision prompt message will appear asking if you wish to add the missing account. If you respond *Yes*, the Chart of Accounts File Maintenance data entry screen will appear, and you will be permitted to add the account to the chart of accounts. After the account has been added and recorded in the computer's memory, the Enter/Correct Journal Entries data entry screen will again appear and you will be permitted to continue. If the account number is in the chart of accounts (or has been added), the account titles and complete edited date (month/day/year) will appear beside the corresponding fields. Also, a proof total will be displayed on the screen. A decision prompt will appear. Strike **C** to change the data. If all of the data is correct, strike **P** to post the transaction. Press Esc to exit and disregard the data.

8. After the computer automatically posts each part of the journal entry, you will be returned to the Journal Entries data entry display screen. The day-of-month value remains from the previous transaction. The purpose of this is to save time and potential keying errors by reducing the number of keystrokes required to enter the journal entry transactions. If the value contained in the *Day of Month* field is the same for the next journal entry transaction, press ENTER/RETURN to move the cursor past the field. If the values are different, key the correct data. Continue keying the additional journal transactions.

9. After all key-entering is complete, press the Esc key without keying any data in the *Day of Month* field to exit this data entry screen and return to the General Ledger Main Menu.

The procedure to correct journal entry transactions is similar to the procedure to correct opening balances you worked with in Chapter 2. Pressing F2 from the Enter/Correct Journal Entries data entry screen will display a window of journal entires for the current batch. To correct previously entered journal entry transactions from the Enter/Correct Journal Entries data entry screen, press the Function 3 key. When this function key is pressed, the data entry screen shown in Figure 3.10 will again appear. This time, instead of the cursor positioned in the *Day of Month* field, it will be positioned in the *Journal Entry Number* field. Remember that during data entry, each transaction is automatically assigned a journal entry number in order for the computer to locate a specific journal entry transaction. These journal entry numbers appear as the first column on the Journal Entries report display or printout and must be used when making corrections. Complete the following steps when making corrections to journal entry transactions:

1. Key-enter the journal entry number for the journal entry transaction you wish to correct or delete, then press the ENTER/RETURN key. The computer will check to see if the journal entry number exists. If the journal entry number exists, all the current data associated with it will be displayed. If the journal entry number does not exist, an error code and message will be displayed, and you will be asked to reference your Journal Entries report to

obtain a valid journal entry number.

2. After the computer verifies the journal entry number and finds and displays the corresponding journal entry, a prompt will appear telling you to strike **C** to change any of the data fields, strike **P** to post the changed data, or strike **D** to delete all the journal entry data that appears on the screen. To make a change, strike **C**, move the cursor to the appropriate field, and key-enter the change. Continue this procedure until all corrections have been made.

3. Press the Esc key to exit this data entry screen and return to a blank Enter/Correct Journal Entries data entry screen to continue making corrections or additional entries.

It is a good idea to display or print another Journal Entries report after making corrections. This will prove that all corrections have been recorded properly, verify that you are in balance, and provide an audit trail (if printed) for future reference.

Journal Entries
Report
Option J

You will find this option similar to the *Opening Balances Report* option introduced in Chapter 2 during general ledger setup. When this option is selected, a decision prompt will appear which consists of three choices: (1) strike **D** to display the Journal Entries report, (2) strike **P** to print the Journal Entries report on an attached printer, or (3) press the Esc key if you wish to exit this option and return to the General Ledger Main Menu. Figure 3.11 illustrates a partially displayed Journal Entries report.

```
RUN DATE: 11/30/--        ADVERTISING SPECIALISTS      JOURNAL ENTRIES BATCH #2
JE#   DATE    ACCOUNT NUMBER & TITLE          DEBIT AMOUNT  CREDIT AMOUNT
----------------------------------------------------------------------------
0008  11/14/-- 1140  Office Equipment            505.00
               1110    Cash                                     505.00
                     DOCUMENT: C407

0009  11/15/-- 5105  Advertising Expense         410.00
               1110    Cash                                     410.00
                     DOCUMENT: C408

0010  11/17/-- 1110  Cash                       3720.20
               4110    Fees Revenue                            3720.20
                     DOCUMENT: R251

0011  11/22/-- 5150  Utilities Expense           117.15
               1110    Cash                                     117.15
                     DOCUMENT: C409

0012  11/25/-- 2120  A-Z Office Supply           353.13
               1110    Cash                                     353.13
                     DOCUMENT: C410
                                                -------------  -------------
               TOTALS                            8694.50        8694.50
                                                =============  =============
               IN BALANCE

Cash Receipts      4687.32
Cash Payments      4007.18

            Press SPACE BAR to continue or press ESC to exit.
```

Figure 3.11   Partially Displayed Journal Entries Report

After the report has been displayed or printed, the program automatically returns to the General Ledger Main Menu. The first column on the report contains the journal entry number. These numbers uniquely identify each journal entry transaction and are used when making corrections. If you find an error on the report, or if the report is out of balance, use the corrections (Function 3 key) feature of the *Enter/Correct Journal Entries* option to make corrections.

Trial Balance Option K

A trial balance of the general ledger data stored in computer memory may be displayed or printed at any time. The Trial Balance report lists the account numbers, titles, and balances of all accounts in the general ledger that currently contain balances. This report is useful in verifying that the general ledger is in balance.

When this option is selected, a decision prompt will appear asking if you wish to display, print, or escape (exit). When the trial balance is finished displaying or printing, you will be returned to the General Ledger Main Menu. A sample trial balance for Advertising Specialists is shown in Figure 3.12.

```
RUN DATE: 11/30/--            ADVERTISING SPECIALISTS              TRIAL BALANCE
ACCOUNT      ACCOUNT
NUMBER       TITLE                        DEBIT AMOUNT      CREDIT AMOUNT
--------------------------------------------------------------------------------
1110         Cash                            1703.69
1120         Office Supplies                 1120.74
1130         Prepaid Insurance                690.00
1140         Office Equipment               11615.00
2120         A-Z Office Supply                                    141.87
2130         Larson Office Equipment                               55.00
3110         Sandra Coleman, Capital                            12474.68
3120         Sandra Coleman, Drawing          850.00
4110         Fees Revenue                                        4687.32
5105         Advertising Expense              410.00
5120         Miscellaneous Expense             45.50
5130         Rent Expense                     610.00
5150         Utilities Expense                313.94
                                          -------------      -------------
             TOTALS                          17358.87           17358.87
                                          =============      =============



                        Press SPACE BAR to continue.
```

Figure 3.12   Trial Balance

General Ledger Report Option L

The purpose of this option is to provide a detailed record of journal entry activity for each account. Each account may be displayed or listed to obtain detailed information regarding all journal entries which have been posted during the accounting cycle. This information is useful in finding errors which may cause the trial balance to be out of balance, for status information about the activity of a specific account, or to identify transactions that were posted to the wrong account.

When this option is selected, a decision prompt will appear which consists of three choices: (1) strike **D** to display the General Ledger report, (2) strike **P** to print the General Ledger report on an attached printer, or (3) press the Esc key if you wish to exit this option and return to the General Ledger Main Menu.

When you strike either **D** (display to screen) or **P** (print to printer), another decision prompt will appear which consists of five choices: (1) strike **A** to display or print all accounts in the general ledger, (2) strike **S** to display or print the status of a specific account, (3) strike **N** to display or print the next account, (4) strike **P** to display or print the previous account, or (5) press Esc to exit and return to the General Ledger Main Menu.

These five decision prompt options are described as follows:

All Accounts. When **A** is chosen, all accounts in the general ledger may be displayed or printed, starting with the first account in the general ledger. Because this option prints the contents of each account in the general ledger, it is a lengthy report and takes some time to display or print.

Specific Account. When **S** is chosen, you will be asked to provide the account number of the specific account you wish to display or print. Key-enter the account number to display or print the account data.

Next Account. After having viewed or printed a specific account, selecting **N** will display or print the next account in sequence in the general ledger. If no account is specified in an earlier selection, then the first account in the general ledger will be displayed or printed. By continually striking this key, you may view the entire general ledger, one account at a time.

Previous Account. After viewing or printing a specific account, select **P** to display or print the preceding account in sequence in the general ledger. If no account is specified in an earlier selection, striking **P** will result in a beginning-of-file error message. By continually striking this key, you may view the entire general ledger in reverse order, one account at a time.

Esc Key to Exit. Pressing the Esc key will exit the General Ledger report and return you to the General Ledger Main Menu.

When the General Ledger report is finished displaying or printing, you will be returned to the General Ledger Main Menu. An example of a printed General Ledger report is shown in Figure 3.13a, and an example of a displayed General Ledger report for the cash account is shown in Figure 3.13b (page 78).

Income Statement Option M   An income statement should be displayed or printed after all transactions for a fiscal period have been key-entered. This report is used to show the progress the company makes over a period of time. The income statement shows the revenue, cost of merchandise sold, gross profit, expenses, and net income or loss for a fiscal period. In addition, a column labeled *% of Net Revenue* has been included to assist management in its analysis of the income statement. The percentages provided in this column are commonly referred to as component percentages. A **component percentage** represents the relationship between each financial statement item (component) and the net revenue. Component

```
RUN DATE: 11/30/--              ADVERTISING SPECIALISTS
                                   GENERAL LEDGER
--------------------------------------------------------------------
ACCOUNT            J.E.  BATCH            DOCUMENT
NUMBER  TITLE      NO.   NUMBER  DATE     NUMBER    DEBIT AMOUNT  CREDIT AMOUNT
--------------------------------------------------------------------
1110    Cash
                   0001   02    11/01/--  C401                        669.61
                   0002   02    11/02/--  C402                        610.00
                   0003   02    11/04/--  C403                        196.79
                   0004   02    11/05/--  R250        967.12
                   0005   02    11/08/--  C404                        850.00
                   0006   02    11/10/--  C405                        250.00
                   0007   02    11/11/--  C406                         45.50
                   0008   02    11/14/--  C407                        505.00
                   0009   02    11/15/--  C408                        410.00
                   0010   02    11/17/--  R251       3720.20
                   0011   02    11/22/--  C409                        117.15
                   0012   02    11/25/--  C410                        353.13
                                          End.Bal.   1703.69

1120    Office Supplies
                   0001   02    11/01/--  C401         669.61
                                          End.Bal.    1120.74

1130    Prepaid Insurance
                   0006   02    11/10/--  C405         250.00
                                          End.Bal.     690.00

1140    Office Equipment
                   0008   02    11/14/--  C407         505.00
                                          End.Bal.   11615.00

2120    A-Z Office Supply
                   0012   02    11/25/--  C410         353.13
                                          End.Bal.                    141.87

2130    Larson Office Equipment         End.Bal.                      55.00

3110    Sandra Coleman, Capital         End.Bal.                   12474.68

3120    Sandra Coleman, Drawing
                   0005   02    11/08/--  C404         850.00
                                          End.Bal.     850.00

3130    Income Summary                  End.Bal.         .00

4110    Fees Revenue
                   0004   02    11/05/--  R250                        967.12
                   0010   02    11/17/--  R251                       3720.20
                                          End.Bal.                   4687.32

5105    Advertising Expense
                   0009   02    11/15/--  C408         410.00
                                          End.Bal.     410.00

5110    Insurance Expense               End.Bal.         .00

5120    Miscellaneous Expense
                   0007   02    11/11/--  C406          45.50
                                          End.Bal.      45.50

5130    Rent Expense
                   0002   02    11/02/--  C402         610.00
                                          End.Bal.     610.00

5140    Office Supplies Expense         End.Bal.         .00

5150    Utilities Expense
                   0003   02    11/04/--  C403         196.79
                   0011   02    11/22/--  C409         117.15
                                          End.Bal.     313.94
```

Figure 3.13a   Printed General Ledger Report

```
RUN DATE: 11/30/--              ADVERTISING SPECIALISTS            GENERAL LEDGER
ACCOUNT          J.E.   BATCH        DOCUMENT
NUMBER  TITLE    NO.    NUMBER  DATE     NUMBER    DEBIT AMOUNT   CREDIT AMOUNT
----------------------------------------------------------------------------------
1110    Cash
                 0001   02     11/01/--  C401                           669.61
                 0002   02     11/02/--  C402                           610.00
                 0003   02     11/04/--  C403                           196.79
                 0004   02     11/05/--  R250          967.12
                 0005   02     11/08/--  C404                           850.00
                 0006   02     11/10/--  C405                           250.00
                 0007   02     11/11/--  C406                            45.50
                 0008   02     11/14/--  C407                           505.00
                 0009   02     11/15/--  C408                           410.00
                 0010   02     11/17/--  R251         3720.20
                 0011   02     11/22/--  C409                           117.15
                 0012   02     11/25/--  C410                           353.13
                                         End.Bal.     1703.69



                 Press SPACE BAR to continue.
```

Figure 3.13b   Displayed General Ledger Report for Cash Account

percentages are calculated by dividing the amount of each component by the net revenue.

When this option is selected, as with all other reports, you will be asked if you wish to display, print, or escape. When the income statement is finished displaying or printing, you will be returned to the General Ledger Main Menu. A sample income statement for Advertising Specialists is shown in Figure 3.14.

Balance Sheet Option N

A balance sheet should be displayed or printed after all transactions for a fiscal period have been key-entered. The balance sheet presents a complete and accurate report of a company's assets and equities. Specifically, it shows the assets, liabilities, and capital for a business on a specific date.

After the *Balance Sheet* option is selected, displayed, or printed, the computer will return to the General Ledger Main Menu. A sample balance sheet for Advertising Specialists is shown in Figure 3.15.

Period-End Closing Option O

In this system, the period-end closing process is performed at the end of every fiscal period. The balances of all the temporary revenue and expense statement accounts are closed to the proper capital accounts, depending on the type of business (sole proprietorship, partnership, or corporation). Since the journal entries are no longer needed after period-end processing is complete, the journal entries are erased and storage space is thereby made available for the next fiscal period.

Before selecting the *Period-End Closing* option, verify that the financial statements are correct. Once this option is chosen, corrections become more difficult. This is why it is a good idea to make a backup copy of the end-of-fiscal-period data prior to performing period-end

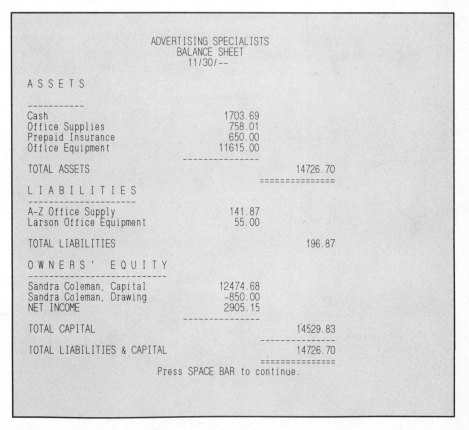

```
                    ADVERTISING SPECIALISTS
                      INCOME STATEMENT
                   FOR PERIOD ENDED 11/30/--
                                                      % OF NET
     R E V E N U E                                    REVENUE
     -------------                                    --------
     Fees Revenue                   4687.32            100.00
                                 ----------------
     NET REVENUE                                4687.32   100.00


     E X P E N S E S
     ---------------
     Advertising Expense            410.00               8.75
     Insurance Expense               40.00                .85
     Miscellaneous Expense           45.50                .97
     Rent Expense                   610.00              13.01
     Office Supplies Expense        362.73               7.74
     Utilities Expense              313.94               6.70
                                 ----------------
     TOTAL EXPENSES                             1782.17   38.02
                                            ----------------
     NET INCOME                                 2905.15   61.98
                                            ================
                   Press SPACE BAR to continue.
```

Figure 3.14   Displayed Income Statement

```
                    ADVERTISING SPECIALISTS
                        BALANCE SHEET
                          11/30/--
     A S S E T S

     -----------
     Cash                          1703.69
     Office Supplies                758.01
     Prepaid Insurance              650.00
     Office Equipment             11615.00
                                 ----------------
     TOTAL ASSETS                              14726.70
                                            ================
     L I A B I L I T I E S
     ---------------------
     A-Z Office Supply              141.87
     Larson Office Equipment         55.00

     TOTAL LIABILITIES                          196.87

     O W N E R S '   E Q U I T Y
     ---------------------------
     Sandra Coleman, Capital      12474.68
     Sandra Coleman, Drawing       -850.00
     NET INCOME                    2905.15
                                 ----------------
     TOTAL CAPITAL                             14529.83
                                            ----------------
     TOTAL LIABILITIES & CAPITAL               14726.70
                                            ================
                   Press SPACE BAR to continue.
```

Figure 3.15   Displayed Balance Sheet

closing. To make a backup, simply instruct the computer to save the data in its memory to your data disk using a different file name.

Prior to key-entering transactions for a new accounting period, the computer must be directed to perform the period-end closing process. Because of the serious consequences of this option, and because of the possibility of striking the wrong key from the menu, when this option is selected, a decision prompt will appear which consists of two choices: (1) *Perform period-end closing (Y or N)?* and (2) *Press the ESC key to exit*. Strike the **Y** (Yes) key to inform the computer to perform period-end closing. Strike the **N** key or press the Esc key to exit and return to the General Ledger Main Menu.

Post-Closing Trial Balance Option P

The purpose of the post-closing trial balance is to provide a screen display or printed report of the account balances immediately after period-end closing. It is prepared to prove the equality of debits and credits in the general ledger after adjusting and closing entries have been made and posted. This report (if printed) acts as an audit trail and reflects the beginning balances of the next fiscal period.

After the *Post-Closing Trial Balance* option has been selected, and the report displayed or printed, you will be returned to the General Ledger Main Menu. A sample post-closing trial balance for Advertising Specialists is shown in Figure 3.16. Notice there are no balances in the temporary revenue and expense accounts.

Save Data to Disk

In Chapter 2, you learned how to save your work to disk as a work in progress file after returning to the System Selection Menu and prior to computer shutdown. Recall that if you fail to follow this procedure, all data key-entered and processed during your computer session will not be recorded (updated) onto your data disk and will, therefore, be lost.

```
RUN DATE: 11/30/--        ADVERTISING SPECIALISTS        POST-CLOSING TRIAL BALANCE
ACCOUNT        ACCOUNT
NUMBER         TITLE                          DEBIT AMOUNT        CREDIT AMOUNT
----------------------------------------------------------------------------------
1110           Cash                              1703.69
1120           Office Supplies                    758.01
1130           Prepaid Insurance                  650.00
1140           Office Equipment                 11615.00
2120           A-Z Office Supply                                     141.87
2130           Larson Office Equipment                                55.00
3110           Sandra Coleman, Capital                            14529.83
                                               ---------------    ---------------
               TOTALS                            14726.70            14726.70
                                               ===============    ===============




                       Press SPACE BAR to continue.
```

Figure 3.16   Displayed Post-Closing Trial Balance

GENERAL LEDGER ACCOUNTING CYCLE (SAMPLE PROBLEM)

The sample problem which follows takes you through an entire fiscal period and general ledger accounting cycle. When you finish this problem, you should be able to use all the options of the General Ledger Main Menu. More importantly, you should be able to describe and demonstrate how a computerized general ledger accounting system functions.

The chart of accounts, control accounts, and opening balances for Advertising Specialists, as discussed and prepared in Chapter 2, will be the basis of this sample problem. The data for Advertising Specialists has been stored on the program disk under the name **AA3-S** (Automated Accounting problem 3-S). To complete this sample problem, you will apply what you have learned in the first three chapters of this text in order to complete the accounting cycle processing for the month of November.

Instructions

Step   1   The following transactions for Advertising Specialists occurred during November of the current year. (Document numbers have been abbreviated as **C** for check and **R** for receipt.) The transactions have been analyzed and recorded for you as Batch No. 2 on a General Ledger input form. The Debit Amount and Credit Amount columns have been added and recorded in the Batch Total boxes at the bottom of the last page. The additions, changes, or deletions in the chart of accounts have been recorded for you on a General Ledger File Maintenance input form. Compare these transactions with the completed input forms shown in Figures 3.17 and 3.18 on the following pages.

Nov 01   Paid cash for office supplies, $669.61 (C401).
   02   Paid cash for the month's rent, $610.00 (C402).
   03   Changed the account title of Fees to Fees Revenue.
   04   Paid cash for the monthly telephone bill (Utilities Expense), $196.79 (C403).
   05   Received cash for design fees, $967.12 (R250).
   08   Owner withdrew $850.00 in cash for personal use (C404).
   10   Paid cash for an insurance premium, $250.00 (C405).
   11   Paid cash for lawn service (Miscellaneous Expense), $45.50 (C406).
   14   Paid cash for new office equipment, $505.00 (C407).
   15   Added Advertising Expense to the chart of accounts as Account No. 5105.

Note: Since the first digit of the account number denotes the classification, the account number assigned to Advertising Expense must begin with the number 5 since it is an expense. Any expense account number that is not already used could have been assigned. Account No. 5105 was chosen in order to maintain the alphabetical order of the expense accounts.

		GENERAL LEDGER FILE MAINTENANCE Input Form	Problem No. _3-S_
RUN DATE _11 , 30 , --_ MM DD YY			FORM GL-1

	ACCOUNT NUMBER	ACCOUNT TITLE	
1	4110	Fees Revenue	1
2	5105	Advertising Expense	2
3	2110	D	3
4			4
5			5
6			6
7			7
8			8
9			9
10			10
11			11
12			12
13			13
14			14
15			15
16			16
17			17
18			18
19			19
20			20
21			21
22			22
23			23
24			24
25			25

Figure 3.17   General Ledger File Maintenance Input Form (Problem 3-S)

15 Paid cash for ad in the local newspaper, $410.00 (C408).
17 Received cash for design fees, $3,720.20 (R251).
22 Paid cash for the electric bill (Utilities Expense), $117.15 (C409).
25 Paid cash on account to A-Z Office Supply, $353.13 (C410).
30 Deleted Winton Office Supply from the chart of accounts.

Step 2 Bring up the System Selection Menu according to the instructions for your microcomputer.

Step 3 Select Option C, *Load Data from Disk*. When the Load Data from Disk menu appears, select Option A, *Load Opening Balances from the Program Disk* (Apple 5 1/4-inch disk users will find their data files on Program Disk 1).

Step 4 When the directory of Opening Balances contained on the program disk appears, select automated accounting problem 3-S by key-entering the

	DAY	DOC. NO.	ACCOUNT NUMBER	DEBIT AMOUNT	CREDIT AMOUNT	
1	01	C401	1120	669 61		1
2			1110		669 61	2
3	02	C402	5130	610 00		3
4			1110		610 00	4
5	04	C403	5150	196 79		5
6			1110		196 79	6
7	05	R250	1110	967 12		7
8			4110		967 12	8
9	08	C404	3120	850 00		9
10			1110		850 00	10
11	10	C405	1130	250 00		11
12			1110		250 00	12
13	11	C406	5120	45 50		13
14			1110		45 50	14
15	14	C407	1140	505 00		15
16			1110		505 00	16
17	15	C408	5105	410 00		17
18			1110		410 00	18
19	17	R251	1110	3720 20		19
20			4110		3720 20	20
21	22	C409	5150	117 15		21
22			1110		117 15	22
23	25	C410	2120	353 13		23
24			1110		353 13	24
25						25
			BATCH TOTALS	8694 50	8694 50	

RUN DATE 11/30/-- MM DD YY

BATCH NO. 2

GENERAL LEDGER
Input Form

Problem No. 3-S

FORM GL-2

Figure 3.18   General Ledger Input Form (Problem 3-S)

file name: **AA3-S**.

Step 5   Select Option D, *Company Information*, and change the run date to: **11/30/--** (use the current year). Record the new company information. Notice that the company name, problem number, and type of business have automatically been set during the problem-selection process. Leave these three fields as they appear.

Step 6   Select Option F, *General Ledger*, from the System Selection Menu.

Step 7   After the General Ledger program has been loaded into the computer's memory, select Option K, *Trial Balance*, from the General Ledger Main Menu, and display a trial balance. Compare the trial balance to the one shown in Figure 3.19 to verify that the correct problem has been selected. If the two reports are not the same, press Esc to Return to the System Selection Menu, and repeat Steps 3-6. If they are the same, press the Space Bar to continue.

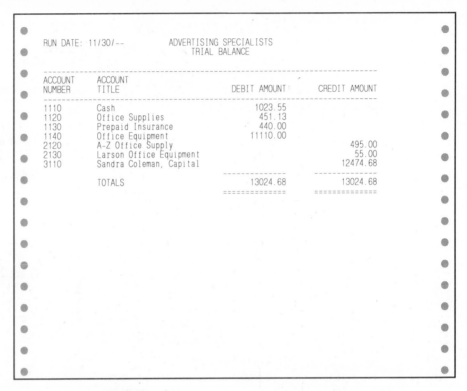

RUN DATE: 11/30/--   ADVERTISING SPECIALISTS
                                           TRIAL BALANCE

```
ACCOUNT    ACCOUNT
NUMBER     TITLE                         DEBIT AMOUNT      CREDIT AMOUNT

1110       Cash                            1023.55
1120       Office Supplies                  451.13
1130       Prepaid Insurance                440.00
1140       Office Equipment               11110.00
2120       A-Z Office Supply                                  495.00
2130       Larson Office Equipment                             55.00
3110       Sandra Coleman, Capital                          12474.68

           TOTALS                         13024.68          13024.68
```

Figure 3.19   Beginning Trial Balance (Problem 3-S)

Step 8   Select Option F, *Chart of Accounts File Maintenance*, from the General Ledger Main Menu, and key-enter the data from the completed General Ledger File Maintenance input form (Figure 3.17). When you are finished, press Esc to return to the General Ledger Main Menu.

Step 9   Select Option G, *Chart of Accounts Report*, and display or print the revised chart of accounts. Verify that the data you key-entered is correct.

Step 10   Select Option H, *Set Run Date and Batch Number*, from the General Ledger Main Menu.

Step 11   Verify that the run date has been set to **November 30** of the current year and that the batch number has been set to **2**. If not, make and record the appropriate changes.

Step 12   Select Option I, *Enter/Correct Journal Entries*.

Step 13   Key-enter and post the data from the completed General Ledger input form shown in Figure 3.18 for Batch 2. When you have finished, press Esc to return to the General Ledger Main Menu.

Step 14   Select Option J, *Journal Entries Report*, and display or print the journal entries. If the Journal Entries report is in balance and you are sure it is correct, proceed to Step 16.

Step 15   If the Journal Entries report is in error, return to the *Enter/Correct Journal Entries* option, select *Corrections* (press the Function 3 key), and key-enter the corrections. Display or print another Journal Entries report. Repeat this step until your journal entries are correct. The correct Journal Entries report is shown in Figure 3.20.

```
RUN DATE: 11/30/--              ADVERTISING SPECIALISTS
                               JOURNAL ENTRIES BATCH #2

------------------------------------------------------------------------
JE#    DATE     ACCOUNT NUMBER & TITLE          DEBIT AMOUNT  CREDIT AMOUNT
------------------------------------------------------------------------
0001  11/01/-- 1120  Office Supplies              669.61
                1110     Cash                                    669.61
                DOCUMENT: C401

0002  11/02/-- 5130  Rent Expense                 610.00
                1110     Cash                                    610.00
                DOCUMENT: C402

0003  11/04/-- 5150  Utilities Expense            196.79
                1110     Cash                                    196.79
                DOCUMENT: C403

0004  11/05/-- 1110  Cash                         967.12
                4110     Fees Revenue                            967.12
                DOCUMENT: R250

0005  11/08/-- 3120  Sandra Coleman, Drawing      850.00
                1110     Cash                                    850.00
                DOCUMENT: C404

0006  11/10/-- 1130  Prepaid Insurance            250.00
                1110     Cash                                    250.00
                DOCUMENT: C405

0007  11/11/-- 5120  Miscellaneous Expense         45.50
                1110     Cash                                     45.50
                DOCUMENT: C406

0008  11/14/-- 1140  Office Equipment             505.00
                1110     Cash                                    505.00
                DOCUMENT: C407

0009  11/15/-- 5105  Advertising Expense.         410.00
                1110     Cash                                    410.00
                DOCUMENT: C408

0010  11/17/-- 1110  Cash                        3720.20
                4110     Fees Revenue                           3720.20
                DOCUMENT: R251

0011  11/22/-- 5150  Utilities Expense            117.15
                1110     Cash                                    117.15
                DOCUMENT: C409

0012  11/25/-- 2120  A-Z Office Supply            353.13
                1110     Cash                                    353.13
                DOCUMENT: C410

                                                 ----------   ----------
                TOTALS                             8694.50      8694.50
                                                 ==========   ==========
                IN BALANCE

Cash Receipts        4687.32
Cash Payments        4007.18
```

Figure 3.20   Journal Entries Report for November Transactions (Problem 3-S)

Step 16   Select Option K, *Trial Balance*, and print or display a trial balance. Compare your trial balance with the correct one which appears in Figure 3.21.

Step 17   Select Option L, *General Ledger Report*.

Step 18   Display or print the data in the Cash account. When prompted to do so, choose Option S, *Specific Account*, and key-enter the Cash account number (1110). To prove cash, verify that the ending cash balance is

```
  RUN DATE: 11/30/--              ADVERTISING SPECIALISTS
                                     TRIAL BALANCE

  -------------------------------------------------------------------------
  ACCOUNT     ACCOUNT
  NUMBER      TITLE                          DEBIT AMOUNT      CREDIT AMOUNT
  -------------------------------------------------------------------------
  1110        Cash                              1703.69
  1120        Office Supplies                   1120.74
  1130        Prepaid Insurance                  690.00
  1140        Office Equipment                 11615.00
  2120        A-Z Office Supply                                      141.87
  2130        Larson Office Equipment                                55.00
  3110        Sandra Coleman, Capital                             12474.68
  3120        Sandra Coleman, Drawing            850.00
  4110        Fees Revenue                                         4687.32
  5105        Advertising Expense               410.00
  5120        Miscellaneous Expense              45.50
  5130        Rent Expense                      610.00
  5150        Utilities Expense                 313.94
                                              ----------         ----------
              TOTALS                           17358.87           17358.87
                                              ==========         ==========
```

Figure 3.21   Trial Balance after November Transactions (Problem 3-S)

equal to the checkbook balance of $1,703.69. Then press Esc to return to the General Ledger Main Menu.

Step 19   The information needed to complete the adjusting entries for November for Advertising Specialists is listed below. The completed General Ledger input form for the adjusting entries is shown in Figure 3.22. Examine these adjusting entries to make sure you understand them.

Adjusting Entries Information, November 30
Office Supplies Inventory ....$758.01.
Value of Insurance Policies ....$650.00.

Step 20   Select Option H, *Set Run Date and Batch Number*. Set the batch number to 3.

Step 21   Select Option I, *Enter/Correct Journal Entries*.

Step 22   Key-enter and post the adjusting entries as Batch No. 3 from the completed General Ledger input form shown in Figure 3.22.

Step 23   Select Option J, *Journal Entries Report*. Print or display the Journal Entries report for the adjustments. If the Journal Entries report for the adjusting entries is in balance, and you are sure everything is correct, proceed to Step 25.

Step 24   If the Journal Entries report is in error, make the necessary corrections. Display or print another Journal Entries report. Repeat this step until your journal entries are correct. The correct Journal Entries report is shown in Figure 3.23 on page 88.

Step 25   Select Option K, *Trial Balance*, and print or display a trial balance. Compare your trial balance with the correct one which appears in Figure 3.24 on page 88.

	DAY	DOC. NO.	ACCOUNT NUMBER	DEBIT AMOUNT	CREDIT AMOUNT	
	1	2	3	4	5	
1	30	ADJ ENTR	5140	362 73		1
2			1120		362 73	2
3	30	ADJ ENTR	5110	40 00		3
4			1130		40 00	4
5						5
6						6
7						7
8						8
9						9
10						10
11						11
12						12
13						13
14						14
15						15
16						16
17						17
18						18
19						19
20						20
21						21
22						22
23						23
24						24
25						25

RUN DATE 11 / 30 / --
MM DD YY

GENERAL LEDGER
Input Form

Problem No. 3-S

FORM GL-2

BATCH NO. 3

BATCH TOTALS   402 73   402 73

Figure 3.22   General Ledger Input Form for Adjusting Entries (Problem 3-S)

Step 26 Select Option M, *Income Statement*, and display or print an income statement. Compare your income statement with the one shown in Figure 3.25 (page 89). If there are errors, make the corrections using the corrections feature of Option I, *Enter/Correct Journal Entries*. Repeat this step until your income statement is correct. It is much more difficult to make corrections after performing the period-end closing.

Step 27 Select Option N, *Balance Sheet*, and print or display a balance sheet. Compare your balance sheet with the one shown in Figure 3.26 (page 89). If there are errors, make the corrections using the corrections feature of Option I, *Enter/Correct Journal Entries*. Repeat this step until your balance sheet is correct. It is much more difficult to make corrections after performing the period-end closing.

Step 28 Select Option O, *Period-End Closing*, and perform the period-end closing process.

```
RUN DATE: 11/30/--            ADVERTISING SPECIALISTS
                             JOURNAL ENTRIES BATCH #3

-----------------------------------------------------------------------
JE#   DATE     ACCOUNT NUMBER & TITLE            DEBIT AMOUNT  CREDIT AMOUNT
-----------------------------------------------------------------------
0013  11/30/-- 5140  Office Supplies Expense         362.73
               1120     Office Supplies                             362.73
                     DOCUMENT: ADJ ENTR

0014  11/30/-- 5110  Insurance Expense                40.00
               1130     Prepaid Insurance                            40.00
                     DOCUMENT: ADJ ENTR

                                                  --------------  --------------
               TOTALS                                 402.73        402.73
                                                  ==============  ==============
               IN BALANCE
```

Figure 3.23   Journal Entries Report for November Adjusting Entries (Problem 3-S)

```
RUN DATE: 11/30/--            ADVERTISING SPECIALISTS
                                  TRIAL BALANCE

-----------------------------------------------------------------------
ACCOUNT    ACCOUNT
NUMBER     TITLE                      DEBIT AMOUNT     CREDIT AMOUNT
-----------------------------------------------------------------------
1110       Cash                          1703.69
1120       Office Supplies                758.01
1130       Prepaid Insurance             650.00
1140       Office Equipment            11615.00
2120       A-Z Office Supply                              141.87
2130       Larson Office Equipment                         55.00
3110       Sandra Coleman, Capital                      12474.68
3120       Sandra Coleman, Drawing       850.00
4110       Fees Revenue                                  4687.32
5105       Advertising Expense           410.00
5110       Insurance Expense              40.00
5120       Miscellaneous Expense          45.50
5130       Rent Expense                  610.00
5140       Office Supplies Expense       362.73
5150       Utilities Expense             313.94
                                       -------------    -------------
           TOTALS                        17358.87         17358.87
                                       =============    =============
```

Figure 3.24   Trial Balance After Adjusting Entries (Problem 3-S)

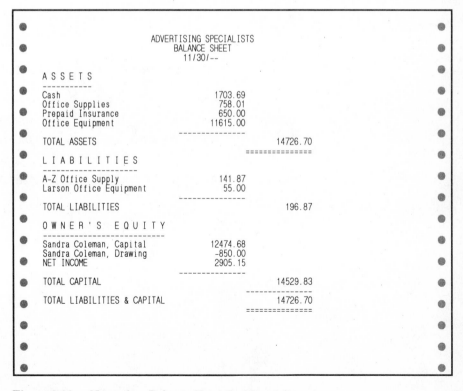

```
                        ADVERTISING SPECIALISTS
                           INCOME STATEMENT
                       FOR PERIOD ENDED 11/30/--
                                                              % OF NET
  R E V E N U E                                               REVENUE
  -------------                                               --------
  Fees Revenue                       4687.32                  100.00
                                  ---------------
  NET REVENUE                                      4687.32    100.00


  E X P E N S E S
  ---------------
  Advertising Expense                 410.00                    8.75
  Insurance Expense                    40.00                     .85
  Miscellaneous Expense                45.50                     .97
  Rent Expense                        610.00                   13.01
  Office Supplies Expense             362.73                    7.74
  Utilities Expense                   313.94                    6.70
                                  ---------------
  TOTAL EXPENSES                                   1782.17     38.02
                                                 ---------------
  NET INCOME                                       2905.15     61.98
                                                 ===============
```

Figure 3.25   November Income Statement for Problem 3-S

```
                        ADVERTISING SPECIALISTS
                             BALANCE SHEET
                               11/30/--

  A S S E T S
  -----------
  Cash                               1703.69
  Office Supplies                     758.01
  Prepaid Insurance                   650.00
  Office Equipment                  11615.00
                                  ---------------
  TOTAL ASSETS                                    14726.70
                                                 ===============
  L I A B I L I T I E S
  ---------------------
  A-Z Office Supply                   141.87
  Larson Office Equipment              55.00
                                  ---------------
  TOTAL LIABILITIES                                196.87

  O W N E R ' S   E Q U I T Y
  ---------------------------
  Sandra Coleman, Capital           12474.68
  Sandra Coleman, Drawing            -850.00
  NET INCOME                         2905.15
                                  ---------------
  TOTAL CAPITAL                                   14529.83
                                                 ---------------
  TOTAL LIABILITIES & CAPITAL                     14726.70
                                                 ===============
```

Figure 3.26   November Balance Sheet Problem 3-S

Step 29   Select Option P, *Post-Closing Trial Balance*, and print or display a post-closing trial balance. If your work has been done accurately, your post-closing trial balance should match the one shown in Figure 3.27. Correct any errors that you find. All corrections that need to be made now must be made via the Enter feature of the *Enter/Correct Journal Entries* option.

```
RUN DATE: 11/30/--              ADVERTISING SPECIALISTS
                                POST-CLOSING TRIAL BALANCE

------------------------------------------------------------------------------
ACCOUNT      ACCOUNT
NUMBER       TITLE                         DEBIT AMOUNT       CREDIT AMOUNT
------------------------------------------------------------------------------
1110         Cash                            1703.69
1120         Office Supplies                  758.01
1130         Prepaid Insurance                650.00
1140         Office Equipment               11615.00
2120         A-Z Office Supply                                    141.87
2130         Larson Office Equipment                              55.00
3110         Sandra Coleman, Capital                           14529.83
                                          ---------------    ---------------
             TOTALS                          14726.70          14726.70
                                          ===============    ===============
```

Figure 3.27   Post-Closing Trial Balance (Problem 3-S)

Step 30   Press Esc to return to the System Selection Menu.

Step 31   Once back in the System Selection Menu, select Option E, *Save Data to Disk*, and save your data as a work in progress file (recommend file name **AA3-S**).

Step 32   Press Esc to end your session. Then complete the student exercise and transaction problem which follow.

Name _____

Class _____ Date _____

CHAPTER 3
STUDENT EXERCISE

I. Matching For each of the following definitions, write the letter of the term which best fits that definition in the space provided.

a. Fiscal period   f. Journal Entries report
b. File maintenance   g. Journal entry number
c. Audit trail   h. Adjusting entry
d. Batch number   i. Component percentage
e. Run date

1. _____ The month, day, and year on which transactions are key-entered and processed by the computer and which will be printed on all computer-generated reports. (Obj. 3)

2. _____ A means whereby a transaction may be traced back to its original source document. (Obj. 5)

3. _____ A regular interval of time for which a business analyzes its financial information. (Obj. 9)

4. _____ A one- or two-digit number used to identify a specific group of journal entries (for example, the first through the fifteenth of the month). (Obj. 3)

5. _____ The process of adding, changing, or deleting records in the chart of accounts. (Obj. 1)

6. _____ A number used to identify each journal entry transaction. (Objs. 4, 5)

7. _____ Percentages included on the income statement that represent the relationship between each financial statement item (component) and the net revenue.

8. _____ An entry that updates account balances that are incorrect at the end of the fiscal period. (Obj. 4)

9. _____ A displayed or printed list of journal entries. (Obj. 5)

II. Short Answer 1. Describe the procedure for making adjusting entries. (Obj. 11)

_____

_____

2. What is the purpose of the batch totals at the bottom of the General Ledger input form? (Obj. 11)

_____

_____

_____

3. Why should another Journal Entries report (proof) be printed after making corrections to the journal entries? (Obj. 4)

_____

_____

_____

4. What is the purpose of the Trial Balance report? (Obj. 6)

_____

_____

5. Why is a worksheet not necessary in an automated accounting system? (Obj. 11)

_____

_____

_____

6. What is the purpose of the *General Ledger Report* option? (Obj. 7)

_____

_____

7. Why must the *Save Data to Disk* option always be chosen prior to system shutdown? (Obj. 11)

_____

_____

_____

_____

_____

8. What is the maximum capacity of the journal entries file? Why are the account balances not lost when that limit is exceeded and the option is selected to erase all the data in the journal entries file? (Obj. 10)

_____

_____

_____

_____

GENERAL LEDGER ACCOUNTING CYCLE
TRANSACTION PROBLEM 3-1

Problem 3-1 is a continuation of Problem 3-S, the sample problem for Chapter 3. Therefore, if you completed the sample problem, it will not be necessary to load the opening balances from the program disk. Instead, you may load your completed problem 3-S work in progress file from your own data disk. If you did not complete the sample problem, you must load the opening balances for file **AA3-1** (Automated Accounting problem 3-1) from the program disk. (Objs. 1-11)

Instructions

Step   1   Remove the blank input forms and the Chapter 3 Audit Test at the end of this chapter. Fill in the answers to the audit test as you work through the following steps.

Step   2   Record the following transactions on the proper input forms. (Document numbers have been abbreviated as **C** for check and **R** for receipt.)

Dec 03   Received cash for design fees, $462.11 (R252).
     04   Paid cash for office rent, $610.00 (C411).
     05   Received cash for design fees, $253.29 (R253).
     06   Paid cash for ad in local newspaper, $221.65 (C412).
     09   Paid cash for amount owed to Larson Office Equipment, $55.00 (C413).
     10   Owner withdrew cash for personal use, $1,250.00 (C414).
     12   Change the title of the Rent Expense account to Office Rent Expense.
     13   Received cash for design fees, $616.99 (R254).
     16   Received cash for design fees, $935.99 (R255).
     18   Paid cash for office supplies, $23.32 (C415).
     20   Paid cash for new drafting table, $585.50 (C416).
     23   Open a new account for Legal Fees Expense, Account No. 5115.
     23   Paid cash for legal fees, $80.00 (C417).
     27   Paid cash for telephone service (Utilities Expense), $187.00 (C418).

Step   3   Bring up the System Selection Menu according to the instructions for your computer.

Step   4   Select Option C, *Load Data from Disk*. If you did not complete Problem 3-S, load file **AA3-1** from the *Load Opening Balances from the Program Disk* option (Apple 5 1/4-inch disk users will find the data files on Program Disk 1). If you did complete Problem 3-S and saved it as a work in progress file, load it from your own data disk.

Step   5   From the System Selection Menu, select Option D, *Company Information*. Set the run date to **December 31** of the current year and make sure the problem number is recorded as **Problem 3-1**.

Step 6   From the System Selection Menu, select Option F, *General Ledger*.

Step 7   Key-enter the data from the General Ledger File Maintenance input form prepared in Step 2.

Step 8   Print or display the chart of accounts.

Step 9   Set the batch number to *4*.

Step 10   Key-enter the journal entries prepared in Step 2.

Step 11   Print or display the Journal Entries report and make any necessary corrections.

Step 12   Print or display the trial balance.

Step 13   Prove cash. The checkbook balance is $959.60.

Step 14   Using the data shown below, record the adjusting entries on the General Ledger input form as Batch No. 5.

Supplies Inventory . . . . $638.50.
Value of Insurance Policies . . . . $609.18.

Step 15   Set the batch number to *5*.

Step 16   Key-enter the adjusting entries prepared in Step 14.

Step 17   Print or display a Journal Entries report. Make any necessary corrections. Repeat this step until the Journal Entries report is correct.

Step 18   Print or display a trial balance. Make any necessary corrections *before proceeding* since corrections are much more difficult to make after the period-end closing has been performed.

Step 19   Print or display an income statement.

Step 20   Print or display a balance sheet.

Step 21   Be certain that all questions have been answered on the Chapter 3 Audit Test sheet before closing the ledger in the following step.

Step 22   Perform the period-end closing.

Step 23   Print or display a post-closing trial balance.

Step 24   Return to the System Selection Menu.

Step 25   Save your work as a work in progress file (recommend file name **AA3-1**) on your own data disk and shut down the computer.

Step 26   Hand in the completed student exercise sheets, input forms, the audit test, and any printouts to your instructor.

You have now completed the computer exercise for Chapter 3.

Name _____

Class _____ Date _____

GENERAL LEDGER
FILE MAINTENANCE
Input Form

Problem No. _____

FORM GL-1

RUN DATE ____ / ____ / ____
MM   DD   YY

	1	2	
	ACCOUNT NUMBER	ACCOUNT TITLE	
1			1
2			2
3			3
4			4
5			5
6			6
7			7
8			8
9			9
10			10
11			11
12			12
13			13
14			14
15			15
16			16
17			17
18			18
19			19
20			20
21			21
22			22
23			23
24			24
25			25

	1	2	3	4	5	
	DAY	DOC. NO.	ACCOUNT NUMBER	DEBIT AMOUNT	CREDIT AMOUNT	
1						1
2						2
3						3
4						4
5						5
6						6
7						7
8						8
9						9
10						10
11						11
12						12
13						13
14						14
15						15
16						16
17						17
18						18
19						19
20						20
21						21
22						22
23						23
24						24
25						25

RUN DATE ___/___/___ MM DD YY

BATCH NO. _____

GENERAL LEDGER
Input Form

Problem No. _____

FORM GL-2

BATCH TOTALS

Name _____

Class _____ Date _____

RUN DATE __/__/__	**GENERAL LEDGER**	Problem No. _____	
MM DD YY	Input Form	**FORM GL-2**	
BATCH NO. [ ]			

	DAY	DOC. NO.	ACCOUNT NUMBER	DEBIT AMOUNT	CREDIT AMOUNT	
1						1
2						2
3						3
4						4
5						5
6						6
7						7
8						8
9						9
10						10
11						11
12						12
13						13
14						14
15						15
16						16
17						17
18						18
19						19
20						20
21						21
22						22
23						23
24						24
25						25
			BATCH TOTALS			

CHAPTER 3
AUDIT TEST

1. What new account title was added to the general ledger this month?

   _____

2. From the General Ledger input form (Form GL-2) for Batch No. 4, what are the total debits and total credits?

   Total debits: _____

   Total credits: _____

3. From the Journal Entries report for Batch No. 4, what is the amount of cash withdrawn by Sandra Coleman?

   _____

4. From the Journal Entries report, to which account was Check No. 418 charged?

   _____

5. What are the total cash receipts for Batch No. 4?

   _____

6. What are the total cash payments for Batch No. 4?

   _____

7. What batch number was assigned to the adjusting entries?

   _____

8. What is the adjustment amount for Office Supplies Expense?

   _____

9. What is the adjustment amount for Insurance Expense?

   _____

10. What is the total of the Debit column from the Trial Balance report?

    _____

11. What is the net revenue for the fiscal period?

    _____

Name ———————————————————————————

Class ——————————————————— Date ———————————

12. What is the amount of advertising expense for the fiscal period?

   ————————————————————————————————

13. What are the total expenses for the fiscal period?

   ————————————————————————————————

14. What is the net income for the fiscal period?

   ————————————————————————————————

15. What are the total assets at the end of the fiscal period?

   ————————————————————————————————

16. What are the total liabilities at the end of the fiscal period?

   ————————————————————————————————

17. What is the balance owed to A-Z Office Supply at the end of the fiscal period?

   ————————————————————————————————

18. What is the total of all the credit balances in the ledger at the end of the fiscal period after the ledger has been closed?

   ————————————————————————————————

19. How many accounts have balances on the post-closing trial balance?

   ————————————————————————————————

20. Why are there fewer accounts with balances on the post-closing trial balance than on the trial balance which was printed before the financial statements?

   ————————————————————————————————

   ————————————————————————————————

4 GENERAL LEDGER FOR A MERCHANDISING BUSINESS

LEARNING OBJECTIVES

Upon completion of this chapter, you will be able to:

1. Complete the system setup process for a merchandising business organized as a partnership.
2. Record transactions for purchases of merchandise.
3. Record the adjusting entries for merchandise inventory.
4. Complete the accounting cycle for a merchandising business using the computerized General Ledger System.
5. Interpret the cost of merchandise sold section of the income statement.

INTRODUCTION

In Chapter 3, you learned how to complete the accounting cycle for a service business using a computerized general ledger system. In this chapter, you will learn how to complete the accounting cycle for a merchandising business. A **merchandising business** is a business that purchases and resells goods. The goods purchased for resale are called merchandise.

The examples used in this chapter are for a merchandising business called Hardware Plus. Hardware Plus is a partnership owned by Dennis Siegel and Ruth Hines. The business purchases and sells microcomputer systems, disk drives, printers, and computer supplies.

CHART OF ACCOUNTS

An asset account titled Merchandise Inventory is included in the chart of accounts for a merchandising business. **Merchandise Inventory** is the account that shows the value of the merchandise on hand. The chart of accounts for a merchandising business includes an additional classification for cost of merchandise accounts. **Cost of merchandise accounts** are those accounts that show the cost or price of merchandise which is purchased for resale to customers. The cost of the merchandise purchased for resale is recorded in the account titled **Purchases**. As you learned in Chapter 1, the first digit of the account number shows the account classification. The accounts for a merchandising business are classified as shown in Figure 4.1.

1 = Assets
2 = Liabilities
3 = Capital
4 = Revenue
5 = Cost of Merchandise
6 = Expenses

Figure 4.1   Account Classifications for a Merchandising Business

The chart of accounts for Hardware Plus is shown in Figure 4.2.

Account Number	Account Title
ASSETS	
110	Cash
120	Accounts Receivable
130	Merchandise Inventory
140	Supplies
150	Prepaid Insurance
LIABILITIES	
210	Accounts Payable
220	Sales Tax Payable
CAPITAL	
310	Dennis Siegel, Capital
320	Dennis Siegel, Drawing
330	Ruth Hines, Capital
340	Ruth Hines, Drawing
350	Income Summary
REVENUE	
410	Sales
COST OF MERCHANDISE	
510	Purchases
EXPENSES	
610	Insurance Expense
620	Legal and Professional Fees Expense
630	Miscellaneous Expense
640	Rent Expense
650	Salary Expense
660	Supplies Expense

Figure 4.2   Chart of Accounts for Hardware Plus

RECORDING PURCHASES OF MERCHANDISE

A purchase invoice is the source document for the purchase of merchandise. The source document data for this type of transaction is then recorded on a General Ledger input form. The General Ledger input form shown in Figure 4.3 shows two entries for purchases of merchandise by Hardware Plus.

The first transaction is a purchase of merchandise on account.

March 6, 19--
Purchased merchandise on account, $4,305.00 (Purchase Invoice No. 210).

In order to record this transaction, Purchases is debited for $4,305.00 and Accounts Payable is credited for $4,305.00. The debit to Purchases, Account No. 510, is shown on line 1. The credit to Accounts Payable, Account No. 210, is shown on line 2.

The second transaction is a purchase of merchandise for cash.

March 16, 19--
Purchased merchandise for cash, $1,250.00 (Check No. 795).

			GENERAL LEDGER Input Form			

RUN DATE _03/31/--_
MM DD YY

BATCH NO. _2_

Problem No. _Sample_

FORM GL-2

	DAY	DOC. NO.	ACCOUNT NUMBER	DEBIT AMOUNT	CREDIT AMOUNT	
1	6	PZ10	510	4305 00		1
2			210		4305 00	2
3	16	C795	510	1250 00		3
4			110		1250 00	4
5						5
6						6
7						7
8						8
9						9
10						10
11						11
12						12
13						13
14						14
15						15
16						16
17						17
18						18
19						19
20						20
21						21
22						22
23						23
24						24
25						25
			BATCH TOTALS	5555 00	5555 00	

Figure 4.3   General Ledger Input Form Showing Purchases of Merchandise

In this transaction, Purchases is debited for $1,250.00, and Cash is credited for $1,250.00. The debit to Purchases, Account No. 510, is shown on line 3. The credit to Cash, Account No. 110, is shown on line 4.

RECORDING WITHDRAWALS BY THE OWNERS For a partnership, the chart of accounts contains a separate drawing account for each partner. The withdrawal of any asset from the business by an owner is recorded in the owner's drawing account. Cash or merchandise withdrawals are recorded in the appropriate partner's drawing account. The General Ledger input form shown in Figure 4.4 shows entries for two withdrawal transactions.

The first transaction is a withdrawal of cash by Dennis Siegel.

March 8, 19--
Dennis Siegel, partner, withdrew cash, $950.00 (Check No. 793).

RUN DATE 03 , 31 , --		GENERAL LEDGER		Problem No. Sample
MM DD YY		Input Form		FORM GL-2
BATCH NO. 2				

	1	2	3	4	5	
	DAY	DOC. NO.	ACCOUNT NUMBER	DEBIT AMOUNT	CREDIT AMOUNT	
1	8	C793	320	950 00		1
2			110		950 00	2
3	19	M51	340	72 45		3
4			510		72 45	4
5						5
6						6
7						7
8						8
9						9
10						10
11						11
12						12
13						13
14						14
15						15
16						16
17						17
18						18
19						19
20						20
21						21
22						22
23						23
24						24
25						25
			BATCH TOTALS	1022 45	1022 45	

Figure 4.4   General Ledger Input Form Showing Withdrawal Transactions

In this transaction, Dennis Siegel, Drawing is debited for $950.00 and Cash is credited for $950.00. The debit to Dennis Siegel, Drawing (Account No. 320) is shown on line 1. The credit to Cash (Account No. 110) is shown on line 2.

The second transaction is a withdrawal of merchandise by Ruth Hines.

March 19, 19--
Ruth Hines, partner, withdrew merchandise, $72.45 (Memorandum No. 51).

To record this transaction, Ruth Hines, Drawing is debited for $72.45 and Purchases is credited for $72.45. The debit to Ruth Hines, Drawing (Account No. 340) is shown on line 3. The credit to Purchases (Account No. 510) is shown on line 4.

ADJUSTING
ENTRIES

An asset account titled Merchandise Inventory is included in the chart of accounts for a merchandising business. Entries are not made to the Merchandise Inventory account during the fiscal period. Purchases of merchandise are recorded in the cost account, Purchases. Sales of merchandise are recorded in the revenue account, Sales. Therefore, the balance in the asset account, Merchandise Inventory, contains the **beginning inventory**, or the value of the merchandise inventory at the beginning of the fiscal period. Consequently, the Merchandise Inventory account must be updated at the end of the fiscal period to show its correct balance so that the financial statements are correct.

To update the Merchandise Inventory account, a physical count is made of the merchandise inventory on hand at the end of the fiscal period to determine its value. Then the difference between the beginning and ending merchandise inventory must be determined. Next, an adjusting entry is made to update the merchandise inventory account. The accounts used for the adjusting entry are Merchandise Inventory and Income Summary. If the ending inventory is larger than the beginning inventory, the balance of the merchandise inventory account must be increased with a debit entry. Income Summary should be credited. If the ending inventory is smaller than the beginning inventory, the balance of the merchandise inventory account must be decreased with a credit entry. Income Summary should be debited. The General Ledger input form shown in Figure 4.5 shows a sample entry for the merchandise inventory adjustment.

March 30, 19--
Record the adjusting entry for merchandise inventory. The balance in the Merchandise Inventory account is $120,855.30. An actual inventory shows an inventory value of $120,477.00.

First, the difference between the beginning merchandise inventory ($120,855.30) and the ending merchandise inventory ($120,477.00) must be determined ($378.30). The ending merchandise inventory is smaller than the beginning inventory. Therefore, the adjusting entry must have a credit to Merchandise Inventory to reduce the balance of the Merchandise Inventory account. The complete adjusting entry for merchandise inventory will have a $378.30 debit to Income Summary and a $378.30 credit to Merchandise Inventory. The entry is shown on lines 1 and 2 of the General Ledger input form in Figure 4.5.

EXPANDED
GENERAL
LEDGER
OPERATIONAL
PROCEDURES

Once the transactions have been recorded on the General Ledger input form, the data must be key-entered into the computer, and various reports may be displayed or printed in order to complete the accounting cycle for the fiscal period. Since most of the operational procedures for processing transactions through the General Ledger System have been covered in earlier chapters, this section will cover only those procedures that are unique to a merchandising business organized as a partnership. Some of the changes in the operating procedures must be made using an option from the System Selection Menu, and others must be made using an option from the General Ledger Main Menu. These changes are described in the following sections.

RUN DATE _03, 31, --_
MM DD YY

BATCH NO. [3]

GENERAL LEDGER
Input Form

Problem No. _Sample_

FORM GL-2

	DAY	DOC. NO.	ACCOUNT NUMBER	DEBIT AMOUNT	CREDIT AMOUNT	
1	30	ADJ ENTR	350	378 30		1
2			130		378 30	2
3						3
4						4
5						5
6						6
7						7
8						8
9						9
10						10
11						11
12						12
13						13
14						14
15						15
16						16
17						17
18						18
19						19
20						20
21						21
22						22
23						23
24						24
25						25
			BATCH TOTALS	378 30	378 30	

Figure 4.5   General Ledger Input Form Showing Adjusting Entries

Accounting System Setup (System Selection Menu) Option B

Option B of the System Selection Menu is *Accounting System Setup*. The first field on the Accounting System Setup data entry screen allows you to set the level of presentation for the General Ledger System. This field allows you to choose between the simplified and expanded versions of the General Ledger System. The expanded version is used for a merchandising business. When the expanded version is selected, merchandise inventory and purchases accounts will appear in the general ledger, and a cost of merchandise sold section will appear on the income statement. For a merchandising business, this field must be set to **E** as shown in Figure 4.6.

Company Information (System Selection Menu) Option D

Option D of the System Selection Menu is *Company Information*. The fourth field on this data entry screen allows you to set the type of business. You may set the type of business as a corporation, a sole proprietorship, or a partnership. For a partnership, the *Type of Business* field must be set to **P** as shown in Figure 4.7.

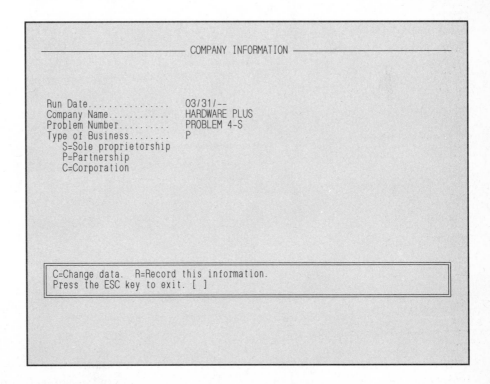

```
 ─────────────────────── ACCOUNTING SYSTEM SETUP ───────────────────────



    Simplified/Expanded General Ledger...... (S/E)   [E]
    Simplified/Expanded Accounts Payable.... (S/E)   [S]
    Simplified/Expanded Accounts Receivable. (S/E)   [S]
    Each report on a new page............... (Y/N)   [Y]
    Checks on preprinted forms.............. (Y/N)   [N]
    Statements on preprinted forms.......... (Y/N)   [N]




   ┌──────────────────────────────────────────────────────────────────┐
   │ Key-enter the data.  Move cursor with arrow keys to correct data.  Press │
   │ ENTER from last field to record.  Press ESC to ignore this entry and exit. │
   └──────────────────────────────────────────────────────────────────┘
```

Figure 4.6   Accounting System Setup Data Entry Screen for Expanded General Ledger

```
 ─────────────────────── COMPANY INFORMATION ───────────────────────



    Run Date................    03/31/--
    Company Name............    HARDWARE PLUS
    Problem Number..........    PROBLEM 4-S
    Type of Business........    P
        S=Sole proprietorship
        P=Partnership
        C=Corporation




   ┌──────────────────────────────────────────────────────────────────┐
   │ C=Change data.  R=Record this information.                         │
   │ Press the ESC key to exit. [ ]                                     │
   └──────────────────────────────────────────────────────────────────┘
```

Figure 4.7   Company Information Data Entry Screen for Partnership

Set Control Accounts (General Ledger Main Menu) Option C

Option C of the General Ledger Main Menu is *Set Control Accounts*. In order for the computer to complete such tasks as preparing the financial statements and performing the period-end closing, it must know the account numbers of certain key accounts. The Cash account number is needed in order to accumulate totals for cash receipts and cash payments. To prepare the cost of merchandise sold section of the income statement in the expanded version, the Merchandise Inventory account number must be entered on this screen. To complete the period-end closing process, the computer must also be supplied with the Income Summary account number. In addition, if the type of business was set for a partnership on the Company Information data entry screen, there is some additional account information that must be supplied in the *Set Control Accounts* option. In order to close the drawing accounts to the respective partner's capital accounts and distribute the net income or loss, the computer must know the account numbers assigned to each partner's capital and drawing accounts. For a partnership, the computer distributes the net income or loss to the respective partner's capital accounts, based on a percentage. This percentage must also be key-entered. The completed Set Control Accounts data entry screen for a merchandising business organized as a partnership with an equal distribution of net income or loss is shown in Figure 4.8.

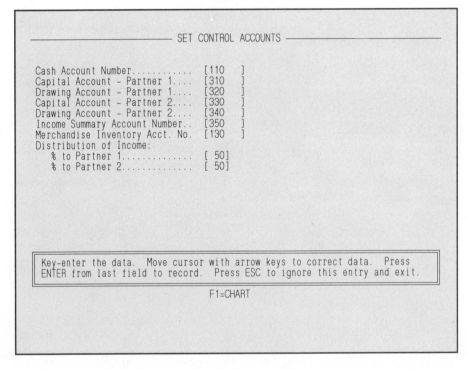

Figure 4.8   Set Control Accounts Data Entry Screen for Equal Distribution of Income

Income Statement for a Merchandising Business

The income statement for a merchandising business includes a cost of merchandise sold section. The **cost of merchandise sold** is the total original cost to the company of all merchandise sold during the fiscal period. The cost of merchandise sold is subtracted from net revenue to obtain gross profit on operations. An income statement for a merchandising business is shown in Figure 4.9.

```
                            HARDWARE PLUS
                           INCOME STATEMENT
                       FOR PERIOD ENDED 03/31/--
                                                              % OF NET
  R E V E N U E                                               REVENUE
  -------------
  Sales                            19820.78                     100.00
                                 ---------------
  NET REVENUE                                      19820.78     100.00

  C O S T   O F   M D S E.   S O L D
  ------------------------------------------
  BEGINNING INVENTORY             120855.30                     609.74
  Purchases                        11313.20                      57.08
                                 ---------------
  MDSE. AVAILABLE FOR SALE        132168.50                     666.82
  LESS ENDING INVENTORY           120477.00                     607.83
                                 ---------------
  COST OF MDSE. SOLD                               11691.50      58.99
                                                 ---------------
  GROSS PROFIT ON OPERATIONS                        8129.28      41.01

  E X P E N S E S
  ----------------
  Insurance Expense                   52.50                        .26
  Legal & Prof. Fees Ex.             220.00                       1.11
  Rent Expense                      1275.00                       6.43
  Salary Expense                    3360.00                      16.95
  Supplies Expense                    97.52                        .49
                                 ---------------
  TOTAL EXPENSES                                    5005.02      25.25
                                                 ---------------
  NET INCOME                                        3124.26      15.76
                                                 ===============
```

Figure 4.9   Income Statement for a Merchandising Business

Notice that in the cost of merchandise sold section, the purchases for the period are added to the beginning merchandise inventory. This sum represents the merchandise available for sale. The ending merchandise inventory value is subtracted from the merchandise available for sale to get the cost of merchandise sold.

GENERAL LEDGER ACCOUNTING CYCLE FOR A MERCHANDISING BUSINESS (SAMPLE PROBLEM)

The sample problem which follows takes you through the accounting cycle for a merchandising business. The chart of accounts, control accounts, and opening balances for Hardware Plus as discussed earlier in this chapter will be the basis of this sample problem. The data for Hardware Plus has been stored as an opening balance file on the program disk under the file name **AA4-S** (Automated Accounting Problem 4-S). You will be completing the accounting cycle for the fiscal period ending March 31 of the current year.

Instructions

Step   1   The following transactions for Hardware Plus occurred during March of the current year. The transactions have been analyzed and recorded as Batch No. 2 on the General Ledger input forms. The completed forms are shown in Figures 4.10a and 4.10b. Compare these transactions with the completed input forms. (Document numbers have been abbreviated as **C** for check, **M** for memorandum, **P** for purchase invoice, **R** for receipt, **S** for sales invoice, and **T** for cash register tape.)

	RUN DATE 03/31/-- MM DD YY		GENERAL LEDGER Input Form		Problem No. 4-S FORM GL-2	
	BATCH NO. 2					
	1	2	3	4	5	
	DAY	DOC. NO.	ACCOUNT NUMBER	DEBIT AMOUNT	CREDIT AMOUNT	
1	01	C790	140	422 23		1
2			110		422 23	2
3	02	S110	120	5512 00		3
4			220		312 00	4
5			410		5200 00	5
6	02	C791	220	882 00		6
7			110		882 00	7
8	03	C792	650	3360 00		8
9			110		3360 00	9
10	06	P210	510	4305 00		10
11			210		4305 00	11
12	08	C793	320	950 00		12
13			110		950 00	13
14	09	C794	210	6457 50		14
15			110		6457 50	15
16	10	P211	510	5830 65		16
17			210		5830 65	17
18	13	S111	120	2438 00		18
19			220		138 00	19
20			410		2300 00	20
21	14	R80	110	18171 30		21
22			120		18171 30	22
23	15	T22	110	3583 10		23
24			220		202 82	24
25			410		3380 28	25
			BATCH TOTALS			

Figure 4.10a   Completed General Ledger Input Form Page 1 (Problem 4-S)

March 01   Paid cash for supplies, $422.23 (C790).
   02   Sold merchandise on account, $5,200.00, plus sales tax, $312.00. Total $5,512.00 (S110).
   02   Paid sales tax to the State Department of Revenue, $882.00 (C791).
   03   Paid salaries, $3,360.00 (C792).
   06   Purchased merchandise on account, $4,305.00 (P210).
   08   Dennis Siegel, partner, withdrew cash, $950.00 (C793).
   09   Paid cash on account, $6,457.50 (C794).

RUN DATE 03/31/--
MM DD YY

GENERAL LEDGER
Input Form

Problem No. 4-S

FORM GL-2

BATCH NO. 2

	DAY	DOC. NO.	ACCOUNT NUMBER	DEBIT AMOUNT	CREDIT AMOUNT	
1	16	C795	510	1250 00		1
2			110		1250 00	2
3	19	M51	340	72 45		3
4			510		72 45	4
5	19	C796	210	5830 65		5
6			110		5830 65	6
7	20	S112	120	4823 00		7
8			220		273 00	8
9			410		4550 00	9
10	21	C797	140	32 00		10
11			110		32 00	11
12	23	C798	340	950 00		12
13			110		950 00	13
14	26	T23	110	4653 93		14
15			220		263 43	15
16			410		4390 50	16
17	28	C799	620	220 00		17
18			110		220 00	18
19	29	C800	640	1275 00		19
20			110		1275 00	20
21						21
22						22
23						23
24						24
25						25
			BATCH TOTALS	71018 81	71018 81	

Figure 4.10b   Completed General Ledger Input Form Page 2 (Problem 4-S)

10   Purchased merchandise on account, $5,830.65 (P211).

13   Sold merchandise on account, $2,300.00, plus sales tax, $138.00. Total, $2,438.00 (S111).

14   Received cash on account, $18,171.30 (R80).

15   Cash sales for the first two weeks, $3,380.28, plus sales tax, $202.82. Total, $3,583.10 (T22).

16   Purchased merchandise for cash, $1,250.00 (C795).

19   Ruth Hines, partner, withdrew merchandise, $72.45 (M51).

19   Paid cash on account, $5,830.65 (C796).

20   Sold merchandise on account, $4,550.00, plus sales tax, $273.00. Total, $4,823.00 (S112).

21   Paid cash for supplies, $32.00 (C797).

23   Ruth Hines, partner, withdrew cash, $950.00 (C798).

26   Cash sales, $4,390.50, plus sales tax, $263.43. Total, $4,653.93 (T23).

28   Paid cash for legal services, $220.00 (C799).

29   Paid cash for rent, $1,275.00 (C800).

Step 2   Bring up the System Selection Menu according to the instructions for your microcomputer.

Step 3   Select Option C, *Load Data from Disk*. When the Load Data from Disk menu appears, select Option A, *Load Opening Balances from the Program Disk*.

Step 4   When the directory of Opening Balances contained on the program disk appears, select Problem 4-S by key-entering the file name: **AA4-S**.

Step 5   Select Option D, *Company Information*, from the System Selection Menu and change the run date to: **03/31/--**. (Use the current year.)

Notice that the company name, problem number, and type of business are automatically set during the problem selection processing. Leave these three fields as they appear.

Step 6   Select Option F, *General Ledger*, from the System Selection Menu.

Step 7   After the General Ledger program has loaded into the computer's memory, select Option K, *Trial Balance*, from the General Ledger Main Menu. Compare the beginning trial balance to the one shown in Figure 4.11 to verify that the correct problem was selected. If the two reports are not the same, press Esc to return to the System Selection Menu, and repeat Steps 3-6. If they are the same, press the Space Bar to continue.

```
RUN DATE: 03/31/--              HARDWARE PLUS
                               TRIAL BALANCE

--------------------------------------------------------------------
ACCOUNT      ACCOUNT
NUMBER       TITLE                 DEBIT AMOUNT      CREDIT AMOUNT
--------------------------------------------------------------------
110          Cash                      2205.00
120          Accounts Receivable      12495.00
130          Merchandise Inventory   120855.30
140          Supplies                   368.00
150          Prepaid Insurance          472.50
210          Accounts Payable                            6457.50
220          Sales Tax Payable                            882.00
310          Dennis Siegel, Capital                      64528.15
330          Ruth Hines, Capital                         64528.15
                                   ---------------   ---------------
             TOTALS                   136395.80         136395.80
                                   ===============   ===============
```

Figure 4.11   Beginning Trial Balance (Problem 4-S)

Step 8   Select Option H, *Set Run Date and Batch Number*, from the General
             Ledger Main Menu. Verify that the run date has been set to **March 31**
             of the current year and the batch number has been set to **2**. If so,
             record the data. If not, make the appropriate changes.

Step 9   Select Option I, *Enter/Correct Journal Entries*, from the General
             Ledger Main Menu. Key-enter and post the data from the two com-
             pleted General Ledger input forms in Figures 4.10a and 4.10b.

Step 10   Select Option J, *Journal Entries Report*, from the General Ledger
             Main Menu. Display or print a Journal Entries report. If the Journal
             Entries report is in balance and you are sure it is correct, proceed to
             Step 11. If the Journal Entries report is in error, make corrections.
             Display or print another Journal Entries report. Repeat this step until
             your journal entries are correct. The correct Journal Entries report for
             the March transactions is shown in Figure 4.12.

```
RUN DATE: 03/31/--                  HARDWARE PLUS
                                 JOURNAL ENTRIES BATCH #2

------------------------------------------------------------------------
JE#   DATE       ACCOUNT NUMBER & TITLE         DEBIT AMOUNT  CREDIT AMOUNT
------------------------------------------------------------------------
0001  03/01/-- 140   Supplies                      422.23
               110      Cash                                      422.23
                     DOCUMENT: C790

0002  03/02/-- 120   Accounts Receivable          5512.00
               220      Sales Tax Payable                         312.00
               410      Sales                                    5200.00
                     DOCUMENT: S110

0003  03/02/-- 220   Sales Tax Payable             882.00
               110      Cash                                      882.00
                     DOCUMENT: C791

0004  03/03/-- 650   Salary Expense               3360.00
               110      Cash                                     3360.00
                     DOCUMENT: C792

0005  03/06/-- 510   Purchases                    4305.00
               210      Accounts Payable                         4305.00
                     DOCUMENT: P210

0006  03/08/-- 320   Dennis Siegel, Drawing        950.00
               110      Cash                                      950.00
                     DOCUMENT: C793

0007  03/09/-- 210   Accounts Payable             6457.50
               110      Cash                                     6457.50
                     DOCUMENT: C794

0008  03/10/-- 510   Purchases                    5830.65
               210      Accounts Payable                         5830.65
                     DOCUMENT: P211

0009  03/13/-- 120   Accounts Receivable          2438.00
               220      Sales Tax Payable                         138.00
               410      Sales                                    2300.00
                     DOCUMENT: S111

0010  03/14/-- 110   Cash                        18171.30
               120      Accounts Receivable                    18171.30
                     DOCUMENT: R80

0011  03/15/-- 110   Cash                         3583.10
               220      Sales Tax Payable                         202.82
               410      Sales                                    3380.28
                     DOCUMENT: T22

0012  03/16/-- 510   Purchases                    1250.00
               110      Cash                                     1250.00
                     DOCUMENT: C795
```

Figure 4.12a   Journal Entries Report for March Transactions, Page 1(Problem 4-S)

```
  RUN DATE: 03/31/--                    HARDWARE PLUS
                                  JOURNAL ENTRIES BATCH #2

  -----------------------------------------------------------------------------
  JE#   DATE      ACCOUNT NUMBER & TITLE          DEBIT AMOUNT  CREDIT AMOUNT
  -----------------------------------------------------------------------------
  0013  03/19/--  340   Ruth Hines, Drawing           72.45
                  510       Purchases                                  72.45
                        DOCUMENT: M51

  0014  03/19/--  210   Accounts Payable            5830.65
                  110       Cash                                     5830.65
                        DOCUMENT: C796

  0015  03/20/--  120   Accounts Receivable         4823.00
                  220       Sales Tax Payable                         273.00
                  410       Sales                                    4550.00
                        DOCUMENT: S112

  0016  03/21/--  140   Supplies                      32.00
                  110       Cash                                       32.00
                        DOCUMENT: C797

  0017  03/23/--  340   Ruth Hines, Drawing          950.00
                  110       Cash                                      950.00
                        DOCUMENT: C798

  0018  03/26/--  110   Cash                        4653.93
                  220       Sales Tax Payable                         263.43
                  410       Sales                                    4390.50
                        DOCUMENT: T23

  0019  03/28/--  620   Legal & Prof. Fees Ex.       220.00
                  110       Cash                                      220.00
                        DOCUMENT: C799

  0020  03/30/--  640   Rent Expense                1275.00
                  110       Cash                                     1275.00
                        DOCUMENT: C800

                                                  -------------- --------------
                        TOTALS                         71018.81      71018.81
                                                  ============== ==============
                        IN BALANCE

  Cash Receipts       26408.33
  Cash Payments       21629.38
```

Figure 4.12b   Journal Entries Report for March Transactions, Page 2
(Problem 4-S)

Step 11   Select Option K, *Trial Balance*, and print or display a trial balance.
Compare your trial balance with the correct one which appears in Figure 4.13.

Step 12   To prove cash, select Option L, *General Ledger Report*, and strike **D** to
display the report. When prompted to do so, choose Option S (*Specific Account*) and key-enter the account number for Cash. Verify that the
ending cash balance is equal to the checkbook balance of $6,983.95.

Step 13   The information needed to complete the adjusting entries for March for
Hardware Plus is listed below. The completed General Ledger input
form for the adjusting entries is shown in Figure 4.14 (page 116).
Examine these adjusting entries to make sure you understand them.

Adjustment Information, March 31
Ending Merchandise Inventory $120,477.00
Supplies Inventory $724.71
Value of Insurance Policies $420.00

Step 14   Select Option H, *Set Run Date and Batch Number*. Set and record the
batch number to **3**.

```
  RUN DATE: 03/31/--                 HARDWARE PLUS
                                     TRIAL BALANCE
  ------------------------------------------------------------------------
  ACCOUNT       ACCOUNT
  NUMBER        TITLE                    DEBIT AMOUNT      CREDIT AMOUNT
  ------------------------------------------------------------------------
  110           Cash                         6983.95
  120           Accounts Receivable          7096.70
  130           Merchandise Inventory      120855.30
  140           Supplies                      822.23
  150           Prepaid Insurance             472.50
  210           Accounts Payable                               4305.00
  220           Sales Tax Payable                              1189.25
  310           Dennis Siegel, Capital                        64528.15
  320           Dennis Siegel, Drawing        950.00
  330           Ruth Hines, Capital                           64528.15
  340           Ruth Hines, Drawing          1022.45
  410           Sales                                         19820.78
  510           Purchases                   11313.20
  620           Legal & Prof. Fees Ex.        220.00
  640           Rent Expense                 1275.00
  650           Salary Expense               3360.00
                                         ------------        ------------
                TOTALS                     154371.33          154371.33
                                         ============        ============
```

Figure 4.13   Trial Balance after March Transactions (Problem 4-S)

Step 15   Select Option I, *Enter/Correct Journal Entries*. Key-enter and post the adjusting entries from the completed General Ledger input form shown in Figure 4.14.

Step 16   Select Option J, *Journal Entries Report*, and print or display the journal entries for the adjustments. The correct Journal Entries report for the March adjusting entries is shown in Figure 4.15 (page 117). If the Journal Entries report for the adjusting entries is in balance and you are sure everything is correct, proceed to Step 18.

Step 17   If the Journal Entries report is in error, make the corrections and print or display another Journal Entries report. Repeat this step until your adjusting entries are correct.

Step 18   Select Option K, *Trial Balance*, and print or display a trial balance. Compare your trial balance with the correct one which appears in Figure 4.16 (page 117).

Step 19   Select Option M, *Income Statement*, from the General Ledger Main Menu, and print or display an income statement. Compare your income statement with the one shown in Figure 4.17 (page 118). If there are differences, determine your mistake and make the necessary correction(s) to Journal Entries. Repeat this step until a correct income statement is printed or displayed. It is much more difficult to make corrections after performing the period-end closing.

Step 20   Select Option N, *Balance Sheet*, and print or display a balance sheet. Compare your balance sheet with the one shown in Figure 4.18 (page 118). If there are differences, determine your mistake and make the necessary correction(s) to Journal Entries. Repeat this step until a cor-

				RUN DATE 03/31/--				GENERAL LEDGER					Problem No. 4-S	

RUN DATE 03 / 31 / --
    MM DD YY

BATCH NO. | 3 |

GENERAL LEDGER
Input Form

Problem No. 4-S

| FORM GL-2 |

	DAY	DOC. NO.	ACCOUNT NUMBER	DEBIT AMOUNT	CREDIT AMOUNT	
1	31	ADJ ENTR	350	378 30		1
2			130		378 30	2
3	31	ADJ ENTR	660	97 52		3
4			140		97 52	4
5	31	ADJ ENTR	610	52 50		5
6			150		52 50	6
7						7
8						8
9						9
10						10
11						11
12						12
13						13
14						14
15						15
16						16
17						17
18						18
19						19
20						20
21						21
22						22
23						23
24						24
25						25
			BATCH TOTALS	528 32	528 32	

Figure 4.14   Completed General Ledger Input Form for March Adjusting Entries
(Problem 4-S)

rect balance sheet is printed or displayed. It is much more difficult to make corrections after performing the period-end closing.

Step 21   Select Option O, *Period-End Closing*, and instruct the computer to perform period-end processing.

Step 22   Select Option P, *Post-Closing Trial Balance*, and print or display a post-closing trial balance. If your work has been done accurately, your post-closing trial balance should match the one shown in Figure 4.19 (page 119). If not, locate your errors and make corrections. All corrections that need to be made now must be made by using the Enter feature of the *Enter/Correct Journal Entries* option.

Step 23   Press Esc to return to the System Selection Menu.

Step 24   Once back in the System Selection Menu, select Option E, *Save Data to Disk*, and save your data as a work in progress file.

Step 25   Press Esc to end your session. Then complete the student exercise and transaction problem which follow.

```
RUN DATE: 03/31/--              HARDWARE PLUS
                             JOURNAL ENTRIES BATCH #3


JE#   DATE    ACCOUNT NUMBER & TITLE          DEBIT AMOUNT  CREDIT AMOUNT

0021  03/31/-- 350    Income Summary              378.30
               130      Merchandise Inventory                   378.30
                     DOCUMENT: ADJ ENTR

0022  03/31/-- 660    Supplies Expense            97.52
               140      Supplies                                 97.52
                     DOCUMENT: ADJ ENTR

0023  03/31/-- 610    Insurance Expense           52.50
               150      Prepaid Insurance                        52.50
                     DOCUMENT: ADJ ENTR


              TOTALS                              528.32         528.32

              IN BALANCE
```

Figure 4.15   Journal Entries Report for March Adjusting Entries (Problem 4-S)

```
RUN DATE: 03/31/--              HARDWARE PLUS
                                TRIAL BALANCE


ACCOUNT   ACCOUNT
NUMBER    TITLE                      DEBIT AMOUNT    CREDIT AMOUNT

110       Cash                         6983.95
120       Accounts Receivable          7096.70
130       Merchandise Inventory      120477.00
140       Supplies                      724.71
150       Prepaid Insurance             420.00
210       Accounts Payable                             4305.00
220       Sales Tax Payable                            1189.25
310       Dennis Siegel, Capital                      64528.15
320       Dennis Siegel, Drawing        950.00
330       Ruth Hines, Capital                         64528.15
340       Ruth Hines, Drawing          1022.45
350       Income Summary                378.30
410       Sales                                       19820.78
510       Purchases                   11313.20
610       Insurance Expense              52.50
620       Legal & Prof. Fees Ex.        220.00
640       Rent Expense                 1275.00
650       Salary Expense               3360.00
660       Supplies Expense               97.52

          TOTALS                      154371.33      154371.33
```

Figure 4.16   Trial Balance after Adjusting Entries (Problem 4-S)

```
                        HARDWARE PLUS
                       INCOME STATEMENT
                    FOR PERIOD ENDED 03/31/--
                                                        % OF NET
                                                        REVENUE
   R E V E N U E
   -------------                                        --------
   Sales                        19820.78                  100.00
                              --------------
   NET REVENUE                               19820.78     100.00

   C O S T   O F   M D S E .   S O L D
   -------------------------------------
   BEGINNING INVENTORY         120855.30                  609.74
   Purchases                    11313.20                   57.08
                              --------------
   MDSE. AVAILABLE FOR SALE    132168.50                  666.82
   LESS ENDING INVENTORY       120477.00                  607.83
                              --------------
   COST OF MDSE. SOLD                        11691.50      58.99
                                           ------------
   GROSS PROFIT ON OPERATIONS                8129.28       41.01

   E X P E N S E S
   ---------------
   Insurance Expense              52.50                      .26
   Legal & Prof. Fees Ex.        220.00                     1.11
   Rent Expense                 1275.00                     6.43
   Salary Expense               3360.00                    16.95
   Supplies Expense               97.52                      .49
                              --------------
   TOTAL EXPENSES                            5005.02       25.25
                                           ------------
   NET INCOME                                3124.26       15.76
                                           ============
```

Figure 4.17   March Income Statement (Problem 4-S)

```
                        HARDWARE PLUS
                        BALANCE SHEET
                          03/31/--

   A S S E T S
   -----------
   Cash                          6983.95
   Accounts Receivable           7096.70
   Merchandise Inventory       120477.00
   Supplies                       724.71
   Prepaid Insurance              420.00
                              --------------
   TOTAL ASSETS                             135702.36
                                           ============
   L I A B I L I T I E S
   ---------------------
   Accounts Payable              4305.00
   Sales Tax Payable             1189.25
                              --------------
   TOTAL LIABILITIES                         5494.25

   O W N E R S '   E Q U I T Y
   ---------------------------
   Dennis Siegel, Capital       64528.15
   Dennis Siegel, Drawing        -950.00
   SHARE OF NET INCOME @ 50%     1562.13
   Ruth Hines, Capital          64528.15
   Ruth Hines, Drawing          -1022.45
   SHARE OF NET INCOME @ 50%     1562.13
                              --------------
   TOTAL CAPITAL                            130208.11
                                           --------------
   TOTAL LIABILITIES & CAPITAL              135702.36
                                           ============
```

Figure 4.18   March 31 Balance Sheet (Problem 4-S)

```
RUN DATE: 03/31/--                    HARDWARE PLUS
                                POST-CLOSING TRIAL BALANCE

----------------------------------------------------------------------------
ACCOUNT    ACCOUNT
NUMBER     TITLE                        DEBIT AMOUNT      CREDIT AMOUNT
----------------------------------------------------------------------------
110        Cash                            6983.95
120        Accounts Receivable             7096.70
130        Merchandise Inventory         120477.00
140        Supplies                         724.71
150        Prepaid Insurance                420.00
210        Accounts Payable                                  4305.00
220        Sales Tax Payable                                 1189.25
310        Dennis Siegel, Capital                           65140.28
330        Ruth Hines, Capital                              65067.83
                                         ---------------   ---------------
           TOTALS                         135702.36         135702.36
                                         ===============   ===============
```

Figure 4.19   Post-Closing Trial Balance (Problem 4-S)

Name _____

Class _____ Date _____

CHAPTER 4
STUDENT EXERCISE

I. Matching   a. Merchandise Inventory   d. Purchases account
             account   e. Cost of merchandise accounts
            b. Merchandising business   f. Beginning inventory
            c. Cost of merchandise sold

1. _____ The value of the merchandise inventory at the beginning of the fiscal period. (Obj. 5)

2. _____ The total original cost to the company of all merchandise sold during the fiscal period. (Obj. 5)

3. _____ The asset account that shows the value of the merchandise on hand. (Obj. 3)

4. _____ A type of business that purchases and resells goods. (Obj. 1)

5. _____ Those accounts that show the cost or price of merchandise which is purchased for resale. (Obj. 1)

6. _____ The account in which the cost of the merchandise purchased for resale is recorded. (Obj. 2)

II. Short Answer   1. List the account classifications and the first digit of each classification used for a merchandising business. (Obj. 1)

_____

_____

_____

_____

_____

_____

2. Which account is debited and which account is credited to record a purchase of merchandise on account? (Obj. 2)

Account debited: _____

Account credited: _____

3. The General Ledger System has simplified and expanded options. Which option must be set to *Expanded* for a merchandising business? (Obj. 1)

_____

4. Which data entry screen is used to set the type of business organiza-
   tion to a partnership? (Obj. 1)

   _____

   _____

5. One of the fields on the Set Control Accounts data entry screen is
   the account number for the Merchandise Inventory account. Why is
   this account number needed by the computer? (Obj. 1)

   _____

   _____

6. List the steps involved in completing the accounting cycle for a merchandising business. (Obj. 4)

   _____

   _____

   _____

   _____

   _____

   _____

   _____

   _____

GENERAL LEDGER ACCOUNTING CYCLE (MERCHANDISING BUSINESS) TRANSACTION PROBLEM 4-1

Problem 4-1 is a continuation of Problem 4-S, the sample problem for Chapter 4. Therefore, if you completed the sample problem, it will not be necessary to load the opening balances from the program disk. Instead, you may load your completed Problem 4-S work in progress file from your own data disk. If you did not complete the sample problem, you must load the opening balances for file **AA4-1** (Automated Accounting Problem 4-1) from the program disk. (Objs. 1-5)

Instructions

Step 1   Remove the blank input forms and the Chapter 4 Audit Test at the end of this chapter. Fill in the answers to the audit test as you work through the following steps.

Step 2   Record the following transactions on the proper input forms. (Document numbers have been abbreviated as **C** for check, **M** for memorandum, **P** for purchase invoice, **R** for receipt, **S** for sales invoice, and **T** for cash register tape.)

April 01   Received cash on account, $4,550.00 (R81).
    02   Sold merchandise on account, $5,380.00, plus sales tax, $322.80. Total, $5,702.80 (S113).
    03   Paid salaries, $3,675.00 (C801).
    04   Paid sales tax to the State Department of Revenue, $1,189.25 (C802).
    05   Purchased merchandise on account, $6,430.04 (P212).
    08   Paid cash on account, $4,525.00 (C803).
    09   Dennis Siegel, partner, withdrew cash, $1,150.00 (C804).
    10   Purchased merchandise on account, $8,530.30 (P213).
    12   Sold merchandise on account, $3,280.40, no sales tax (S114).
    15   Cash sales for the first two weeks, $4,313.61, plus sales tax, $258.82. Total, $4,572.43 (T24).
    16   Received cash on account, $5,702.80 (R82).
    17   Purchased merchandise on account, $2,296.25 (P214).
    19   Ruth Hines, partner, withdrew cash, $1,250.00 (C805).
    22   Paid cash for supplies, $87.05 (C806).
    23   Paid cash on account, $8,530.30 (C807).
    24   Received cash on account, $3,280.40 (R83).
    26   Paid cash for rent, $1,275.00 (C808).
    29   Sold merchandise on account, $5,457.00, plus sales tax, $327.42. Total, $5784.42 (S115).
    30   Purchased merchandise for cash, $211.16 (C809).
    30   Paid cash for legal services, $190.00 (C810).
    30   Cash sales for the last two weeks, $4570.20, plus sales tax, $274.21. Total, $4844.41 (T25).

Step 3   Bring up the System Selection Menu.

Step   4   Select Option C, *Load Data from Disk*. If you did not complete Problem 4-S, load file **AA4-1** from the *Load Opening Balances from the Program Disk* option. If you did complete Problem 4-S and saved it as a work in progress file, load it from your own data disk.

Step   5   From the System Selection Menu, select Option D, *Company Information*. Set the run date to **April 30** of the current year and make sure the problem number is recorded as **Problem 4-1**.

Step   6   From the System Selection Menu, select the *General Ledger System*.

Step   7   Set the batch number to 4.

Step   8   Key-enter as Batch No. 4 the journal entries prepared in Step 2.

Step   9   Print or display a Journal Entries report.

Step 10   Make corrections if necessary.

Step 11   Print or display a trial balance.

Step 12   Prove cash. The checkbook balance is $7,851.23.

Step 13   Using the data shown below, record the adjusting entries on the General Ledger input form as Batch No. 5.

Adjustment Information, April 30

Ending Merchandise Inventory $127,260.00
Supplies Inventory.. $546.00
Value of Insurance Policies.................................. $367.50

Step 14   Set the batch number to **5**.

Step 15   Key-enter the adjusting entries prepared in Step 13.

Step 16   Print or display a Journal Entries report. Make corrections if necessary. Repeat this step until a correct Journal Entries report is obtained.

Step 17   Print or display a trial balance. Make any necessary corrections before proceeding. Corrections are much more difficult to make after the period-end closing has been performed.

Step 18   Print or display an income statement.

Step 19   Print or display a balance sheet.

Step 20   Be certain that all questions have been answered on the Chapter 4 Audit Test sheet before closing the ledger in the following step.

Step 21   Perform the period-end closing.

Step 22   Print or display a post-closing trial balance.

Step 23   Return to the System Selection Menu. Save your data to a work in progress file, and perform system shutdown.

Step 24   Hand in the completed student exercise sheets, input forms, the audit test, and any printouts to your instructor.

You have now completed the computer exercise for Chapter 4.

Name _____

Class _____ Date _____

RUN DATE __ / __ / __		GENERAL LEDGER	Problem No. _____	
MM DD YY		Input Form	FORM GL-2	
BATCH NO. [ ]				

	1	2	3	4	5	
	DAY	DOC. NO.	ACCOUNT NUMBER	DEBIT AMOUNT	CREDIT AMOUNT	
1						1
2						2
3						3
4						4
5						5
6						6
7						7
8						8
9						9
10						10
11						11
12						12
13						13
14						14
15						15
16						16
17						17
18						18
19						19
20						20
21						21
22						22
23						23
24						24
25						25

BATCH TOTALS

RUN DATE ___/___/___
MM DD YY

BATCH NO. [   ]

Problem No. _____

GENERAL LEDGER
Input Form

FORM GL-2

	1	2	3	4	5	
	DAY	DOC. NO.	ACCOUNT NUMBER	DEBIT AMOUNT	CREDIT AMOUNT	
1						1
2						2
3						3
4						4
5						5
6						6
7						7
8						8
9						9
10						10
11						11
12						12
13						13
14						14
15						15
16						16
17						17
18						18
19						19
20						20
21						21
22						22
23						23
24						24
25						25

BATCH TOTALS [   ]

Name _____

Class _____ Date _____

RUN DATE __/__/__ MM DD YY	GENERAL LEDGER Input Form	Problem No. _____ FORM GL-2
BATCH NO. [____]		

	DAY	DOC. NO.	ACCOUNT NUMBER	DEBIT AMOUNT	CREDIT AMOUNT	
	1	2	3	4	5	
1						1
2						2
3						3
4						4
5						5
6						6
7						7
8						8
9						9
10						10
11						11
12						12
13						13
14						14
15						15
16						16
17						17
18						18
19						19
20						20
21						21
22						22
23						23
24						24
25						25

BATCH TOTALS [_____] [_____]

CHAPTER 4
AUDIT TEST

1. What is the run date printed on the Journal Entries report for the monthly transactions?

   _____

2. What is the batch number printed on the Journal Entries report for the monthly transactions?

   _____

3. What were the total cash receipts for April?

   _____

4. What were the total cash payments for April?

   _____

5. The totals of the *Debit* and *Credit* columns for each batch of transactions should be equal. What are the totals for Batch No. 4 (monthly transactions)?

   _____

6. What is the amount of the adjustment to Merchandise Inventory?

   _____

7. What is the amount of the adjustment to Supplies?

   _____

8. What is the amount of the adjustment to Prepaid Insurance?

   _____

9. What are the debit and credit totals for the adjusting entries?

   _____

10. What are the totals of the *Debit* and *Credit* columns on the Trial Balance report after the adjusting entries have been entered and posted?

    _____

11. How many journal entries were posted to the cash account during the month?

    _____

Name _____

Class _____ Date _____

12. How many times during the month did the company purchase merchandise?

_____

13. What are the total sales for the fiscal period?

_____

14. What were the total purchases for the fiscal period?

_____

15. What was the cost of merchandise sold for the fiscal period?

_____

16. What was the gross profit on operations for the fiscal period?

_____

17. What were the total expenses for the fiscal period?

_____

18. What was the net income for the fiscal period?

_____

19. What are the total assets at the end of the fiscal period?

_____

20. What are the total liabilities at the end of the fiscal period?

_____

21. What is the total capital at the end of the fiscal period?

_____

22. What is the balance in the Cash account at the end of the fiscal period after the ledger has been closed?

_____

23. What is the balance in the Merchandise Inventory account at the end of the fiscal period after the ledger has been closed?

_____

24. What is the total of the debit balances in the ledger after the ledger has been closed?

_____

25. How many capital accounts had balances after all work was completed at the end of the fiscal period?

_____

Part 2

ACCOUNTS PAYABLE

5 ACCOUNTS PAYABLE SETUP

Upon completion of this chapter, you will be able to:

1. Describe the differences between manual and computerized accounts payable methods.
2. Enter vendor data.
3. Display or print a vendor list.
4. Set control account.
5. Set the beginning check number.
6. Enter/correct opening balances.
7. Display or print opening balances.
8. Save data to disk.
9. Perform system shutdown.
10. Identify the components of and procedures for accounts payable setup.

INTRODUCTION

In a manual accounting system, purchases of merchandise are recorded in a purchases journal and posted from the purchases journal to individual creditor or vendor accounts in the accounts payable subsidiary ledger. Periodically, column totals are posted from the purchases journal to the accounts payable account in the general ledger. When checks are written, they are recorded in the cash payments journal and posted to individual creditor or vendor accounts in the accounts payable subsidiary ledger. Entries are also posted from the cash payments journal to the appropriate accounts in the general ledger. Periodically, totals are posted from the cash payments journal to the general ledger accounts. At the end of the month, a schedule of accounts payable is prepared from the accounts payable subsidiary ledger. The total of the schedule of accounts payable must equal the balance of the accounts payable account in the general ledger.

Computerized accounts payable systems are designed to keep track of everything purchased from vendors automatically. The computerized Accounts Payable System produces reports that tell management when payment is due, to whom payment is owed, and the cash requirements for paying all invoices due. The system also writes checks to the vendors and updates the appropriate general ledger and subsidiary ledger accounts.

The computer stores two different types of information in an accounts payable data file: (1) the vendor data and (2) the accounts payable ledger data. Recall that the **accounts payable data file** (similar to the general ledger data file) contains all the data required by the computer to process accounts payable transactions. This data file is a part of the entire automated accounting database.

The **vendor data** consists of a record for each vendor with whom the company does business. Each of these records typically contains fields for the vendor number, name, and mailing address. In order to limit the amount of keying necessary, the vendor data used in this system is limited to fields for vendor number and name. The **accounts payable ledger data** consists of a record for each item for which a check is to be printed. Each of these records contains fields for the purchase invoice number, vendor number, date purchased, general ledger account number, invoice amount, cash payment date, disposition code, and manual check number. The contents of these records are similar to the contents of accounts payable subsidiary ledgers in a manual accounting system.

In order to set up the accounts payable data file, vendor and accounts payable opening balance ledger information must be recorded on the appropriate input forms. This data is then key-entered into the computer and stored in computer memory. After all key-entering is completed, the data may be saved to disk as a work in progress file for future reference and updating.

The accounts payable setup procedures are a set of steps which provide the computer with information that it requires before it can work with Accounts Payable as an ongoing system. The steps of the accounts payable setup procedure are: (1) setup the vendor data, (2) inform the computer of special account numbers it needs in order to update the appropriate accounts in the general ledger, (3) establish a beginning check number, and (4) enter opening vendor balances. Menu options for screen displays or printouts of the vendors and opening balances are provided to assist you in verifying the accuracy of your work. In addition, an option to make corrections to opening balances is available in case you make an error. Accounts payable setup activities are required only when establishing a new company. This setup procedure, as illustrated in Figure 5.1, will not be required again until another company is to be created.

Account numbers that require special handling by the computer, called **control accounts**, must be established, or set, during the accounts payable setup process. As accounts payable transactions are entered or corrected in the Accounts Payable System, the journal entries resulting from those transactions are automatically integrated into the General Ledger System by the computer. In order to integrate these entries, the computer must know the account numbers you have assigned to the general ledger accounts involved. You must provide the computer with the needed control account numbers by entering them using the *Set Control Account* option as part of the accounts payable setup procedures.

COMPLETING THE INPUT FORMS

The data required to perform accounts payable setup is recorded on two different forms. These forms are the Accounts Payable File Maintenance input form (Form AP-1) and the Accounts Payable input form (Form AP-2). In this chapter you will learn how each of these forms is used to record the data required to setup the accounts payable data file.

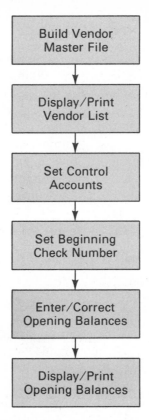

Figure 5.1   Accounts Payable Setup

Accounts Payable File Maintenance Input Form (Form AP-1)

The **Accounts Payable File Maintenance input form** serves two separate functions. First, it is used to record the vendors to be established during accounts payable setup. Second, it is used to record additions, changes, and deletions to the vendors after accounts payable setup has been completed and during the ongoing process of the accounting cycle. The second use of this form will be discussed further in Chapter 6.

The Accounts Payable File Maintenance input form shown in Figure 5.2 illustrates how the vendor numbers and corresponding vendor names are recorded to set up the vendor data for Hardware Plus.

The run date recorded in the upper left corner of the form, 05/01/--, is the month, day, and year the form was completed and key-entered into the computer. The ideal time to start an accounts payable system is the first day of a new fiscal period (start of an accounting cycle). The body of the form contains the vendor numbers and vendor names which are to be used to set up the vendor data.

Accounts Payable Input Form (Form AP-2)

The **Accounts Payable input form** also serves two separate functions. First, it is used to record opening balances which are to be key-entered into the computer during accounts payable setup. Second, it is used to record various accounts payable transactions, such as purchases on account and cash payments which occur during the ongoing process of the Accounts Payable System. The second use of this form will be discussed further in Chapter 6. After the vendor data has been set up, the control accounts have been set, and the beginning check number has been set, the opening balances must be established or set up for each

RUN DATE 05/01/--		ACCOUNTS PAYABLE FILE MAINTENANCE Input Form	Problem No. *Sample* FORM AP-1	
	1	**2**		
	VENDOR NUMBER	VENDOR NAME		
1	010	DataPro Paper Supply		1
2	020	Computer Distribution Co.		2
3	030	Metro Computer Store		3
4	040	Computer Executive Ltd.		4
5	050	A+K Advertising		5
6	060	Hightech Ribbon Co.		6
7	070	Inntouch Marketing		7
8	080	Modern Printing		8
9	090	Dakota County Power		9
10				10
11				11
12				12
13				13
14				14
15				15
16				16
17				17
18				18
19				19
20				20
21				21
22				22
23				23
24				24
25				25

Figure 5.2   Accounts Payable File Maintenance Input Form

vendor with a beginning balance. These opening balances are stored in the accounts payable data file.

An Accounts Payable input form should be completed and used as the source document from which the opening balances are keyed. The Accounts Payable input form shown in Figure 5.3 illustrates how to record the opening balances for Hardware Plus.

The run date (05/01/--), located in the upper left corner of the form, is usually the first day of the fiscal period, or the start of an accounting cycle. The batch number specifically reserved for all the opening balances, Batch No. 1, is located beneath the run date in the upper left corner of the form. The computer will automatically assign this batch number to the opening balances as they are key-entered into the computer. By using Batch No. 1 to identify all the opening balances, it will later be possible to distinguish opening balance entries from other key-entered transactions.

RUN DATE 05 01 11-- (MM DD YY)   BATCH NO. 1

ACCOUNTS PAYABLE
Input Form

Problem No. Sample   FORM AP-2

| | 1 PURCH. INVOICE NO. | PURCHASES | | | | CASH PAYMENTS | | | |
		2 VEND. NO.	3 DATE (MO. DAY YR.)	4 GEN. LEDGER ACCT. NO.	5 INVOICE AMOUNT	6 DATE (MO. DAY YR.)	7 DISP. CODE	8 MANUAL CHECK NO.	
1	352	010	04 05 --	510	1812 83		A		1
2	353	020	04 10 --	510	478 99		A		2
3	354	030	04 12 --	510	761 25		A		3
4	355	040	04 16 --	510	1275 47		A		4
5	356	060	04 18 --	510	1522 25		A		5
6	357	070	04 22 --	510	2320 00		A		6
7	358	080	04 25 --	510	335 50		A		7
8									8
9									9
10									10
11									11
12									12
13									13
14									14
15									15
16									16
17									17
18									18
19									19
20									20
21									21
22									22
23									23
24									24
25									25

BATCH TOTALS   850629

DISPOSITION CODE:
A = ON ACCOUNT
M = MANUAL CHECK
P = PAY THIS ITEM
(COMPUTER WRITES CHECK)

Figure 5.3   Accounts Payable Input Form

The Accounts Payable input form consists of two major sections: (1) the Purchases section and (2) the Cash Payments section. When performing accounts payable setup, the Purchase Invoice No. (which must be specified when using either of the two sections), the data fields in the purchases section, and the disposition code in the cash payments section will be used. The remaining data fields are used in an ongoing system and will be discussed in Chapter 6.

Each line on the body of the form contains data required to establish an opening balance. Recorded in the Purchase Invoice Number column is a three-digit number assigned consecutively to each opening balance recorded. The Vendor Number column contains the numbers of those vendors which have opening balances. These vendor numbers can be located by referring to the Accounts Payable File Maintenance input form prepared earlier. The Purchases Date column contains the date of the opening balance in the MM/DD/YY format. The General Ledger

Account Number column contains the number of the general ledger account debited as a result of the transaction. The Invoice Amount column contains the amount of the opening balance. The second to the last column (under the Cash Payment section), Disposition Code, contains the letter **A** to indicate that each opening balance is on account. The total of the amounts in the Invoice Amount column should be determined using a calculator, and the total should be written in the Batch Totals space provided at the bottom of the column.

ACCOUNTS PAYABLE SETUP OPERATIONAL PROCEDURES

Once the Accounts Payable input forms are completed, the data contained on them must be key-entered into the computer, and various reports may be displayed or printed. However, several steps must be followed before you may begin work in the Accounts Payable System. First, after the initial start-up procedures have been performed, Option B, *Accounting System Setup*, must be selected from the System Selection Menu. Using this option, the correct data fields must be set if this has not been done previously. Second, Option C, *Load Data from Disk*, must be selected. When the Load Data from Disk menu appears, Option D, *Create Empty File*, must be chosen to inform the computer that you will be creating new general ledger and accounts payable data files. Third, Option D, *Company Information*, must be selected from the System Selection Menu, and the correct data fields must be established. Fourth, Option F, *General Ledger*, must be selected from the System Selection Menu, and the general ledger chart of accounts and opening balances must be established. Finally, Option G, *Accounts Payable*, must be selected from the System Selection Menu. Once the *Accounts Payable* option is selected, it will be loaded from the program disk into computer memory, and the Accounts Payable Main Menu will appear on the screen as shown in Figure 5.4.

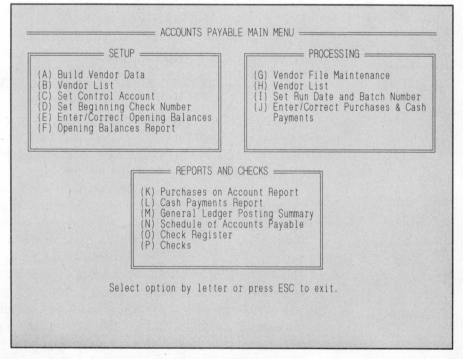

```
================== ACCOUNTS PAYABLE MAIN MENU ==================

===== SETUP =====                      ===== PROCESSING =====

(A) Build Vendor Data                  (G) Vendor File Maintenance
(B) Vendor List                        (H) Vendor List
(C) Set Control Account                (I) Set Run Date and Batch Number
(D) Set Beginning Check Number         (J) Enter/Correct Purchases & Cash
(E) Enter/Correct Opening Balances         Payments
(F) Opening Balances Report


================ REPORTS AND CHECKS ================

(K) Purchases on Account Report
(L) Cash Payments Report
(M) General Ledger Posting Summary
(N) Schedule of Accounts Payable
(O) Check Register
(P) Checks


Select option by letter or press ESC to exit.
```

Figure 5.4   Accounts Payable Main Menu

Any option may be selected from the Accounts Payable Main Menu by simply keying the appropriate letter. Subsequently, a new display will appear on the screen that will allow you to enter appropriate data or choose a course of action. The following sections explain how Options A through F (the setup options) can be used to create a new accounts payable data file containing vendors and opening balance ledger data. Each of these options should be performed in sequence in order to complete the accounts payable setup process.

Build Vendor Data Option A

When you select Option A from the Accounts Payable Main Menu, the Build Vendor Data screen shown in Figure 5.5 will appear.

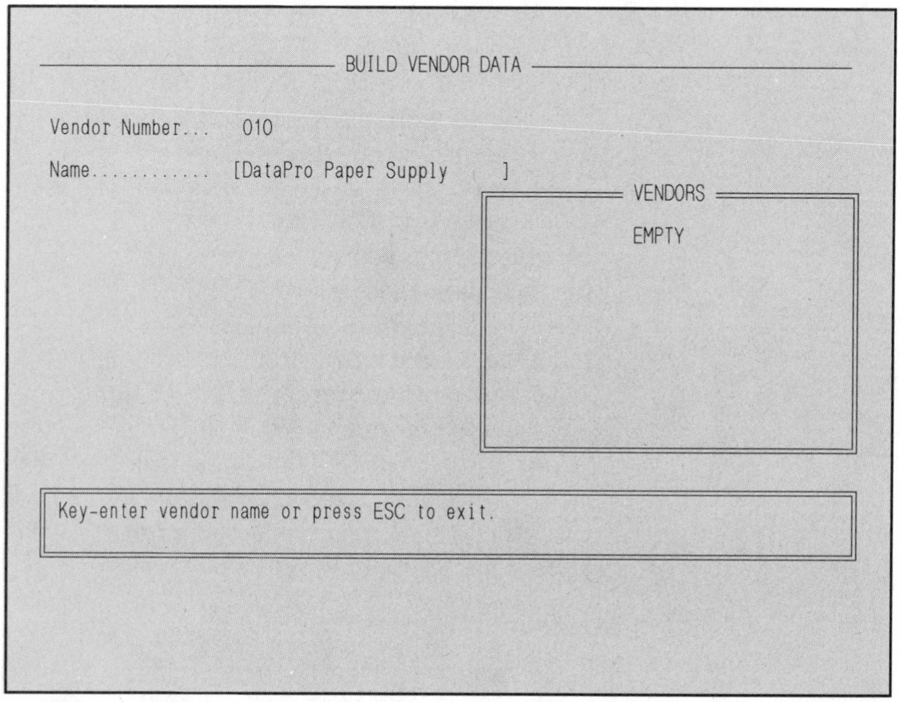

```
┌──────────────────────────────────────────────────────────────────────┐
│                                                                        │
│  ───────────────────────── BUILD VENDOR DATA ───────────────────────  │
│                                                                        │
│                                                                        │
│   Vendor Number...   010                                               │
│                                                                        │
│   Name...........  [DataPro Paper Supply    ]                          │
│                                           ┌═══════ VENDORS ═══════┐     │
│                                           │  EMPTY                 │    │
│                                           │                        │    │
│                                           │                        │    │
│                                           │                        │    │
│                                           │                        │    │
│                                           │                        │    │
│                                           └────────────────────────┘    │
│   ┌────────────────────────────────────────────────────────────────┐  │
│   │ Key-enter vendor name or press ESC to exit.                      │  │
│   └────────────────────────────────────────────────────────────────┘  │
│                                                                        │
└──────────────────────────────────────────────────────────────────────┘
```

Figure 5.5   Build Vendor Data Screen

Notice, the Vendors window displays **EMPTY** to indicate that there are no vendors currently in the computer memory. However, if the computer detects vendors currently stored in the computer's memory, a decision prompt message will appear, and you will be asked to strike the **Y** key (for Yes) or **N** (for No) to erase the vendor data currently in memory. Also, because of the serious consequences of selecting this option, a warning decision prompt message is displayed on the screen when the option is selected. The **N** option should be selected if you were unable to key-enter all of your vendor data during a previous work session. When you are ready to complete entering the vendor data, you may select the *Build Vendor Data* option, choose the **N** option, and key-enter the remaining vendor data. Strike the **Y** key to erase all previous data and proceed.

The Accounts Payable File Maintenance input form is to be used as the source document from which the vendor numbers and names are keyed. In order to key-enter the vendor number and names, complete the following steps:

1. Key-enter a vendor number from one to three digits in length. The cursor will then move to the first position of the corresponding name field.
2. Key-enter the vendor name which corresponds to the vendor number just keyed.

   Note: After the vendor name is key-entered, the vendor number and name will appear in the Vendors window, indicating that it has been created.

3. Continue key-entering vendor numbers and names until all fields have been entered.

If you detect an error or wish to delete a previously entered vendor, simply key-enter the vendor number of the vendor to be changed or deleted. The computer will check to see if the vendor number already exists. If the vendor number already exists, the computer will display the vendor name and number and assume that you wish to either change the vendor name or delete the vendor. In this case, a decision prompt will ask you to strike **C** if you want to change the vendor name, **R** to record the name as it appears on the screen, or **D** to delete this vendor. If the vendor already exists and you wish to change the vendor name, strike **C** for change, key-enter the correct vendor name, and then strike **R** to record the vendor data. If the vendor already exists and you wish to delete it, strike **D**, and the vendor will be deleted. You may press Esc to exit and not make any changes. *Note: A vendor cannot be deleted if it has any transaction activity. Even though a vendor's balance is zero, it cannot be deleted if it has transaction data. For example, if an invoice is paid and the balance is zero, the associated vendor cannot be deleted until the file is purged or period-end closing is performed.*

Vendor List Option B

When you select Option B from the Accounts Payable Main Menu, you will be able to get a printout or screen display of the list of vendors. When this option is chosen, a decision prompt will appear which consists of three choices: (1) strike **D** to display the vendor list, (2) strike **P** to print the vendor list, or (3) press Esc if you wish to exit this option (do nothing) and return to the Accounts Payable Main Menu. To display the vendor list on the screen, strike **D**. In order to print the vendor list on an attached printer, check to see that the printer is properly connected to the computer, turn on the printer power switch, align the paper if necessary, and strike **P**. If you want to interrupt the printer and return to the Accounts Payable Main Menu during printing, press the Esc key. Figure 5.6 illustrates a displayed vendor list for Hardware Plus.

Set Control Account Option C

There are certain account numbers that require special identification and handling by the computer. These account numbers must be established or setup through the Accounts Payable Main Menu Option C, *Set Control Account*. This setup should be performed immediately after the vendors are built and a vendor list is displayed or printed. The control accounts may also be changed at any time. When this option is selected, the account titles displayed for which numbers must be set

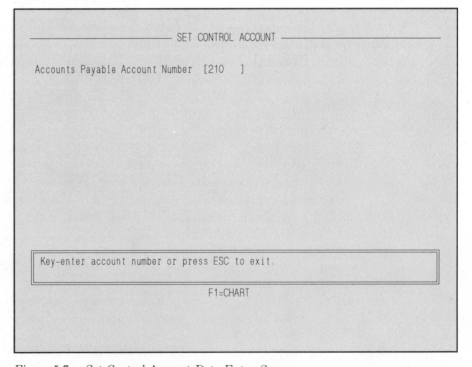

```
RUN DATE: 05/01/--                    HARDWARE PLUS                    VENDOR LIST
VENDOR      VENDOR
NUMBER      NAME
------------------
010         DataPro Paper Supply
020         Computer Distribution Co.
030         Metro Computer Store
040         Computer Executive Ltd.
050         A & K Advertising Co.
060         Hightech Ribbon Co.
070         Inntouch Marketing
080         Modern Printing
090         Dakota County Power Co.




                        Press SPACE BAR to continue.
```

Figure 5.6   Vendor List

will depend on whether you selected simplified or expanded accounts payable during accounting system setup (Option A of the System Selection Menu). Once the set control accounts data is key-entered, it is recorded in the computer's memory. Figure 5.7 shows the completed Set Control Account data entry screen for Hardware Plus using the simplified Accounts Payable System.

```
───────────────── SET CONTROL ACCOUNT ─────────────────


  Accounts Payable Account Number  [210   ]









  ┌───────────────────────────────────────────────────────┐
  │ Key-enter account number or press ESC to exit.        │
  └───────────────────────────────────────────────────────┘
                        F1=CHART
```

Figure 5.7   Set Control Account Data Entry Screen

The data recorded on the General Ledger input form or the Chart of Accounts report may be used as a source document from which the control accounts are keyed. A window may be opened (by pressing the Function 1 key) to view your chart of accounts if you wish to verify an account number. To set the control account(s) or to change a current value(s), complete the following steps.

1. Key-enter the appropriate account number for each of the control account titles displayed.
2. After all control accounts have been key-entered, visually check to verify the accuracy of your keying. If you detect an error, move the cursor to the error and make the correction. When finished, move the cursor to the last field and press ENTER/RETURN to indicate you want the computer to accept your data.
3. At this time, the computer will match the account numbers just key-entered to the chart of accounts to verify that they exist. If an account number cannot be found, an error message will be displayed and you will be permitted to make a correction. If all the account numbers match, the computer will display them along with their assigned titles. In addition, a decision prompt will appear at the bottom of the screen. Strike **C** to change the data, **R** to record the account numbers, or press Esc to exit (ignore the data) and return to the Accounts Payable Main Menu.

Set Beginning Check Number Option D

The purpose of this option is to allow you to establish a starting check number. This check number will then be assigned to the first accounts payable check printed. The checks will be numbered consecutively thereafter. The Set Beginning Check Number data entry screen is shown in Figure 5.8.

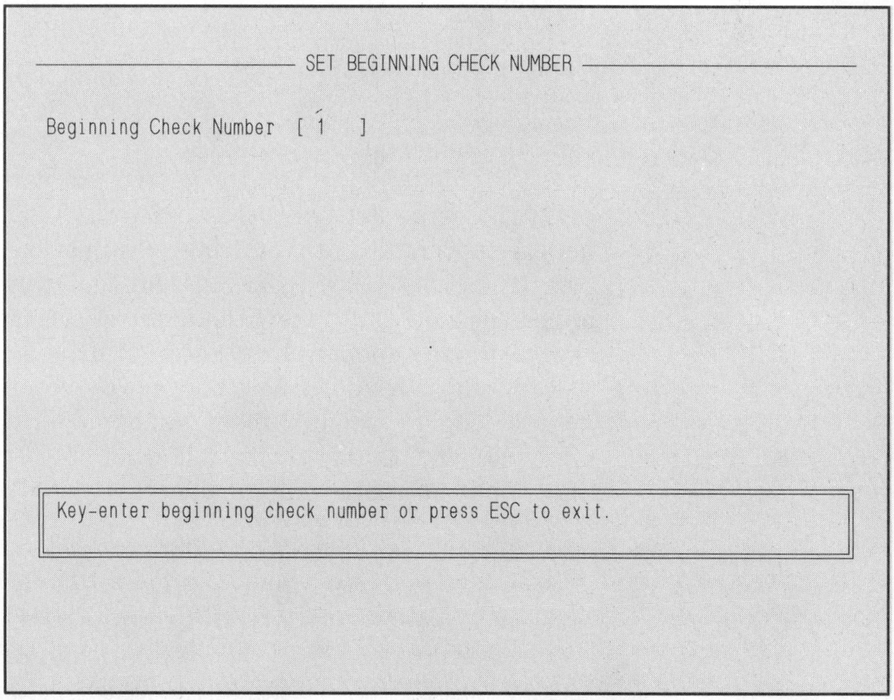

```
┌──────────────────── SET BEGINNING CHECK NUMBER ────────────────────┐
│                                                                     │
│  Beginning Check Number  [ 1   ]                                    │
│                                                                     │
│                                                                     │
│                                                                     │
│   ┌─────────────────────────────────────────────────────────────┐  │
│   │ Key-enter beginning check number or press ESC to exit.        │  │
│   └─────────────────────────────────────────────────────────────┘  │
│                                                                     │
└─────────────────────────────────────────────────────────────────────┘
```

Figure 5.8   Set Beginning Check Number Data Entry Screen

When Option D, *Set Beginning Check Number*, is chosen from the Accounts Payable Main Menu, a prompt message will appear asking you to key-enter a beginning check number or press Esc to exit. If a beginning check number is key-entered, a decision prompt will appear which consists of three choices: (1) strike **C** to change data, (2) strike **R** to record the check number which appears, or (3) press the Esc key to exit (do nothing) and return to the Accounts Payable Main Menu. To change the beginning check number just entered, strike **C** to indicate to the computer that you wish to change the existing data, then key-enter the beginning check number desired. Strike the **R** key to record the check number that appears and return to the Accounts Payable Main Menu.

The beginning check number is the check number with which you would like to begin numbering checks the next time checks are displayed and/or printed. When you display or print the check register or checks, the computer begins with this number. In an ongoing system, the computer will automatically update the next check number to be used whenever the batch number (see Option I—*Set Run Date and Batch Number*) is changed. Therefore, if you correct transactions after you have displayed or printed checks, you should check to be certain that the *Next Check No.* field is correct before proceeding.

Enter/Correct Opening Balances Option E

After the vendor data has been built, the control accounts have been set, and the beginning check number has been established, the opening balances must be key-entered for each vendor with a balance. An Accounts Payable input form should be completed and used as the source document from which these opening balances are keyed. When Option E is selected and a new invoice number is key-entered, the Enter/Correct Opening Balances data entry screen shown in Figure 5.9 will appear. This data entry screen is used to enter, and make corrections to, the opening balances.

The Enter/Correct Opening Balances data entry screen allows you to key opening balances from the Accounts Payable input form. In addition, this menu option can be used to make corrections to opening balances which were previously keyed. At various points during data entry, three windows may be displayed. The first window option that appears permits you to view invoices previously entered into the system (Function 3 key). The second and third window options that appear permit you to view the chart of accounts (Function 1 key) and the vendors (Function 2 key) stored in the computer's memory. You will find these windows helpful in verifying previously keyed invoices, general ledger account numbers, and vendor numbers during this data entry activity. Complete the following steps to establish opening balances or to correct opening balances:

1. Key-enter the purchase invoice number.

   Note: At this time, the computer will check to see if the purchase invoice number just keyed already exists. If the purchase invoice number does exist, all the opening balance data will be displayed, and you will be permitted to make corrections (proceed to No. 8). If no opening balance data exists for the designated purchase invoice

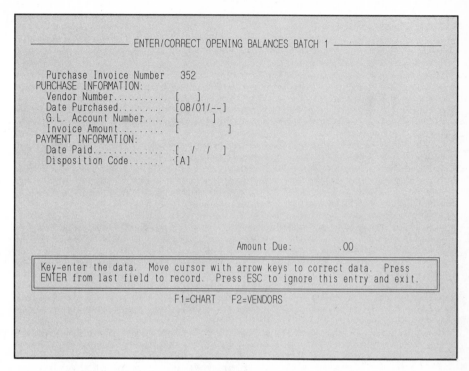

```
──────────────────── ENTER/CORRECT OPENING BALANCES BATCH 1 ────────────────────


    Purchase Invoice Number    352
  PURCHASE INFORMATION:
    Vendor Number..........    [   ]
    Date Purchased.........    [08/01/--]
    G.L. Account Number....    [       ]
    Invoice Amount.........    [           ]
  PAYMENT INFORMATION:
    Date Paid..............    [  /  /  ]
    Disposition Code.......    [A]





                                      Amount Due:          .00
  ┌──────────────────────────────────────────────────────────────────────────┐
  │ Key-enter the data.  Move cursor with arrow keys to correct data.  Press   │
  │ ENTER from last field to record.  Press ESC to ignore this entry and exit. │
  └──────────────────────────────────────────────────────────────────────────┘
                      F1=CHART    F2=VENDORS
```

Figure 5.9   Enter/Correct Opening Balances Data Entry Screen

number, the computer will assume you wish to set up an opening balance for that invoice.

2. Key-enter the vendor number.
3. Key-enter the date of the opening balance in the MMDDYY format (without the slashes).
4. Key-enter the general ledger account number of the account to be charged for the invoice. Most often this account will be Purchases because the invoice was for merchandise. However, this is not always the case. It may be an expense account or some other account.
5. Key-enter the opening balance in the *Invoice Amount* field.
6. Move the cursor past the *Date Paid* field to the *Disposition Code* field by pressing the Down Arrow or the ENTER/RETURN key.
7. The *Disposition Code* field contains the letter **A**, indicating that the invoice for the opening balance is on account. Since all opening balances are on account, leave this field as is and press the ENTER/RETURN key.
8. A decision prompt will appear asking if you wish to make a change, post the transaction, or ignore the displayed data (do nothing). Strike **C** to make changes or corrections. Strike **P** to post and record the opening balance data as displayed. Press Esc to ignore the data and display a blank Enter/Correct Opening Balances data entry screen. If the purchase invoice had previously been entered into the system, and you are making a correction, a decision prompt message permitting you to strike **D** to delete the transaction would also appear.

Note: At this time the computer will check the data you have entered to verify its accuracy. If errors are detected, you will be given a *chance to make corrections. If the vendor number does not exist, a decision prompt message will appear asking if you wish to set up this vendor. If you respond **Yes**, the Build Vendor Data screen will appear and you will be permitted to set up the vendor. After the vendor has been set up and recorded in the computer's memory, the Enter/Correct Opening Balances data entry screen will again appear, and you will be permitted to continue.*

9. Continue this procedure until all opening balances and/or corrections have been key-entered. When finished, press the Esc key to exit this data entry screen and return to the Accounts Payable Main Menu.

Opening Balances Report Option F

When you select Option F, *Opening Balances Report*, from the Accounts Payable Main Menu, you will be able to get a printout or screen display of the Opening Balances report. This report consists of the vendor numbers, vendor names, purchase invoice numbers, dates, amounts of the opening vendor account balances, and the total of all the individual vendor opening balances.

When this option is selected, a decision prompt will appear which will permit you to strike **D** to display the Opening Balances report on the screen or to strike **P** to print the Opening Balances report. Press the Esc key if you wish to exit this option and return to the Accounts Payable Main Menu. Figure 5.10 illustrates a displayed Opening Balances report for Hardware Plus.

It is recommended that the *Opening Balances Report* option be selected and run after the opening balances are set up and after making any corrections. Examining this report and comparing the computer

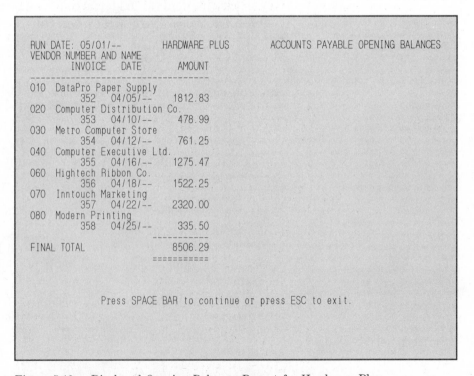

```
RUN DATE: 05/01/--        HARDWARE PLUS      ACCOUNTS PAYABLE OPENING BALANCES
VENDOR NUMBER AND NAME
        INVOICE    DATE        AMOUNT
-------------------------------------------
010  DataPro Paper Supply
          352    04/05/--    1812.83
020  Computer Distribution Co.
          353    04/10/--     478.99
030  Metro Computer Store
          354    04/12/--     761.25
040  Computer Executive Ltd.
          355    04/16/--    1275.47
060  Hightech Ribbon Co.
          356    04/18/--    1522.25
070  Inntouch Marketing
          357    04/22/--    2320.00
080  Modern Printing
          358    04/25/--     335.50
                            -----------
FINAL TOTAL                  8506.29
                            ===========


          Press SPACE BAR to continue or press ESC to exit.
```

Figure 5.10   Displayed Opening Balances Report for Hardware Plus

total with the batch total at the bottom of the Accounts Payable input form will help verify that all data has been recorded properly and provide an audit trail (if printed) for future reference.

Save Data to Disk   After the accounts payable setup has been completed (Options A through F), press Esc to return to the System Selection Menu. Choose Option E, *Save Data to Disk*, and save your newly created data to disk as a work in progress file. This option *must* be the last option selected prior to ending the automated accounting session. If you fail to perform this procedure prior to computer shut-down, before loading another problem, or before creating empty files, all data keyed and processed during the session will be lost.

ACCOUNTS PAYABLE SETUP (SAMPLE PROBLEM)

Setting up a business on a computerized accounting system involves several one-time activities to initially establish (set up) the required computer files. You will be completing this setup procedure for Hardware Plus in this computer exercise.

The vendor data for Hardware Plus has been recorded for you on the Accounts Payable File Maintenance input form (Form AP-1) shown in Figure 5.11. Each vendor has been assigned a number from one to three digits in length. The vendor name is limited to 25 characters in length. The opening balances for all vendors who have opening balances have been recorded on the Accounts Payable input form (Form AP-2) shown in Figure 5.12.

Instructions

Step   1   Bring up the System Selection Menu according to the instructions for your microcomputer.

Step   2   From the System Selection Menu, select Option C (*Load Data from Disk*). When the Load Data from Disk menu appears, select Option A, *Load Opening Balances from the Program Disk*.

Step   3   When the directory of Opening Balances contained on the disk appears, select Problem 5-S by key-entering the file name: **AA5-S**.

Step   4   Select Option B, *Accounting System Setup*, and set each field as follows. You may wish to set *Each Report on New Page* to **N** (for No) if your instructor wishes. After you have key-entered all of the settings, strike **R** to record your data and return to the System Selection Menu.

Simplified/Expanded General Ledger ....S
Simplified/Expanded Accounts Payable ....S
Simplified/Expanded Accounts Receivable .....S
Each Report on New Page ....Y
Checks on Preprinted Forms ....N
Statements on Preprinted Forms...........N

	ACCOUNTS PAYABLE FILE MAINTENANCE Input Form	Problem No. _5-S_
RUN DATE _05/01/--_ MM DD YY		FORM AP-1

	1 VENDOR NUMBER	2 VENDOR NAME	
1	010	DataPro Paper Supply	1
2	020	Computer Distribution Co.	2
3	030	Metro Computer Store	3
4	040	Computer Executive Ltd.	4
5	050	A+K Advertising	5
6	060	Hightech Ribbon Co.	6
7	070	Inntouch Marketing	7
8	080	Modern Printing	8
9	090	Dakota County Power	9
10			10
11			11
12			12
13			13
14			14
15			15
16			16
17			17
18			18
19			19
20			20
21			21
22			22
23			23
24			24
25			25

Figure 5.11   Accounts Payable File Maintenance Input Form (Problem 5-S)

Step 5   Select Option D, *Company Information*, from the System Selection Menu. Set the run date to **May 1** of the current year. Verify that the *Company Name* field contains **Hardware Plus** and that the *Problem Number* field contains **Problem 5-S**. If not, you may have loaded the wrong opening balance data, and you should therefore return to Step 3. Notice the company name, problem number, and type of business are automatically set during the problem selection process. Leave these three fields as they appear. When the data is correct, strike **R** to record this information and return to the System Selection Menu.

Step 6   Select Option G, *Accounts Payable*, from the System Selection Menu.

Step 7   After the Accounts Payable System has finished loading, select Option A, *Build Vendor Master File*, from the Accounts Payable Main Menu.

Step 8   Key-enter the data from the Accounts Payable File Maintenance input form shown in Figure 5.11 on the Build Vendor Data screen.

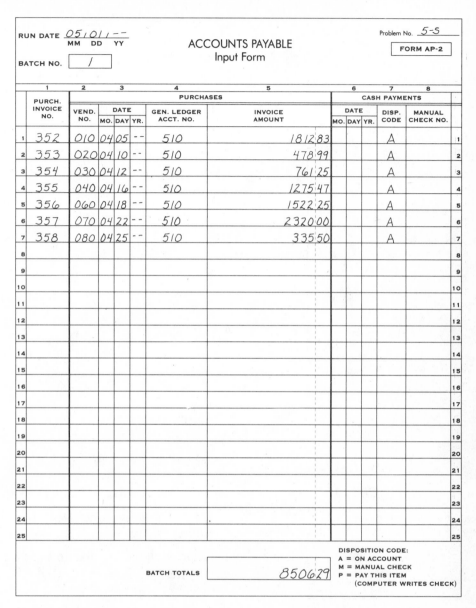

RUN DATE 05/01/-- MM DD YY			ACCOUNTS PAYABLE Input Form					Problem No. 5-S FORM AP-2	

Figure 5.12   Accounts Payable Input Form (Problem 5-S)

Step 9 If you must exit before all entries have been key-entered, save your work as Work in Progress. The remaining entries may be key-entered at a later time by completing the following steps:

1. Load your work in progress.
2. Select Option A, *Build Vendor Master File,* from the Accounts Payable Main Menu.
3. When the decision prompt *Erase accounts payable files (Y or N)?* appears, strike **N**.
4. Key-enter the remainder of the vendors.

Step 10 Select Option B, *Vendor List,* from the Accounts Payable Main Menu.

Step 11 Strike **D** to display or **P** to print the vendor list.

Step 12 Compare your vendor list with the correct one shown in Figure 5.13. If you detect an error on the vendor list, return to the *Build Vendor*

Data option, strike **N** so the vendor list will not be erased, and key-enter the missing or correct data.

```
RUN DATE: 05/01/--                 HARDWARE PLUS
                                   VENDOR LIST

------------------
VENDOR    VENDOR
NUMBER    NAME
------------------
010       DataPro Paper Supply
020       Computer Distribution Co.
030       Metro Computer Store
040       Computer Executive Ltd.
050       A & K Advertising Co.
060       Hightech Ribbon Co.
070       Inntouch Marketing
080       Modern Printing
090       Dakota County Power Co.
```

Figure 5.13   Vendor List (Problem 5-S)

Step 13   Select Option C, *Set Control Account*, and key-enter the following control account.

Accounts Payable Account No.............. 210

Step 14   If you make an error, strike **C** to change the data and make the correction. If the account number is correct, strike **R** to record the accounts payable control account number.

Step 15   Select Option D, *Set Beginning Check Number*.

Step 16   Key-enter **301** as the beginning check number, then strike **R** to record the data.

Step 17   Select Option E, *Enter/Correct Opening Balances*, from the Accounts Payable Main Menu.

Step 18   Key-enter the opening balances from the Accounts Payable input form shown in Figure 5.12. After each part of the entry is key-entered, examine it for accuracy. If there are any errors, strike **C** to change the data and make the corrections. If the data is correct, strike **P** to post this opening accounts payable vendor balance.

Step 19   After all vendor opening balances have been key-entered, press Esc to exit and return to the Accounts Payable Main Menu.

Step 20   Select Option F, *Opening Balances Report*, from the Accounts Payable Main Menu.

Step 21   Strike **D** to display or **P** to print the Opening Balances report. Compare your Opening Balances report with the correct one for Hardware Plus shown in Figure 5.14. The computer total should be the same as the batch total at the bottom of the Accounts Payable input form.

```
RUN DATE: 05/01/--                        HARDWARE PLUS
                            ACCOUNTS PAYABLE OPENING BALANCES

----------------------------------------
VENDOR NUMBER AND NAME
          INVOICE    DATE        AMOUNT
----------------------------------------
010  DataPro Paper Supply
          352    04/05/--       1812.83
020  Computer Distribution Co.
          353    04/10/--        478.99
030  Metro Computer Store
          354    04/12/--        761.25
040  Computer Executive Ltd.
          355    04/16/--       1275.47
060  Hightech Ribbon Co.
          356    04/18/--       1522.25
070  Inntouch Marketing
          357    04/22/--       2320.00
080  Modern Printing
          358    04/25/--        335.50
                               -----------
FINAL TOTAL                     8506.29
                               ===========
```

Figure 5.14   Opening Balances Report (Problem 5-S)

Step 22   If your Opening Balances report is out of balance, or if errors are detected, select Option E, *Enter/Correct Opening Balances*, from the Accounts Payable Main Menu. Make the necessary corrections to the opening balances by key-entering the purchase invoice number of the incorrect opening balance. Key-enter and post the correct data for each part of the opening entry that is in error. When all corrections have been made, press Esc to return to the Accounts Payable Main Menu. Display or print a new Opening Balances report. Repeat this procedure until all data in the Opening Balances report is correct.

Step 23   Press Esc to exit from the Accounts Payable Main Menu and return to the System Selection Menu.

Step 24   From the System Selection Menu, select Option E, *Save Data to Disk*, and save your data as a work in progress file (recommend file name **AA5-S**).

Step 25   Press Esc to end your automated accounting session. Then complete the student exercise and transaction problem which follow.

Name _____

Class _____ Date _____

CHAPTER 5
STUDENT EXERCISE

I. Matching For each of the following definitions, write the letter of the term which best fits that definition in the space provided.

a. Accounts payable ledger data   d. Accounts payable file mainte-
b. Accounts payable input form   nance input form
c. Vendor data   e. Accounts payable data file

1. _____ Consists of a record for each item for which a check is to be printed. (Obj. 6)

2. _____ An input form used to record the vendors to be established during accounts payable setup and to record additions, changes, and deletions to the vendor records. (Objs. 2, 10)

3. _____ Consists of a separate record for each vendor with whom the company does business. (Obj. 2)

4. _____ An input form used to record opening vendor account balances and to record accounts payable transactions. (Objs. 6, 10)

5. _____ The part of the automated accounting database that contains all the data required by the computer to process accounts payable transactions. (Obj. 10)

II. Short Answer 1. Identify and describe the steps involved in accounts payable setup. (Objs. 1, 10)

_____

_____

_____

_____

2. Describe the differences between a manual and a computerized accounts payable system. (Obj. 1)

_____

_____

_____

_____

3. Why must the *Save Data to Disk* menu option be the last option selection prior to ending your computer session? (Obj. 8)

_____

_____

_____

_____

4. What is shown on a vendor list? (Obj. 3)

_____

_____

5. What is the purpose of the Opening Balances report? (Obj. 7)

_____

_____

_____

ACCOUNTS PAYABLE SETUP
TRANSACTION PROBLEM 5-1

As of August 1, 19-- (use current year), Wilderness Camping Center lists the following vendors and the outstanding opening balances (purchases on account) for those vendors from whom it has purchased merchandise. Wilderness Camping Center is a small store which sells backpacking and family camping equipment. It is organized as a partnership. Its general ledger accounts and account opening balances have already been established for you. Your task is to set up the Accounts Payable System for Wilderness Camping Center. (Objs. 2-10)

Purchase Inv. No.	Vendor Number	Vendor Name	Date Purchased	Gen. Led. Acct. No.	Invoice Amount	Disp. Code
255	110	Outdoor Supplies	07/07/--	510	1557.80	A
264	120	Camping Supply Co.	07/12/--	510	83.50	A
272	130	Factory Supply, Inc.	07/15/--	510	565.28	A
288	140	Scout Outdoors Supply	07/21/--	510	2782.50	A
289	150	Camper's Depot	07/28/--	510	289.22	A

Instructions

Step 1 Remove the blank input forms and the Chapter 5 Audit Test at the end of this chapter. Complete the questions on the audit test as you work through the steps which follow.

Step 2 Using the data in the previous table, record the vendor numbers and names on the Accounts Payable File Maintenance input form (Form AP-1).

Step 3 Using the data above, record as Batch No. 1 the vendor opening balances (purchases on account) on the Accounts Payable input form (Form AP-2). Be sure to take a calculator total for the Invoice Amount column and write it in the Batch Total box at the bottom of the form.

Step 4 Bring up the System Selection Menu.

Step 5 From the System Selection Menu, select Option C (*Load Data from Disk*). When the Load Data from Disk menu appears, select Option A, *Load Opening Balances from the Program Disk*.

Step 6 When the directory of Opening Balances contained on the disk appears, select Problem 5-1 by key-entering the file name: **AA5-1.**

Step 7 Select Option B, *Accounting System Setup*, and set each field as follows. You may wish to set *Each Report on New Page* to **N** (for No) if your instructor wishes. After you have key-entered all of the settings, strike **R** to record your data and return to the System Selection Menu.

Simplified/Expanded General Ledger . . . . S
Simplified/Expanded Accounts Payable . . . . S
Simplified/Expanded Accounts Receivable . . . . . S
Each Report on New Page . . . . Y
Checks on Preprinted Forms . . . . N
Statements on Preprinted Forms . . . . N

Step 8 Select Option D, *Company Information*, from the System Selection Menu. Set the run date to **August 1** of the current year. Verify that the *Company Name* field contains **Wilderness Camping Center** and that the *Problem Number* field contains **Problem 5-1**. If not, you may have loaded the wrong opening balance data, and you should therefore return to Step 5. Notice the company name, problem number, and type of business are automatically set during the problem selection process. Leave these three fields as they appear. When the data is correct, strike **R** to record this information and return to the System Selection Menu.

Step 9 Select Option G, *Accounts Payable*, from the System Selection Menu.

Step 10 After the Accounts Payable System has finished loading, select Option A, *Build Vendor Data*, from the Accounts Payable Main Menu. Key-enter the data from the Accounts Payable File Maintenance input form prepared in Step 2.

Step 11 Select Option B, *Vendor List*, and print or display a vendor list. If errors are detected on the vendor list, return to the Build Vendor Data screen, strike **N**, and key-enter the missing or incorrect vendors.

Step 12 Select Option C, *Set Control Account*, and key-enter and record the following control account:

Accounts Payable Account No. 210

Step 13 Select Option D, *Set Beginning Check Number*, and key-enter and record the starting check number as 701.

Step 14 Select Option E, *Enter/Correct Opening Balances*. Key-enter and post the opening balances from the Accounts Payable input form prepared in Step 3.

Step 15 Select Option F, *Opening Balances Report*, and print or display an accounts payable Opening Balances report. Examine this report and compare the computer total with the batch total at the bottom of the Accounts Payable input form. If errors are detected on your Opening Balances report, select the *Enter/Correct Opening Balances* option, and make the necessary corrections.

Step 16 Press Esc to exit from the Accounts Payable Main Menu and return to the System Selection Menu.

Step 17 From the System Selection Menu, select Option E, *Save Data to Disk*, and save your data as a work in progress file (recommend file name **AA5-1**).

Step 18 Press Esc to end your automated accounting session.

Step 19 Hand in the completed student exercise sheets, input forms, the audit test, and any printouts to your instructor.

    You have now completed the computer exercise for Chapter 5.

Name _____

Class _____ Date _____

	VENDOR NUMBER	VENDOR NAME	

ACCOUNTS PAYABLE
FILE MAINTENANCE
Input Form

Problem No. _____

FORM AP-1

RUN DATE ____/____/____
MM   DD   YY

	1	2	
	VENDOR NUMBER	**VENDOR NAME**	
1			1
2			2
3			3
4			4
5			5
6			6
7			7
8			8
9			9
10			10
11			11
12			12
13			13
14			14
15			15
16			16
17			17
18			18
19			19
20			20
21			21
22			22
23			23
24			24
25			25

RUN DATE ___/___/___
MM   DD   YY

BATCH NO. [   ]

ACCOUNTS PAYABLE
Input Form

Problem No. _____

FORM AP-2

	1	2	3			4	5		6			7	8	
	PURCH. INVOICE NO.	VEND. NO.	DATE			GEN. LEDGER ACCT. NO.	INVOICE AMOUNT		DATE			DISP. CODE	MANUAL CHECK NO.	
			MO.	DAY	YR.				MO.	DAY	YR.			
1														1
2														2
3														3
4														4
5														5
6														6
7														7
8														8
9														9
10														10
11														11
12														12
13														13
14														14
15														15
16														16
17														17
18														18
19														19
20														20
21														21
22														22
23														23
24														24
25														25

BATCH TOTALS [   ]

DISPOSITION CODE:
A = ON ACCOUNT
M = MANUAL CHECK
P = PAY THIS ITEM
     (COMPUTER WRITES CHECK)

Name _____

Class _____ Date _____

CHAPTER 5
AUDIT TEST

1. What is the run date shown on the Vendor List report?

   _____

2. What vendor number has been assigned to Camping Supply Co.?

   _____

3. Which vendor has been assigned Vendor No. 140?

   _____

4. How many vendors did the company owe money to at the beginning of the fiscal period?

   _____

5. What is the total amount that the company owed to all vendors at the beginning of the fiscal period?

   _____

6 ACCOUNTS PAYABLE TRANSACTIONS AND REPORTS

Upon completion of this chapter, you will be able to:

1. Perform vendor file maintenance.
2. Display or print a vendor list.
3. Set the run date and batch number.
4. Enter/correct purchases and cash payments.
5. Display or print a Purchases on Account report.
6. Display or print a Cash Payments report.
7. Display or print a general ledger posting summary.
8. Display or print a schedule of accounts payable.
9. Display or print a check register.
10. Display or print checks.
11. Save data to disk and perform the system shutdown procedure.
12. Identify the components and procedures required to process accounts payable transactions and generate Accounts Payable reports.

INTRODUCTION

In Chapter 5, you learned how to set up vendors and their opening balances in the accounts payable data file. This chapter will cover the accounts payable accounting cycle used in an automated accounting system. You will soon see how transaction data is used to update the computer's files and, in turn, generate the Accounts Payable reports required to keep track of a company's purchases and cash payments. The procedures used in *Automated Accounting for the Microcomputer* to perform accounts payable processing are illustrated in Figure 6.1.

Vendor data changes constantly during the operation of a business. Changes may occur because a business makes purchases from new vendors, vendor names change, or the company decides to no longer buy from a particular vendor. Therefore, the computer's vendor data must be updated to show these changes. This process of adding, changing, and deleting vendor records is called **vendor file maintenance**.

Each transaction for which cash is to be paid is called an **accounts payable transaction**. Each accounts payable transaction must be assigned a number to identify that transaction. *Automated Accounting for the Microcomputer* uses a **purchase invoice number** to identify each accounts payable transaction. This purchase invoice number must be recorded on the Accounts Payable input form (Form AP-2) with each transaction. The purchases on account and cash payment transactions are then key-entered from the input form into the computer. All transactions for a specific period of time are grouped together, and each group of transactions is assigned a batch number. These transac-

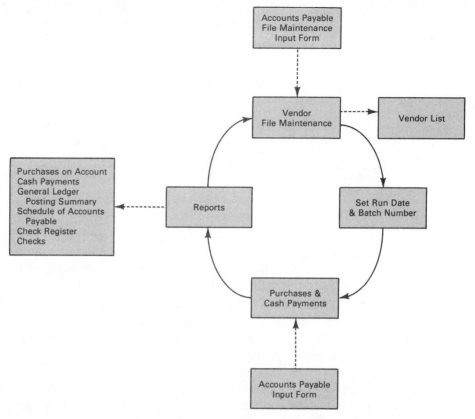

Figure 6.1   Accounts Payable Transaction Processing Procedure

tions are then stored in their respective batches in the accounts payable data file.

Accounts payable transactions may be recorded on the input form and key-entered with three different disposition codes that inform the computer how they are to be processed. A transaction may be recorded with Disposition Code A, **on account**, to indicate that a purchase of an item has been made on account for which the company now owes money. A transaction may also be recorded with Disposition Code M, **manual check**, to indicate to the computer that a manual check has already been issued in payment of the purchase invoice. A manual check is a check written by hand. Finally, a transaction may be recorded with Disposition Code P, **pay this item**, to indicate to the computer to print a check the next time checks are printed. In all three cases, processing occurs based on the batch number which is assigned at the time the transaction was key-entered. Therefore, all Purchases on Account and Cash Payments reports are generated for the specific batch of transactions desired. Each batch of accounts payable transactions remains stored in the accounts payable data file. If an error is detected after a report for a specific batch is printed, it can be corrected, and the report can be rerun. The accounts payable data file has a maximum capacity of 50 transactions. If this limit is exceeded, the paid transactions from all previous batches stored in the file will be erased, thereby freeing up additional space for the current batch of transactions. This process is called **purging**. Since only the paid transactions are erased, no data will be lost when this file is purged.

ACCOUNTS PAYABLE INTEGRATION

As accounts payable transactions are entered or corrected in the Accounts Payable System, the journal entries resulting from the transactions are automatically integrated into the General Ledger System by the computer. In order to integrate these entries, the computer must know the control account numbers you have assigned to the general ledger accounts involved. In Chapter 5, you learned how to provide these control account numbers during accounts payable setup. When the *simplified* accounts payable option is being used, the account number for Accounts Payable is set when Option C, *Set Control Account*, is selected from the Accounts Payable Main Menu. In addition, the account numbers for Purchases Returns and Allowances and Purchases Discount are set if the expanded accounts payable option is being used. By supplying these control account numbers, only the account number to be debited for the transaction need be provided at the time an accounts payable transaction is entered.

When a new purchase transaction is entered, the computer will (1) debit the account which is included as part of the transaction and (2) credit Accounts Payable. When a transaction is released for payment (or entered with an indication that a manual check has already been written), the computer will (1) debit Accounts Payable and (2) credit Cash. If a transaction is found to be in error and is corrected, the computer will make the necessary correcting journal entries.

COMPLETING THE INPUT FORMS

Accounts payable input is recorded on two different input forms: the Accounts Payable File Maintenance input form (Form AP-1) and the Accounts Payable input form (Form AP-2). You have already worked with each of these forms in Chapter 5 to build the vendor data and establish their opening balances in the accounts payable data file. In this chapter, you will learn how the Accounts Payable File Maintenance input form and the Accounts Payable input form are used to record the data the computer needs to keep track of a company's vendors, purchases, and cash payments.

Accounts Payable File Maintenance Input Form (Form AP-1)

The vendor data must be kept current by adding new vendors, making corrections to existing vendors, and deleting vendors with whom the company no longer does business. The vendors established for Hardware Plus in Chapter 5 are illustrated in Figure 6.2.

Vendor Number	Vendor Name
010	DataPro Paper Supply
020	Computer Distribution Co.
030	Metro Computer Store
040	Computer Executive Ltd.
050	A & K Advertising Co.
060	Hightech Ribbon Co.
070	Inntouch Marketing
080	Modern Printing
090	Dakota County Power Co.

Figure 6.2   The Hardware Plus Vendors

Let's suppose that during the course of the month, Vendor No. 100, Digital Electronics Co., needs to be added; the vendor name for Vendor No. 060, Hightech Ribbon Co., needs to be changed to Quality Ribbon Co.; and Vendor No. 070, Inntouch Marketing, has become inactive and should be deleted. In order to record these changes, the Accounts Payable File Maintenance input form (Form AP-1) shown in Figure 6.3 must be completed. Notice that this form is the same form you used to build the vendor data during accounts payable setup activities.

	VENDOR NUMBER	VENDOR NAME	
1	100	Digital Electronics Co.	1
2	060	Quality Ribbon Co.	2
3	070	D	3
4			4
5			5
6			6
7			7
8			8
9			9
10			10
11			11
12			12
13			13
14			14
15			15
16			16
17			17
18			18
19			19
20			20
21			21
22			22
23			23
24			24
25			25

ACCOUNTS PAYABLE FILE MAINTENANCE Input Form

RUN DATE 02/15/-- MM DD YY

Problem No. Sample

FORM AP-1

Figure 6.3   Accounts Payable File Maintenance Input Form

The first entry involves adding a vendor, and the second entry involves changing a vendor's name. Notice that in either case, you simply record the vendor number and the vendor name. The third entry involves deleting a vendor. To delete a vendor, merely record the vendor number to be deleted and place a **D** (for Delete) in the Vendor Name column. Only vendors which are inactive (have no outstanding balance and transaction activity) can be deleted. Vendor No. 070 has been inactive and does not have any existing balances in the accounts payable data file. Therefore, the computer will allow this vendor to be deleted.

Accounts Payable Input Form (Form AP-2)

In a computerized accounts payable system, purchases on account and cash payments must be analyzed, recorded on an Accounts Payable input form, and key-entered into the computer by batch number. As you have already seen, the accounts payable transactions data is stored by batch number as the transactions are entered. The accounts payable transactions remain in the accounts payable data file until the maximum capacity of the file is reached. At that time, the computer will automatically purge the paid invoices from all previous batches.

In the Accounts Payable System, purchases and cash payments are recorded on the Accounts Payable input form (Form AP-2). This form can accommodate any type of accounts payable transaction. Figure 6.4 illustrates a completed Accounts Payable input form.

	PURCH. INVOICE NO.	VEND. NO.	DATE MO.	DATE DAY	DATE YR.	GEN. LEDGER ACCT. NO.	INVOICE AMOUNT	DATE MO.	DATE DAY	DATE YR.	DISP. CODE	MANUAL CHECK NO.	
1	292	010	02	01	--	510	1484 42				A		1
2	294							02	10	--	M	3344	2
3	297	020	02	11	--	510	228 50	02	11	--	P		3
4	288							02	12	--	P		4

RUN DATE 02 / 15 / -- (MM DD YY)   ACCOUNTS PAYABLE Input Form   Problem No. *Sample*   FORM AP-2

BATCH NO. 2

BATCH TOTALS   1712 92

DISPOSITION CODE:
A = ON ACCOUNT
M = MANUAL CHECK
P = PAY THIS ITEM
(COMPUTER WRITES CHECK)

Figure 6.4   Accounts Payable Input Form

In Figure 6.4, the accounts payable transactions to be key-entered into the computer for Hardware Plus occurred during the month of February, as indicated by the run date located in the upper left corner of the form. The batch number, located beneath the run date, should contain a one- or two-digit number which identifies a specific group of accounts payable transactions. Remember that Batch No. 1 is reserved for the opening balances you worked with in Chapter 5 during accounts payable setup. In this example, the accounts payable transactions are identified as Batch No. 2. Succeeding batch numbers (3, 4, . . .) should be assigned to subsequent monthly groupings of transactions. The use of batch numbers is helpful in finding and isolating errors by providing a convenient method of tracing an error back to its source.

As you learned in Chapter 5, the Accounts Payable input form consists of two major sections: (1) the purchases section and (2) the cash payments section. When using this form in an ongoing system to process accounts payable transactions, purchases data is recorded in the purchases section, and cash payment data is recorded in the cash payment section.

Each line on the Accounts Payable input form represents one accounts payable transaction. Recorded in the Purchase Invoice Number column is a number from one to four digits used by the computer to identify each accounts payable transaction. The purchase invoice number *must* be supplied for each accounts payable transaction, whether it is a purchase or a cash payment.

In the Purchases section of the form, the Vendor Number column represents the number from the vendor list, or vendor window, which identifies the vendor to whom the transaction data belongs. The Purchases Date column contains spaces for the date of the purchases invoice in the MM/DD/YY format. The General Ledger Account Number column is used by the computer to perform the integration with the General Ledger System. The account number entered will be debited. For example, if the transaction is for the purchase of supplies, the Supplies account number is recorded. If merchandise is purchased, the Purchases account number is recorded. The next column, Invoice Amount, contains the gross amount of the transaction.

In the Cash Payments section of the form, the Date column contains spaces for the date of the cash payment in the MM/DD/YY format. The Disposition Code column is used to indicate that the transaction is on account (Code A), a manual check has already been written (Code M), or a transaction is on account and is to be paid by the computer the next time checks are printed (Code P). If a disposition code of M (Manual Check) is entered, you must supply the check number in the Manual Check Number column.

At the bottom of the form, the total of the amounts in the Invoice Amount column should be determined using a calculator, and this total should be written in the Batch Totals space provided at the bottom of the column. This total will be used to help verify the accuracy of data entry activities during transaction processing.

Four different types of accounts payable transactions are illustrated in Figure 6.4, the Accounts Payable input form for Hardware Plus.

The first transaction is an example of a purchase of merchandise on account.

February 1, 19--
Purchased merchandise on account from DataPro Paper Supply, $1,484.42 (Purchase Invoice No. 292).

The entry to record this transaction is shown on line 1 of the Accounts Payable input form. The purchase invoice number, 292, is recorded in the Purchase Invoice Number column. The vendor number for DataPro Paper Supply, 010, is recorded in the Vendor Number column. The month, day, and year of the purchase are recorded in the Purchases Date column. Because merchandise was purchased, the Purchases account number, 510, is debited and, therefore, recorded in the General Ledger Account Number column. The total or gross amount of the invoice, $1,484.42, is entered in the Invoice Amount column. The Disposition Code column contains the letter **A** to indicate that the purchase is on account and will be paid for by check at a later date.

The second transaction is an example of a purchase in which a manual check was written for a payment on account rather than having the computer write the check.

February 10, 19--
Paid on account (manual check) to Metro Computer Store, $310.00, for Purchase Invoice No. 294 (Check No. 3344).

The entry to record this transaction is shown on line 2 of the Accounts Payable input form. Notice that only the purchase invoice number, date the check was written, disposition code (M), and manual check number are required. The rest of the columns need not be filled in because the information was recorded previously as a purchase on account transaction.

The third transaction is an example of a purchase for which the computer is to print a check the next time checks are printed.

February 11, 19--
Purchased merchandise from Computer Distribution Co., $228.50 (Purchase Invoice No. 297). Released this purchase invoice for payment.

The entry to record this transaction is shown on line 3 of the Accounts Payable input form. The Purchases account (Account No. 510) is to be debited and is therefore recorded in the General Ledger Account Number column. Notice the Disposition Code column contains the letter **P** to indicate that this invoice is to be paid the next time checks are printed by the computer.

The fourth and final transaction is an example of a release for payment.

February 12, 19--
Released Purchase Invoice No. 288 to Computer Distribution Co. for payment.

The entry to record this transaction is shown on line 4 of the Accounts Payable input form. Purchase Invoice No. 288 is an unpaid purchase invoice recorded for the previous month and is now being released for payment. Notice that only the purchase invoice number, cash payment date, and disposition code (**P**) are required. The rest of the columns need not be filled in because the information was recorded with the first transaction, the original purchase.

ACCOUNTS PAYABLE OPERATIONAL PROCEDURES

Once the Accounts Payable File Maintenance input form(s) and the Accounts Payable input form(s) are completed, the data contained on them must be key-entered into the computer. Various reports may then be printed or displayed in order to complete the processing of accounts payable transactions. The following sections explain how Options G through P of the Accounts Payable Main Menu (illustrated in Figure 6.5) are used to accomplish this task.

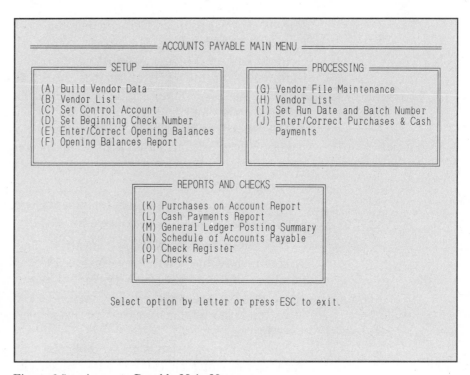

Figure 6.5   Accounts Payable Main Menu

The options on the Accounts Payable Main Menu should be completed in sequence during the accounts payable operational procedures. As you learned in Chapter 5, the Accounts Payable Main Menu is divided into three sections: The first section, Setup, contains Options A through F; the second section, Processing, contains Options G through J; and the third section, Reports and Checks, contains Options K through P. The sections which follow explain how Options G through P are used to complete accounts payable transaction processing in an ongoing system.

Vendor File Maintenance Option G

The *Vendor File Maintenance* option permits additions, changes, and deletions to the existing vendor data. When this option is selected, and a vendor number is key-entered, the Vendor File Maintenance data entry screen shown in Figure 6.6 will appear.

In order to add, change, or delete vendors, complete the following steps:

1. Key-enter a vendor number. The computer will check to see if the vendor number already exists in its memory. If not, the computer

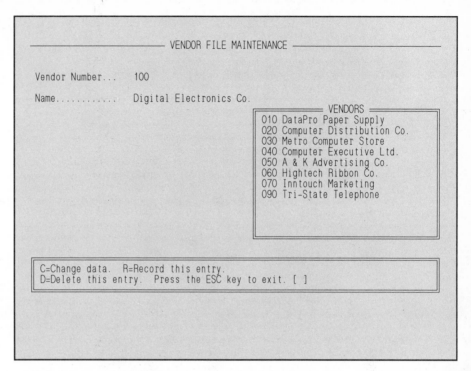

Figure 6.6   Vendor File Maintenance Data Entry Screen

will assume that you wish to add a new vendor (proceed to No. 2). If the vendor number already exists, the computer will assume that you wish to delete the vendor or change its name. In either case, a decision prompt will appear asking you to strike **C** if you want to change the vendor name, **R** if you wish to record the name as it appears on the screen, or **D** if you wish to delete this vendor. Remember that a vendor cannot be deleted if it has activity.

2. If you are adding a new account, key-enter the name of the vendor. A decision prompt will appear asking you to strike **C** to correct the vendor name if entered incorrectly, **R** to record the vendor number and name as keyed, or **D** to delete the entry.

3. If the account already exists and you wish to change the vendor name, strike **C** for change, key-enter the correct vendor name, and strike **R** to record the account data.

4. If the vendor account already exists and you wish to delete it, strike **D**, and the account will be deleted.

5. Repeat this procedure until all additions, changes, and deletions have been key-entered from the Accounts Payable File Maintenance input form. After all data has been key-entered, press the Esc key without keying any data in the *Vendor Number* field to exit this menu and return to the Accounts Payable Main Menu.

Vendor List Option H   A **vendor list** is a report showing data that is stored in the computer's memory. The vendor list may be displayed or printed at any time and is used to verify file maintenance data which has been entered into the Accounts Payable System. Whenever an addition, change, or deletion of a vendor takes place, an updated vendor list should be generated.

This option is identical to the *Vendor List* option you used in Chapter

5 during accounts payable setup. When this option is chosen, a decision prompt will appear that will permit you to display, print, or exit the vendor list. Select the option desired. Figure 6.7 illustrates a displayed vendor list for Hardware Plus.

```
RUN DATE: 02/15/--               HARDWARE PLUS                VENDOR LIST
VENDOR      VENDOR
NUMBER      NAME
-----------------
010         DataPro Paper Supply
020         Computer Distribution Co.
030         Metro Computer Store
040         Computer Executive Ltd.
050         A & K Advertising Co.
060         Quality Ribbon Co.
070         Inntouch Marketing
090         Tri-State Telephone
100         Digital Electronics Co.
110         Park Ave. Development
120         Rocket Delivery Service
130         Dennis Siegel
140         Ruth Hines
150         A-1 Electronics Supply




                       Press SPACE BAR to continue.
```

Figure 6.7   Hardware Plus Vendor List

Set Run Date and Batch Number Option I

The purpose of Option I, *Set Run Date and Batch Number*, is to provide the computer with the run date to be used on reports and a batch number that will identify a group of accounts payable transactions. The run date that is key-entered should correspond with the run date recorded on the upper left corner of the Accounts Payable input form. This date must contain the month and year the purchases and cash payments occurred. The day should be the day of the month the transactions were key-entered. The batch number that is key-entered should correspond to the batch number located on the upper left corner of the Accounts Payable input form. Remember that Batch No. 1 is reserved for the opening balances you entered in Chapter 5 during accounts payable setup. Succeeding batch numbers (2, 3, . . .) should be assigned to subsequent groups of accounts payable transactions as discussed earlier. The batch number will prove helpful in locating errors and providing an audit trail by which you will be able to trace a transaction to its source. The data entry screen to set the run date and batch number is shown in Figure 6.8.

In order to key-enter the run date and batch number, complete the following steps:

1. Check the run date and batch number displayed. If both data fields are correct as displayed, exit this menu and return to the Accounts Payable Main Menu by pressing the Esc key.

```
┌─────────────────────────────────────────────────────────────┐
│                                                               │
│  ─────────────────── SET RUN DATE AND BATCH NUMBER ─────────  │
│                                                               │
│   Run Date............   02/15/--                             │
│                                                               │
│   Batch Number........   2                                    │
│                                                               │
│                                                               │
│                                                               │
│                                                               │
│                                                               │
│                                                               │
│                                                               │
│                                                               │
│     ┌─────────────────────────────────────────────────────┐  │
│     │ C=Change data.  R=Record this information.           │  │
│     │ Press the ESC key to exit. [ ]                       │  │
│     └─────────────────────────────────────────────────────┘  │
│                                                               │
└─────────────────────────────────────────────────────────────┘
```

Figure 6.8   Set Run Date and Batch Number Data Entry Screen

2. Position the cursor in the data field you wish to change and key-enter the correct date (in the format MMDDYY without slashes) or batch number. Press the ENTER/RETURN key after changes are complete.

3. Verify the accuracy of the run date and batch number, then strike **R** to record your changes and return to the Accounts Payable Main Menu.

Enter/Correct Purchases & Cash Payments Option J

The purpose of the *Purchases & Cash Payments* option (accounts payable transactions) is to permit you to: (1) enter new accounts payable transactions, (2) make corrections to previously entered transactions, (3) release transactions for payment, and (4) delete previously entered transactions. The procedure for key-entering this data from the Accounts Payable input form is identical to the procedure introduced in Chapter 5 for key-entering the opening balances during accounts payable setup. Windows may be opened using the function keys to enable you to reference the chart of accounts (Function 1 key), vendors (Function 2 key), or active invoices (Function 3 key) in case you need to verify a particular account, vendor number, or active invoice.

If the last option selected was not the *Set Run Date and Batch Number* option, a window display will appear that allows you to verify the current settings of the run date and batch number. If these data fields are correct, press the Space Bar to continue. If these data fields are incorrect, press Esc to exit back to the Accounts Payable Main Menu, select the *Set Run Date and Batch Number* option, and enter the correct data.

The Enter/Correct Purchases & Cash Payments data entry screen (with a purchase and release for payment transaction already keyed) is shown in Figure 6.9.

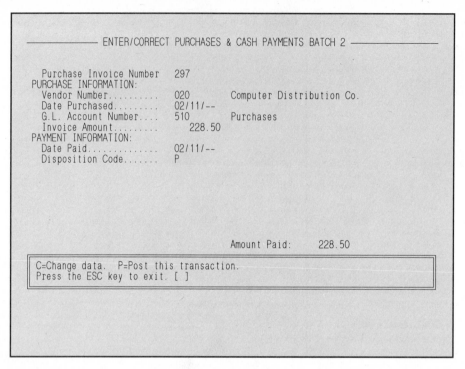

```
─────────── ENTER/CORRECT PURCHASES & CASH PAYMENTS BATCH 2 ───────────


        Purchase Invoice Number   297
      PURCHASE INFORMATION:
        Vendor Number.........    020         Computer Distribution Co.
        Date Purchased........    02/11/--
        G.L. Account Number....   510         Purchases
        Invoice Amount.........      228.50
      PAYMENT INFORMATION:
        Date Paid.............    02/11/--
        Disposition Code.......   P




                                            Amount Paid:     228.50

      ┌──────────────────────────────────────────────────────────────┐
      │ C=Change data.   P=Post this transaction.                    │
      │ Press the ESC key to exit. [ ]                               │
      └──────────────────────────────────────────────────────────────┘
```

Figure 6.9   Enter/Correct Purchases and Cash Payments Data Entry Screen

Complete the following procedure when key-entering accounts payable transactions or making corrections to errors:

1. Key-enter the purchase invoice number. At this time, the computer will check to see if the purchase invoice number just keyed already exists. If the invoice number exists and the disposition code is **A**, the cursor will position itself in the *Date Paid* field (it will assume you are going to pay it). Also, if the invoice exists, and the disposition code is **P** or **M**, all transaction data will be displayed and a prompt will appear. Strike **C** to change the data, **D** to delete the transaction, or press Esc to exit this screen, leaving the data unchanged. If no transaction data exists, the computer will assume you wish to enter a new accounts payable transaction for the purchase invoice number, and empty data fields will be displayed. If data fields should appear for discount and debit data (fields which do not appear on your input document) you have somehow selected the expanded accounts payable mode. Leave these fields blank by pressing ENTER/RETURN without entering any data. These fields will be explained further in a later chapter.

2. Key-enter the vendor number.
3. Key-enter the date of the purchase invoice.
4. Key-enter the general ledger account number (account to be debited).
5. Key-enter the amount of the transaction.
6. Key-enter the date of the cash payment.
7. Key-enter the disposition code.

   *Note: if the disposition code is **M** (for Manual Check), a* Manual Check Number *field will appear below the disposition code in which you may key-enter the check number.*

8. A decision prompt will appear asking if you wish to make a change, delete the transaction, post the transaction, or ignore the displayed data (do nothing). Strike **C** if you wish to make changes or corrections, **D** if you wish to delete the transaction, **P** if you wish to post and record the transaction data as displayed, or press Esc to exit and disregard the data on the screen.

   *Note: At this time the computer will check the data you have entered to verify its accuracy. If errors are detected, you will be given a chance to make corrections. If the vendor number does not exist, a decision prompt message will appear asking if you wish to add this vendor. If you respond **Yes**, the Vendor File Maintenance data entry screen will appear and you will be permitted to add the vendor. After the vendor has been added and recorded in the computer's memory, the Enter/Correct Purchases and Cash Payments data entry screen will again appear and you will be permitted to continue.*

9. Continue this procedure until all transactions or corrections have been key-entered. When finished, press the Esc key to exit this data entry screen and return to the Accounts Payable Main Menu.

When key-entering accounts payable transactions, all errors may not be discovered as the transactions are being entered on the data entry screen. It is easy to correct these errors even though they are not discovered until later. The following sections describe two examples of typical errors and the methods for correcting them:

Error 1: A data field in a transaction from a previous batch is in error.

To correct this error, select Option J, *Enter/Correct Purchases and Cash Payments*, from the Accounts Payable Main Menu. Key-enter the purchase invoice number. Follow the procedure for making corrections explained previously in Step 1. Corrections may be made to a transaction even though it has already been released for payment and a check has been printed. After the correction has been made, all the Accounts Payable reports for the batch (including the checks) can be reprinted.

Error 2: A transaction is key-entered with an incorrect purchase invoice number.

To correct this error, select Option I, *Set Run Date and Batch Number*, from the Accounts Payable Main Menu. Set the batch number to the number of the batch which contains the error. Key the incorrect purchase invoice number. The computer will display the transaction in error. When the decision prompt described in Step 1 appears, strike **D** to delete the entire transaction. Finally, key-enter the transaction with the correct purchase invoice number.

Purchases on Account Report Option K
The **Purchases on Account report** lists all transactions, by batch, in which cash is to be paid out. This report should be printed or displayed after purchases on account transactions are key-entered into the computer and after making any corrections. Examining this report and comparing the computer total with the batch total at the bottom of the Accounts Payable input form will help verify that all data has been

recorded properly and provide an audit trail (if printed) for future reference. When this option is selected, a decision prompt will appear which permits you to print or display the Purchases on Account report or to exit. Select the option of your choice. Figure 6.10 illustrates a displayed Purchases on Account report for Hardware Plus. Notice that only the transactions from the batch number which has been set are included on the report.

```
RUN DATE: 02/15/--        HARDWARE PLUS        PURCHASES ON ACCOUNT BATCH #2
VENDOR                       PURCH.      G.L.
NO. NAME                     INV.  DATE  ACCOUNT    AMOUNT
------------------------------------------------------------------------------
010 DataPro Paper Supply     292  02/01/-- 510      1484.42
150 A-1 Electronics Supply   293  02/04/-- 140        30.85
030 Metro Computer Store     294  02/05/-- 510       310.00
060 Quality Ribbon Co.       295  02/09/-- 510       545.95
130 Dennis Siegel            296  02/10/-- 320      1050.00
020 Computer Distribution Co. 297 02/11/-- 510       228.50
140 Ruth Hines               298  02/12/-- 340      1300.00
030 Metro Computer Store     299  02/15/-- 510      1280.20
020 Computer Distribution Co. 300 02/15/-- 510      2072.90
060 Quality Ribbon Co.       301  02/15/-- 510       305.48
                                                  ----------
   TOTALS                                           8608.30
                                                  ==========




            Press SPACE BAR to continue.
```

Figure 6.10   Purchases on Account Report

Cash Payments Report Option L

Cash payments are payments for purchase invoices. The **Cash Payments report** lists all the transactions (including those paid by manual check), by batch number, which have been released to be paid the next time checks are printed by the computer. This report should be run after cash payment transactions are key-entered and after any corrections have been made. This will help verify that all data has been recorded properly and provide an audit trail (if printed) for future reference. The procedure to display or print the Cash Payments report is similar to that of the Purchases on Account report. Figure 6.11 illustrates a displayed Cash Payments report for Hardware Plus. Notice that only transactions from the batch number which has been set are included on the report.

General Ledger Posting Summary Option M

The **general ledger posting summary** summarizes the changes in general ledger accounts resulting from the journal entries generated *only* for the current batch of accounts payable transactions. When this option is selected, the usual decision prompt will appear which permits you to display, print, or to exit the General Ledger Posting Summary data entry screen. Select the option of your choice. If a printer is attached to your computer, it is recommended that the general ledger

```
RUN DATE: 02/15/--              HARDWARE PLUS              CASH PAYMENTS BATCH #2
VENDOR                        INVOICE                                  MAN.
NO. NAME                        NO.  DATE         AMOUNT  TYPE         CHK.
-----------------------------------------------------------------------------
020 Computer Distribution Co.  288 02/12/--       2005.00 Payment
030 Metro Computer Store        291 02/02/--        930.00 Payment
060 Quality Ribbon Co.          290 02/05/--       1160.00 Payment
010 DataPro Paper Supply        292 02/11/--       1484.42 Payment
150 A-1 Electronics Supply      293 02/08/--         30.85 Payment
030 Metro Computer Store        294 02/10/--        310.00 Payment       3344
130 Dennis Siegel               296 02/10/--       1050.00 Payment
020 Computer Distribution Co.  297 02/11/--        228.50 Payment
140 Ruth Hines                  298 02/12/--       1300.00 Payment

    TOTAL CASH PAYMENTS    8498.77




                          Press SPACE BAR to continue.
```

Figure 6.11   Cash Payments Report

posting summary be printed so that it will be available for future reference. Figure 6.12 illustrates a displayed general ledger posting summary for Hardware Plus. Notice, the Accounts Payable account (account number 210) appears twice in order to show the total debits and credits integrated into the general ledger system during the current computer session. The $8,608.30 Accounts Payable credit amount represents the total amount of purchases during the current computer session (see Figure 6.10). The $8,498.77 Accounts Payable debit amount represents the total amount of cash payments during the current computer session (see Figure 6.11).

Schedule of Accounts Payable Option N

The schedule of accounts payable lists all unpaid invoices by vendor, the total amount due each vendor, and the total amount due all vendors. This report should be run after all current transactions are key-entered and posted. When the *Schedule of Accounts Payable* option is selected, the usual decision prompt will appear which permits you to display or print the Schedule of Accounts Payable or to exit. Select the option of your choice. A displayed schedule of accounts payable for Hardware Plus is illustrated in Figure 6.13.

Check Register Option O

The **check register** lists each check for the current batch that is to be printed by the computer as well as any manual checks previously entered. This report contains the check number, vendor number, vendor name, check amount, and the total amount paid to all vendors. It provides an audit trail (if printed) for future reference. After you select this option, a decision prompt will appear on your screen which allows you to display or print the check register or exit. Select the option of your choice. A displayed check register for Hardware Plus is shown in

```
RUN DATE: 02/15/--          HARDWARE PLUS          G.L. POSTING SUMMARY BATCH #2
ACCOUNT ACCOUNT
NUMBER  TITLE                              DEBIT     CREDIT
-----------------------------------------------------------
110     Cash                                          8498.77
140     Supplies                           30.85
210     Accounts Payable                 8498.77
210     Accounts Payable                              8608.30
320     Dennis Siegel, Drawing           1050.00
340     Ruth Hines, Drawing              1300.00
510     Purchases                        6227.45
                                        ----------  ----------
        TOTALS                           17107.07   17107.07
                                        ==========  ==========




                      Press SPACE BAR to continue.
```

Figure 6.12   General Ledger Posting Summary

```
RUN DATE: 02/15/--          HARDWARE PLUS          SCHEDULE OF ACCOUNTS PAYABLE
VENDOR NUMBER AND NAME
        INVOICE    DATE        AMOUNT
----------------------------------------
020  Computer Distribution Co.
        300    02/15/--     2072.90
     VENDOR TOTAL           2072.90

030  Metro Computer Store
        299    02/15/--     1280.20
     VENDOR TOTAL           1280.20

060  Quality Ribbon Co.
        295    02/09/--      545.95
        301    02/15/--      305.48
     VENDOR TOTAL            851.43

                          ----------
FINAL TOTAL                 4204.53
                          ==========

                Press SPACE BAR to continue.
```

Figure 6.13   Schedule of Accounts Payable

Figure 6.14. Notice that the first line of the report contains information from a manual check.

```
RUN DATE: 02/15/--              HARDWARE PLUS          CHECK REGISTER BATCH #2
CHECK   VENDOR VENDOR                        CHECK
NUMBER  NUMBER NAME                          AMOUNT
--------------------------------------------------------
 3344    030   Metro Computer Store           310.00
 2245    010   DataPro Paper Supply          1484.42
 2253    020   Computer Distribution Co.     2233.50
 2254    030   Metro Computer Store           930.00
 2255    060   Quality Ribbon Co.            1160.00
 2256    130   Dennis Siegel                 1050.00
 2257    140   Ruth Hines                    1300.00
 2258    150   A-1 Electronics Supply          30.85
                                             --------
               FINAL TOTAL                   8498.77
                                             ========




               Press SPACE BAR to continue.
```

Figure 6.14   Check Register

Checks Option P

When this option is selected, the computer will print checks by batch number for all transactions that have been released for payment. If several transactions have been released for one vendor, all payments for that vendor are combined into one check with each transaction shown separately on the remittance advice stub. When this option is selected, the usual decision prompt will appear which permits you to display, print, or exit the checks option. If the option to print checks is chosen, the computer will check to see if preprinted check forms are required (as specified during accounting system setup). If preprinted check forms are required, the computer will prompt you to insert the forms before continuing. If not, the computer will draw an outline of a check as it prints the data on standard continuous form paper. Examples of a remittance advice stub and check, both on a preprinted check form and a computer-drawn check, are illustrated in Figure 6.15.

Save Data to Disk

Be sure to save your data to disk as a work in progress file after returning to the System Selection Menu prior to computer shutdown. This option must be the last option selected prior to ending the automated accounting session or before loading another file from disk into your computer's memory. If you fail to run this option, all data keyed and processed during this session will not be recorded onto your data disk and will be lost.

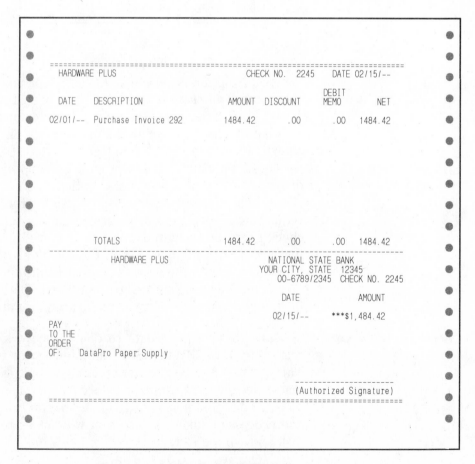

Figure 6.15   Remittance Advice Stub and Check

ACCOUNTS PAYABLE TRANSACTIONS AND REPORTS (SAMPLE PROBLEM)

This sample problem illustrates the principles and procedures required to process accounts payable transactions using an automated accounting system. The chart of accounts, control accounts, vendors, and opening balances for Hardware Plus will be the basis of this sample problem. The data for this sample problem has been stored on disk under the file name **AA6-S**. In this problem, you will process accounts payable transactions for the first half of February.

Instructions

Step 1   The following accounts payable transactions for Hardware Plus occurred during the first half of February of the current year. Additions, changes, and deletions to vendor data for Problem 6-S have been recorded on the Accounts Payable File Maintenance input form shown in Figure 6.16. The transactions have been analyzed and recorded for you as Batch No. 2 on the Accounts Payable input form for Problem 6-S shown in Figure 6.17. Compare the transactions with the completed forms shown on the following pages.

Feb 01   Purchased merchandise on account from DataPro Paper Supply, $1,484.42 (Purchase Invoice No. 292).

02   Released Purchase Invoice No. 291 to Metro Computer Store for payment.

04   Bought supplies on account from A-1 Electronics Supply, $30.85 (Purchase Invoice No. 293).

A-1 Electronics Supply is recorded on the Accounts Payable File Maintenance input form (Figure 6.16) as a new vendor. Because vendor numbers are usually assigned in increments of ten, this vendor has been assigned Vendor No. 150. Purchase Invoice No. 293 is recorded on the Accounts Payable input form (Figure 6.17) using the vendor number for A-1 Electronics Supply.

05   Purchased merchandise on account from Metro Computer Store, $310.00 (Purchase Invoice No. 294).

05   Released Purchase Invoice No. 290 to Hightech Ribbon Co. for payment.

08   Released Purchase Invoice No. 293 to A-1 Electronics Supply for payment.

09   Changed the vendor name of Hightech Ribbon Co. to Quality Ribbon Co.

09   Purchased merchandise on account from Quality Ribbon Co., $545.95 (Purchase Invoice No. 295).

10   Paid on account (manual check) to Metro Computer Store, $310.00, for Purchase Invoice No. 294 (Check No. 3344).

Since a manual check was written to pay this account, record an **M** in the Disposition Code column and the check number in the Manual Check Number column.

	1	2	

ACCOUNTS PAYABLE
FILE MAINTENANCE
Input Form

RUN DATE _02, 15 , --_
  MM   DD   YY

Problem No. _6-S_

FORM AP-1

	VENDOR NUMBER	VENDOR NAME	
1	150	A-1 Electronics Supply	1
2	060	Quality Ribbon Co.	2
3			3
4			4
5			5
6			6
7			7
8			8
9			9
10			10
11			11
12			12
13			13
14			14
15			15
16			16
17			17
18			18
19			19
20			20
21			21
22			22
23			23
24			24
25			25

Figure 6.16   Accounts Payable File Maintenance Input Form (Problem 6-S)

10   Dennis Siegel, partner, wishes to withdraw $1,050.00 for personal use (Purchase Invoice No. 296). Released this purchase invoice for payment.

Use the general ledger account number for the Drawing account. Include a **P** in the Disposition Code column.

11   Released Purchase Invoice No. 292 to DataPro Paper Supply for payment.

11   Purchased merchandise from Computer Distribution Co., $228.50 (Purchase Invoice No. 297). Released this purchase invoice for payment.

12   Released Purchase Invoice No. 288 to Computer Distribution Co. for payment.

12   Ruth Hines, partner, wishes to withdraw cash for personal use, $1,300.00 (Purchase Invoice No. 298). Released this purchase invoice for payment.

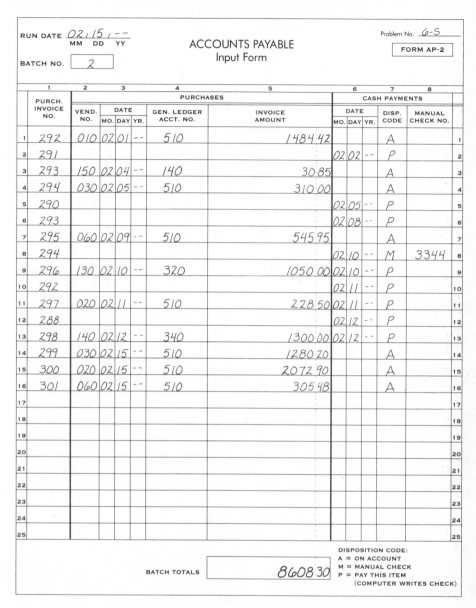

Figure 6.17   Accounts Payable Input Form (Problem 6-S)

15   Purchased merchandise on account from Metro Computer Store, $1,280.20 (Purchase Invoice No. 299).

15   Purchased merchandise on account from Computer Distribution Co., $2,072.90 (Purchase Invoice No. 300).

15   Purchased merchandise on account from Quality Ribbon Co., $305.48 (Purchase Invoice No. 301).

Step 2   Bring up the System Selection Menu according to the instructions for your microcomputer.

Step 3   Select Option C, *Load Data From Disk*, from the System Selection Menu.

Step 4   Select Problem 6-S from *Load Data from the Program Disk* by key-entering **AA6-S** when the directory list appears.

Step **5** Select Option D, *Company Information*, from the System Selection Menu. Verify that the *Problem Number* field contains **Problem 6-S**, that the *Company Name* field contains **Hardware Plus**, and that the *Type of Business* field is set to **P**. If these data fields are correct, set the run date to **February 15** of the current year, record the correct data, and proceed to Step 6. If these data fields are not correct, the wrong file has been loaded into your computer's memory. Repeat Steps 3 and 4 above.

Step **6** Select Option G, *Accounts Payable*, from the System Selection Menu.

Step **7** Select Option G, *Vendor File Maintenance*, from the Accounts Payable Main Menu. Key-enter and record the vendor file maintenance transactions from the Accounts Payable File Maintenance input form (Figure 6.16.)

Step **8** Select Option H, *Vendor List*, and display or print a revised vendor list. Verify that the data you key-entered is correct. The correct revised vendor list is shown in Figure 6.18.

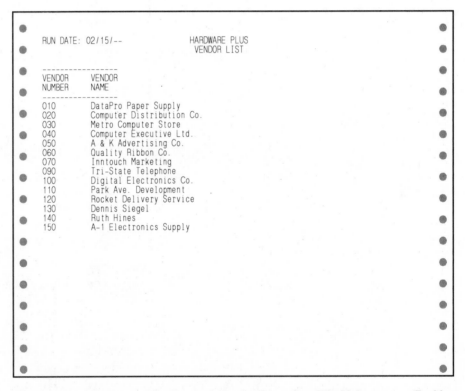

```
RUN DATE: 02/15/--              HARDWARE PLUS
                                 VENDOR LIST


-----------------
VENDOR    VENDOR
NUMBER    NAME
-----------------
010       DataPro Paper Supply
020       Computer Distribution Co.
030       Metro Computer Store
040       Computer Executive Ltd.
050       A & K Advertising Co.
060       Quality Ribbon Co.
070       Inntouch Marketing
090       Tri-State Telephone
100       Digital Electronics Co.
110       Park Ave. Development
120       Rocket Delivery Service
130       Dennis Siegel
140       Ruth Hines
150       A-1 Electronics Supply
```

Figure 6.18   Hardware Plus Revised Vendor List after File Maintenance (Problem 6-S)

Step **9** Select Option I, *Set Run Date and Batch Number*, from the Accounts Payable Main Menu. Verify that the run date has been set to **February 15** of the current year and that the batch number has been set to **2**. If not, make the appropriate changes and strike **R** to record the data.

Step **10** Select Option J, *Enter/Correct Purchases & Cash Payments*, from the Accounts Payable Main Menu. When the Purchases & Cash Payments data entry screen for Batch 2 appears, key-enter and post the purchases and cash payments transactions from the Accounts Payable input form in Figure 6.17.

Step 11   Select Option K, *Purchases on Account Report*, from the Accounts Payable Main Menu. Display or print the Purchases on Account report. Compare your Purchases on Account report with the correct one shown in Figure 6.19. The computer total should match the batch total at the bottom of the Accounts Payable input form. If the Purchases on Account report is correct, proceed to Step 13.

```
RUN DATE: 02/15/--                    HARDWARE PLUS
                              PURCHASES ON ACCOUNT BATCH #2

--------------------------------------------------------------------
VENDOR                          PURCH.          G.L.
NO.  NAME                       INV.  DATE      ACCOUNT    AMOUNT
--------------------------------------------------------------------
010  DataPro Paper Supply       292   02/01/--  510        1484.42
150  A-1 Electronics Supply     293   02/04/--  140          30.85
030  Metro Computer Store       294   02/05/--  510         310.00
060  Quality Ribbon Co.         295   02/09/--  510         545.95
130  Dennis Siegel              296   02/10/--  320        1050.00
020  Computer Distribution Co.  297   02/11/--  510         228.50
140  Ruth Hines                 298   02/12/--  340        1300.00
030  Metro Computer Store       299   02/15/--  510        1280.20
020  Computer Distribution Co.  300   02/15/--  510        2072.90
060  Quality Ribbon Co.         301   02/15/--  510         305.48
                                                          ----------
     TOTALS                                                8608.30
                                                          ==========
```

Figure 6.19   Purchases on Account Report (Problem 6-S)

Step 12   If the Purchases on Account report is in error, select Option J, *Enter/ Correct Purchases & Cash Payments*. Key-enter and post the corrections, then display or print another Purchases on Account report. Repeat this step until your Purchases on Account data is correct.

Step 13   Select Option L, *Cash Payments Report*, from the Accounts Payable Main Menu. Display or print your Cash Payments report and compare it to the correct one shown in Figure 6.20. If your Cash Payments report is correct, proceed to Step 15.

Step 14   If the Cash Payments report is in error, select Option J, *Enter/Correct Purchases & Cash Payments*. Key-enter and post the corrections, then display or print another Cash Payments report. Repeat this step until your Cash Payments report is correct.

Step 15   Select Option M, *General Ledger Posting Summary*, from the Accounts Payable Main Menu, and display or print a general ledger posting summary. The correct general ledger posting summary is shown in Figure 6.21. Notice that the posting summary is for all trans-

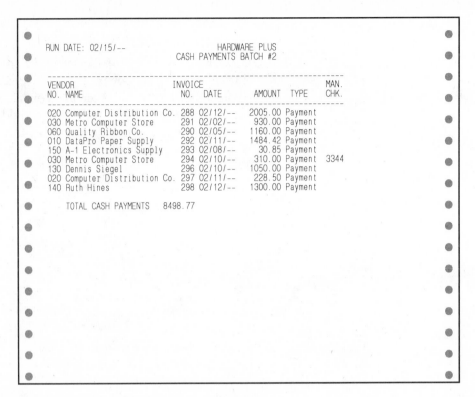

```
RUN DATE: 02/15/--                    HARDWARE PLUS
                                 CASH PAYMENTS BATCH #2

      ------------------------------------------------------------------
      VENDOR                     INVOICE                            MAN.
      NO. NAME                   NO.  DATE      AMOUNT  TYPE        CHK.
      ------------------------------------------------------------------
      020 Computer Distribution Co. 288 02/12/--  2005.00 Payment
      030 Metro Computer Store      291 02/02/--   930.00 Payment
      060 Quality Ribbon Co.        290 02/05/--  1160.00 Payment
      010 DataPro Paper Supply      292 02/11/--  1484.42 Payment
      150 A-1 Electronics Supply    293 02/08/--    30.85 Payment
      030 Metro Computer Store      294 02/10/--   310.00 Payment   3344
      130 Dennis Siegel             296 02/10/--  1050.00 Payment
      020 Computer Distribution Co. 297 02/11/--   228.50 Payment
      140 Ruth Hines                298 02/12/--  1300.00 Payment

         TOTAL CASH PAYMENTS    8498.77
```

Figure 6.20   Cash Payments Report (Problem 6-S)

```
RUN DATE: 02/15/--                       HARDWARE PLUS
                            GENERAL LEDGER POSTING SUMMARY BATCH #2

      --------------------------------------------------------------
      ACCOUNT ACCOUNT
      NUMBER  TITLE                        DEBIT       CREDIT
      --------------------------------------------------------------
      110     Cash                                     8498.77
      140     Supplies                      30.85
      210     Accounts Payable            8498.77
      210     Accounts Payable                         8608.30
      320     Dennis Siegel, Drawing      1050.00
      340     Ruth Hines, Drawing         1300.00
      510     Purchases                   6227.45
                                         ---------   ---------
              TOTALS                     17107.07    17107.07
                                         =========   =========
```

Figure 6.21   General Ledger Posting Summary (Problem 6-S)

actions in the current batch number. Therefore, if you entered transactions or made corrections during more than one work session, your posting summary will still reflect all the transactions in that particular batch number.

Step 16   Select Option N, *Schedule of Accounts Payable*, from the Accounts Payable Main Menu. Display or print a schedule of accounts payable. The correct schedule of accounts payable is shown in Figure 6.22.

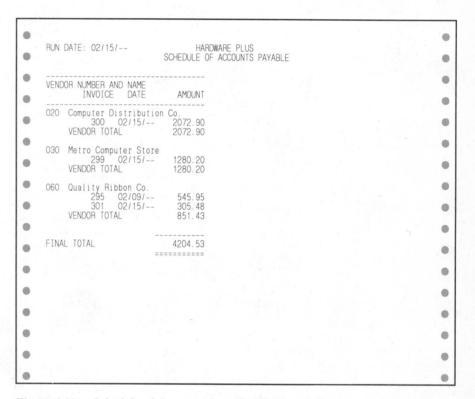

```
RUN DATE: 02/15/--                    HARDWARE PLUS
                              SCHEDULE OF ACCOUNTS PAYABLE


------------------------------------
VENDOR NUMBER AND NAME
          INVOICE    DATE        AMOUNT
------------------------------------
020  Computer Distribution Co.
         300   02/15/--     2072.90
         VENDOR TOTAL       2072.90

030  Metro Computer Store
         299   02/15/--     1280.20
         VENDOR TOTAL       1280.20

060  Quality Ribbon Co.
         295   02/09/--      545.95
         301   02/15/--      305.48
         VENDOR TOTAL        851.43

                           ----------
FINAL TOTAL                 4204.53
                           ==========
```

Figure 6.22   Schedule of Accounts Payable (Problem 6-S)

Step 17   Select Option O, *Check Register*, from the Accounts Payable Main Menu. Display or print a check register. The correct check register is shown in Figure 6.23.

Step 18   Select Option P, *Checks*, from the Accounts Payable Main Menu. Display or print the checks. As discussed earlier, the checks can be printed on preprinted check forms or on standard paper, depending on the option selected during accounting system setup. If you wish to print the checks on the special preprinted check forms, align the check forms on the printer so that the first line of print will fall between the two short black lines shown in the upper left corner of the check stub. The two short horizontal lines are printed at the left edge of the paper, outside the tractor feed perforation. The checks shown in Figure 6.24 (page 185) are printed on preprinted check forms.

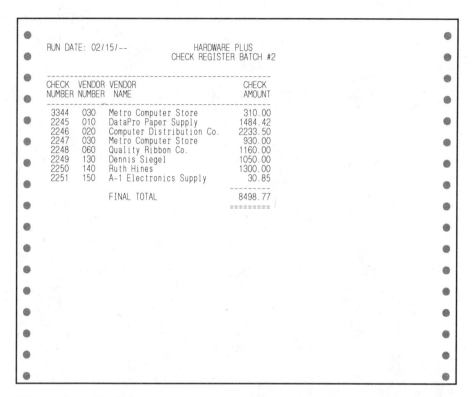

```
  RUN DATE: 02/15/--                    HARDWARE PLUS
                                    CHECK REGISTER BATCH #2

  -------------------------------------------------------------
  CHECK   VENDOR  VENDOR                              CHECK
  NUMBER  NUMBER  NAME                                AMOUNT
  -------------------------------------------------------------
  3344    030     Metro Computer Store                 310.00
  2245    010     DataPro Paper Supply                1484.42
  2246    020     Computer Distribution Co.           2233.50
  2247    030     Metro Computer Store                 930.00
  2248    060     Quality Ribbon Co.                  1160.00
  2249    130     Dennis Siegel                       1050.00
  2250    140     Ruth Hines                          1300.00
  2251    150     A-1 Electronics Supply                30.85
                                                     ---------
                  FINAL TOTAL                         8498.77
                                                     =========
```

Figure 6.23   Check Register (Problem 6-S)

Step 19   Return to the System Selection Menu.

Step 20   Select Option F, *General Ledger*, from the System Selection Menu.

Step 21   Select Option K, *Trial Balance*, from the General Ledger Main Menu.
Display or print a trial balance. The correct trial balance is shown in
Figure 6.25. Notice that the accounts which were affected by transac-
tions have been updated through the integration with the Accounts
Payable System. The accounts payable balance should be the same as
the final total on the schedule of accounts payable prepared in Step 16.

Step 22   Return to the System Selection Menu.

Step 23   Save your work as a work in progress file on your own data disk (recommend file name **AA6-S**) and shut down the computer. Then complete
the student exercise and transaction problem which follow.

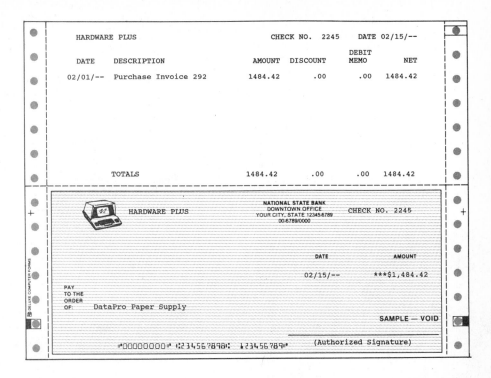

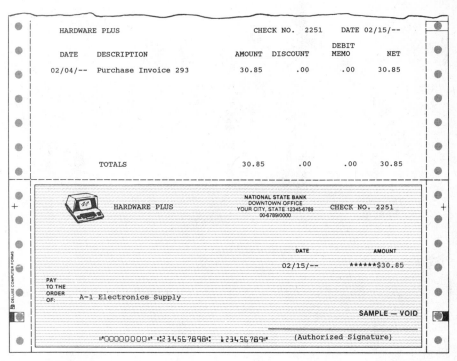

Figure 6.24   Checks on Preprinted Forms (Problem 6-S)

```
    RUN DATE: 02/15/--                    HARDWARE PLUS
                                          TRIAL BALANCE

    ---------------------------------------------------------------------------
    ACCOUNT    ACCOUNT
    NUMBER     TITLE                      DEBIT AMOUNT      CREDIT AMOUNT
    ---------------------------------------------------------------------------
    110        Cash                         7243.01
    120        Accounts Receivable          6445.00
    130        Merchandise Inventory      111141.57
    140        Supplies                      680.85
    150        Prepaid Insurance             320.00
    210        Accounts Payable                                 4204.53
    220        Sales Tax Payable                                1072.35
    310        Dennis Siegel, Capital                          64565.50
    320        Dennis Siegel, Drawing       1050.00
    330        Ruth Hines, Capital                             64565.50
    340        Ruth Hines, Drawing          1300.00
    510        Purchases                    6227.45
                                          --------------    --------------
               TOTALS                     134407.88          134407.88
                                          ==============    ==============
```

Figure 6.25   Trial Balance (Problem 6-S)

Name _____

Class _____ Date _____

CHAPTER 6
STUDENT EXERCISE

I. Matching   For each of the following definitions, write the letter of the term which best fits that definition in the space provided.

a. On account
b. Vendor file maintenance
c. Vendor list
d. Cash Payments report
e. Check Register report
f. Manual check

g. Purchase invoice number
h. Purchases on Account report
i. General ledger posting summary
j. Purging

1. _____ An assigned number used by the computer to identify each accounts payable transaction. (Obj. 12)

2. _____ The process of adding, changing, or deleting vendor records. (Obj. 1)

3. _____ An accounts payable transaction recorded to indicate that a purchase of an item has been made on account for which the company owes money. (Obj. 4)

4. _____ A check written by hand from a checkbook. (Obj. 4)

5. _____ A report which lists all the transactions, by batch number, which have been released to be paid the next time checks are printed by the computer. A report used to help verify that all payments made in cash have been key-entered into the computer correctly. (Obj. 6)

6. _____ A report which lists all transactions, by batch, in which cash is to be paid out. (Obj. 5)

7. _____ A report which shows, in summary form, the changes in general ledger accounts resulting from the journal entries generated *only* for the current batch of accounts payable transactions. (Obj. 7)

8. _____ A report showing vendor data that is stored in the computer's memory. (Obj. 2)

9. _____ A process by which the paid transactions from all previous batches stored in the file are erased, thereby freeing up additional space for the current batch of transactions. (Obj. 10)

10. _____ A report which lists each check which is to be printed by the computer. (Obj. 9)

II. Short Answer   1. Explain the purpose of the general ledger account number on the Accounts Payable input form. (Obj. 12)

_____

_____

2. Explain the accounts payable/general ledger integration process in the following situations. (Obj. 12)

A new transaction is entered: _____

_____

A transaction is released for payment: _____

_____

3. Why must the _Save Data to Disk_ option be the last option selected prior to loading another file into memory or shutting down the computer system? (Obj. 11)

_____

_____

_____

_____

4. Identify the procedures used in _Automated Accounting for the Microcomputer_ to perform accounts payable processing. (Obj. 12)

_____

_____

_____

ACCOUNTS PAYABLE TRANSACTIONS AND REPORTS
TRANSACTION PROBLEM 6-1

Problem 6-1 is a continuation of Problem 6-S. Problem 6-S contained the accounts payable transactions for the first half of February. Problem 6-1 contains the accounts payable transactions for the last half of February. Therefore, if you did not complete the sample problem, you must load the opening balances for Problem 6-1. (Objs. 1-11)

Instructions

Step 1 Remove the blank input forms and the Chapter 6 Audit Test from the end of this chapter. Complete the questions on the audit test as you work through Problem 6-1.

Step 2 The following accounts payable transactions for Hardware Plus occurred during the last half of February. Record the transactions on the proper input forms.

Feb 18 Purchased merchandise on account from A-1 Electronics Supply, $1,140.05 (Purchase Invoice No. 302).

19 Recorded Purchase Invoice No. 303 to Park Ave. Developers for rent, $1,050.00. Released this purchase invoice for payment.

20 Released Purchase Invoice No. 299 to Metro Computer Store for payment.

22 Recorded Purchase Invoice No. 304 (on account) to Rocket Delivery Service for delivery charges, $75.25.

You will need to add Delivery Expense to the general ledger as a new account. Record the new account as Account No. 605 on the General Ledger File Maintenance input form provided.

25 Recorded Purchase Invoice No. 305 (on account) to Etter and Panozza for legal services, $200.00.

You will need to add a new vendor account for Etter and Panozza. Record the new account as Account No. 160 on the Accounts Payable File Maintenance input form provided.

26 Purchased merchandise on account from Digital Electronics Co., $475.00 (Purchase Invoice No. 306).

27 Purchased merchandise on account from Computer Distribution Co., $330.00. (Purchase Invoice No. 307).

28 Released Purchase Invoice No. 300 to Computer Distribution Co. for payment.

28 Released Purchase Invoice No. 295 to Quality Ribbon Co. for payment.

28 Bought supplies on account from A-1 Electronics Supply, $25.00 (Purchase Invoice No. 308).

Step 3 Bring up the System Selection Menu.

Step 4 If you did not complete Problem 6-S, select the *Load Data from Disk* option and choose Problem 6-1 by key-entering the file name **AA6-1** when the directory list appears. If you did complete Problem 6-S, load the data from your work in progress file.

Step 5   Set the run date to **February 28** of the current year. Set the problem number to **Problem 6-1**.

Step 6   Select the *General Ledger* option.

Step 7   Key-enter the chart of accounts file maintenance transactions from the General Ledger File Maintenance input form.

Step 8   Display or print a Chart of Accounts report and verify the entries key-entered in Step 7.

Step 9   Return to the System Selection Menu.

Step 10   Select the *Accounts Payable* option.

Step 11   Key-enter and record the vendor file maintenance transactions from the Accounts Payable File Maintenance input form.

Step 12   Display or print a vendor list and verify the data key-entered in Step 11.

Step 13   Set the batch number to 3.

Step 14   Key-enter and post the purchases and cash payments transactions from the Accounts Payable input form.

Step 15   Display or print the Purchases on Account report and check the computer total against the batch total on your input document.

Step 16   Display or print the Cash Payments report.

Step 17   Verify the data you key-entered. If errors are detected, make corrections and print new Purchases on Account and Cash Payments reports.

Step 18   Display or print a general ledger posting summary.

Step 19   Display or print a schedule of accounts payable. Make any necessary corrections before proceeding.

Step 20   Display or print a check register.

Step 21   Display or print checks.

Step 22   Return to the System Selection Menu.

Step 23   Select the *General Ledger* option.

Step 24   Display or print a trial balance. The accounts payable account balance on the Trial Balance report should be the same as the final total on the schedule of accounts payable prepared in Step 19.

Step 25   Return to the *System Selection Menu* option.

Step 26   Save your work as a work in progress file (recommend file name **AA6-1**). Then shut down the computer.

Step 27   Hand in the completed student exercise sheets, input forms, the audit test, and any printouts to your instructor. You have now completed the computer exercise for Chapter 6.

Name _____

Class _____ Date _____

	ACCOUNTS PAYABLE FILE MAINTENANCE Input Form	Problem No. _____
RUN DATE ___/___/___ MM DD YY		FORM AP-1

	1	2	
	VENDOR NUMBER	VENDOR NAME	
1			1
2			2
3			3
4			4
5			5
6			6
7			7
8			8
9			9
10			10
11			11
12			12
13			13
14			14
15			15
16			16
17			17
18			18
19			19
20			20
21			21
22			22
23			23
24			24
25			25

RUN DATE ___/___/___
MM DD YY

ACCOUNTS PAYABLE
Input Form

Problem No. _____

FORM AP-2

BATCH NO. ☐

	1	2	3			4	5		6			7	8	
	PURCH. INVOICE NO.	PURCHASES							CASH PAYMENTS					
		VEND. NO.	DATE			GEN. LEDGER ACCT. NO.	INVOICE AMOUNT		DATE			DISP. CODE	MANUAL CHECK NO.	
			MO.	DAY	YR.				MO.	DAY	YR.			
1														1
2														2
3														3
4														4
5														5
6														6
7														7
8														8
9														9
10														10
11														11
12														12
13														13
14														14
15														15
16														16
17														17
18														18
19														19
20														20
21														21
22														22
23														23
24														24
25														25

BATCH TOTALS ☐

DISPOSITION CODE:
A = ON ACCOUNT
M = MANUAL CHECK
P = PAY THIS ITEM
   (COMPUTER WRITES CHECK)

Name _____

Class _____ Date _____

	GENERAL LEDGER FILE MAINTENANCE Input Form	Problem No. _____ FORM GL-1

RUN DATE ___/___/___
MM DD YY

	1	2	
	ACCOUNT NUMBER	ACCOUNT TITLE	
1			1
2			2
3			3
4			4
5			5
6			6
7			7
8			8
9			9
10			10
11			11
12			12
13			13
14			14
15			15
16			16
17			17
18			18
19			19
20			20
21			21
22			22
23			23
24			24
25			25

CHAPTER 6
AUDIT TEST

1. What is the account number and account title of the general ledger account added to the chart of accounts this month?

   Account number: _____

   Account title: _____

2. What is the vendor number and name of the vendor added to the vendor file this month?

   Vendor number: _____

   Vendor name: _____

3. What is the batch number of the accounts payable transactions?

   _____

4. Why does Purchase Invoice No. 303 have both an amount in the Invoice Amount column and a **P** in the Disposition Code column? (Refer to the Accounts Payable input form.)

   _____

   _____

5. What is the account number for Miscellaneous Expenses?

   _____

6. Which vendor has been assigned to Vendor No. 140?

   _____

7. To what company is Purchase Invoice No. 306 owed?

   _____

8. To what general ledger account number and title is Purchase Invoice No. 304 charged?

   Account number: _____

   Account title: _____

9. What is the total of the purchases on account for Batch No. 3?

   _____

10. What is the run date printed on the Cash Payments report for Batch No. 3?

   _____

Name _____

Class _____ Date _____

11. What is the amount paid to Park Ave. Development for Purchase Invoice No. 303?

   _____

12. What are the total cash payments for Batch No. 3?

   _____

13. Why do all invoices on the Cash Payments report show Payment in the Type column?

   _____

   _____

   _____

   _____

14. What are the total debits and total credits shown on the general ledger posting summary?

   Total debits: _____

   Total credits: _____

15. Why does Vendor No. 150, A-1 Electronics Supply, have two separate items shown on the schedule of accounts payable?

   _____

16. To how many different vendors does Hardware Plus owe money at the end of the month?

   _____

17. What is the total amount owed to all vendors by Hardware Plus at the end of the month?

   _____

18. What is the check number assigned to the check written to Computer Distribution Co.?

   _____

19. What is the balance in the accounts payable account at the end of the month?

   _____

20. What are the totals of the Debit and Credit columns on the Trial Balance report at the end of the month?

Total debits: _____

Total credits: _____

Part 3

ACCOUNTS RECEIVABLE

7 ACCOUNTS RECEIVABLE SETUP

LEARNING OBJECTIVES

Upon completion of this chapter, you will be able to:

1. Describe the differences between manual and computerized accounts receivable methods.
2. Build customer data.
3. Display or print a customer list.
4. Set control accounts.
5. Enter/correct opening balances.
6. Display or print opening balances.
7. Save data to disk.
8. Perform system shutdown.
9. Identify the components and procedures for accounts receivable setup.

INTRODUCTION

In a manual accounting system, accounts receivable transactions involving a sale of merchandise on account are recorded in a sales journal and posted from the sales journal to individual accounts in an accounts receivable ledger. Periodically, column totals are posted from the sales journal to accounts in the general ledger. Cash receipts on account are recorded in a cash receipts journal and posted to individual accounts in the accounts receivable subsidiary ledger. Entries are also posted from the cash receipts journal to accounts in the general ledger. Periodically, column totals are posted from the cash receipts journal to accounts in the general ledger. At the end of the month, statements of account and a schedule of accounts receivable are prepared from the subsidiary ledger. The total of the schedule of accounts receivable must equal the balance of the accounts receivable account in the general ledger.

A computerized accounts receivable system provides management with information about the company's credit sales and cash receipts. This information includes what the customers bought, how much they owe, when payment is due, and a list of any payments past due. Based on this information, the system prepares a monthly statement of account for each customer who has an outstanding (unpaid) balance. Information produced by the computerized accounts receivable system is summarized, and the appropriate accounts in both the subsidiary and general ledgers are updated.

Another important part of a computerized accounts receivable system is cash flow information. This information is very important to management because it shows how much cash the company is receiving from its customers. Management must have this information to determine if the company has enough money to pay its bills.

There are two approaches to computerized accounts receivable: (1) the balance forward method and (2) the open item method. In the balance forward method, the balance owed is kept by the computer for each customer. Sales on account increase the balance; payments and returns and allowances decrease the balance. With this method, the monthly statement shows only a balance due. The statement does not indicate what invoices or credit memorandums are included. In the open item method, the computer keeps a separate record for each open item (unpaid invoice). When cash is received from a customer, the credit is applied to the appropriate invoice. The monthly statement of account shows the balance due by invoice. The open item method is used in *Automated Accounting for the Microcomputer*.

The computer stores two different types of information in an accounts receivable data file: (1) the customer data and (2) the accounts receivable ledger data. The **accounts receivable data file** (similar to the general ledger and accounts payable data files) contains all the data required by the computer to process accounts receivable transactions. This data file is a part of the entire automated accounting database.

The **customer data** consists of a record for each customer with whom the company does business. Each of these records typically contains a field for the customer number, name, and mailing address. In order to limit the amount of keying necessary, the customer data used in this system is limited to fields for customer number and name. The **accounts receivable ledger data** consists of a record for each sales invoice. Each of these records contains a field for sales invoice number, customer number, sales invoice date, general ledger account number, invoice amount, sales tax percentage, cash received date, document number, and cash received amount. This information is used to print monthly statements and management reports. The contents of these records are similar to the contents of an accounts receivable subsidiary ledger and journals in a manual accounting system.

In order to set up the accounts receivable data file, customer and accounts receivable opening balance ledger information must be recorded on the appropriate input forms. This data is then key-entered into the computer and stored in computer memory. After all key-entering is completed, the data may be saved to disk as a work in progress file for future reference and updating.

The accounts receivable setup procedures consist of several steps which must be carried out before beginning to work with the accounts receivable system. The steps of the accounts receivable setup procedures are as follows: (1) set up customer data, (2) inform the computer of special account numbers it needs in order to update the appropriate accounts in the general ledger, and (3) key-enter the opening balance data for each customer. Menu options for screen displays or printouts of the customers and opening balances are provided to assist you in verifying your work. In addition, an option to make corrections to opening balances is available in case you make a mistake. Accounts receivable setup activities are required only when establishing a new company. This setup procedure, as illustrated in Figure 7.1, will not be required again until another company is created.

Account numbers that require special handling by the computer, called **control accounts**, must be set during the accounts receivable setup process. As accounts receivable transactions are entered or cor-

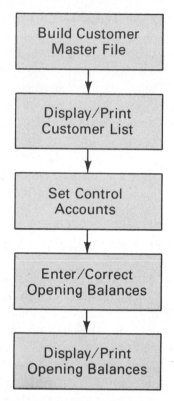

Figure 7.1   Accounts Receivable Setup Procedure

rected in the Accounts Receivable System, the journal entries resulting from those transactions are automatically integrated into the General Ledger System by the computer. In order to integrate these entries, the computer must know the account numbers you have assigned to the general ledger accounts involved. These control account numbers are set using the *Set Control Accounts* option.

COMPLETING THE INPUT FORMS

The data required to perform accounts receivable setup is recorded on two different forms: the Accounts Receivable File Maintenance input form (Form AR-1) and the Accounts Receivable input form (Form AR-2). In this chapter, you will learn how each of these forms is used to record the data required to set up the accounts receivable data file.

Accounts Receivable File Maintenance Input Form (Form AR-1)

The **Accounts Receivable File Maintenance input form** is used to set up and maintain customer data. This form contains fields for the customer number and the customer name. The Accounts Receivable File Maintenance input form serves two separate functions. First, it is used to record the customers to be established during accounts receivable setup. Second, it is used to record additions, changes, and deletions to the customers after accounts receivable setup has been completed and during the ongoing process of the accounting cycle. The second use of this form will be discussed further in Chapter 8.

The Accounts Receivable File Maintenance input form shown in Figure 7.2 illustrates how the customer numbers and corresponding customer names are recorded in order to set up the customer data for Hardware Plus.

	ACCOUNTS RECEIVABLE FILE MAINTENANCE Input Form	Problem No. *Sample* FORM AR-1

RUN DATE 10/01/--
MM DD YY

	CUSTOMER NUMBER	CUSTOMER NAME	
1	010	Dakota County Inquirer	1
2	020	Janice Meyer	2
3	030	Superior New & Used Autos	3
4	040	Sounds Around, Inc.	4
5	050	Linda's Exercise Center	5
6	060	Greenthumb Florists	6
7	070	Harmon Furniture Co.	7
8	080	Galactic Insurance	8
9	090	Paddock Realty Co.	9
10	100	Robert Fox	10
11			11
12			12
13			13
14			14
15			15
16			16
17			17
18			18
19			19
20			20
21			21
22			22
23			23
24			24
25			25

Figure 7.2   Accounts Receivable File Maintenance Input Form (Form AR-1)

The run date recorded in the upper left corner of the form, 10/01/--, is the month, day, and year the form was completed and key-entered into the computer. The ideal time to start an accounts receivable system is the first day of the fiscal period (start of an accounting cycle). The body of the form contains the customer numbers and customer names which are to be used to set up the customer data.

Accounts Receivable Input Form (Form AR-2)

The **Accounts Receivable input form** is an input form used to record the opening balance data for each customer and to record accounts receivable transactions. This form has a field for the sales invoice number, customer number, sales invoice date, general ledger account number, invoice amount, sales tax percentage, cash receipt date, document number, and cash received amount. The Accounts Receivable input form also serves two separate functions. First, it is used to record opening account balances which are to be key-entered into the computer during accounts receivable setup. Second, it is used to record various accounts receivable transactions, such as sales invoices and cash receipts, which occur during the ongoing process of the accounts receivable system. The second use of this form will be discussed further in Chapter 8. After the customer data has been set up and the control accounts set, the opening balance data must be set up for each customer with a beginning balance. These opening balances are recorded in the accounts receivable data file.

An Accounts Receivable input form should be completed and used as the source document from which opening balances are key-entered. The Accounts Receivable input form in Figure 7.3 shows the opening balances for customers of Hardware Plus.

The run date (10/01/--), located in the upper left corner of the form, is usually the first day of the month (the start of the accounting cycle). The batch number, located beneath the run date in the upper left corner of the form, is recorded as Batch No. 1. Recall that this is the batch

RUN DATE 10/01/--									Problem No. Sample
ACCOUNTS RECEIVABLE Input Form									FORM AR-2
BATCH NO. 1									

	1	2	3	4	5	6	7	8	9	
	SALES INVOICE NO.	SALES					CASH RECEIPTS			
		CUST. NO.	DATE MO. DAY YR.	GEN. LEDGER ACCT. NO.	INVOICE AMOUNT	SALES TAX %	DATE MO. DAY YR.	DOC. NO.	CASH RECEIVED	
1	747	010	09 02 --	410	507 24	6				1
2	748	020	09 05 --	410	305 50	6				2
3	749	030	09 08 --	410	1114 50	6				3
4	750	040	09 12 --	410	275 50	6				4
5	751	070	09 18 --	410	1734 46	6				5
6	752	080	09 26 --	410	722 00	6				6
7	753	100	09 27 --	410	1885 80	6				7
8										8
9										9
10										10
11										11
12										12
13										13
14										14
15										15
16										16
17										17
18										18
19										19
20										20
21										21
22										22
23										23
24										24
25										25
				BATCH TOTALS	6545 00					

Figure 7.3   Accounts Receivable Input Form (Form AR-2)

number specifically reserved for opening balances. The computer will automatically assign Batch No. 1 to the opening balances as they are key-entered into the computer. By using Batch No. 1 to identify the opening balances, it will later be possible to distinguish opening balance entries from other transactions.

The Accounts Receivable input form consists of two major sections: (1) the sales section and (2) the cash receipts section. When performing accounts receivable setup, the sales invoice number (which must be specified when using either of the two sections) and the data fields in the sales section will be used. The remaining data fields are used in an ongoing system and will be discussed in Chapter 8.

The body of the form represents data required to establish the opening balances. Recorded in the Sales Invoice Number column is a three-digit sales invoice number consecutively assigned to each opening balance recorded. The Customer Number column contains the number of each customer who has an opening balance. These customer numbers can be located by referring to the Accounts Receivable File Maintenance input form prepared earlier. The Date column contains the date of the opening balance in the MM/DD/YY format. The General Ledger Account Number column contains the sales account number established in the chart of accounts during general ledger setup. The Invoice Amount column contains the amount of the opening balance. The Sales Tax Percentage column contains the sales tax percentage recorded in decimal format. For example, sales tax of 5 1/2 percent is recorded as 5.50. The Cash Receipts section is left blank when this form is used to record opening balances. The total of the amounts in the Invoice Amount column should be determined using a calculator and should be written in the space provided at the bottom of this column.

ACCOUNTS RECEIVABLE SETUP OPERATIONAL PROCEDURES

Once the Accounts Receivable input forms are completed, the data contained on them must be key-entered into the computer and various reports may be generated. However, several steps must be followed before you begin working in the Accounts Receivable System. First, after the initial start-up procedures have been performed, Option A, *Accounting System Setup*, must be selected from the System Selection Menu, and the correct data fields must be set if this has not been done previously. Second, Option C, *Load Data from Disk*, must be selected. When the Load Data from Disk menu appears, Option D, *Create Empty File*, must be chosen to inform the computer that you will be creating new general ledger and accounts receivable data fields. Third, Option D, *Company Information*, must be selected from the System Selection Menu, and the correct data fields must be established. Fourth, Option F, *General Ledger*, must be selected from the System Selection Menu, and the general ledger chart of accounts and opening balances must be established. Finally, Option H, *Accounts Receivable*, must be selected from the System Selection Menu. Once the *Accounts Receivable* option is selected, the Accounts Receivable Main Menu shown in Figure 7.4. will appear on the screen.

Any option may be selected from the Accounts Receivable Main Menu by simply keying the appropriate letter. Subsequently, a new display will appear on the screen that will allow you to enter appropri-

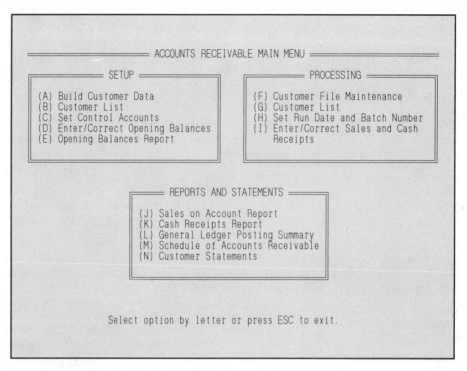

Figure 7.4   Accounts Receivable Main Menu

ate data or choose a course of action. The following sections explain how Options A through E (the setup options) can be used to create a new accounts receivable data file containing customers and opening balance ledger data. Each of these options should be performed in sequence in order to complete the accounts receivable setup process.

Build Customer Data Option A

When you select Option A from the Accounts Receivable Main Menu, the Build Customer Data screen shown in Figure 7.5 will appear.

Notice that the Customers window displays **EMPTY** to indicate that there are no customers currently in computer memory. However, if the computer detects customers currently stored in its memory, a decision prompt message will appear and you will be asked to strike the **Y** key (for Yes) or **N** (for No) to erase the customer data currently in memory. Also, because of the serious consequences of selecting this option, a warning decision prompt message is displayed on the screen when the option is selected. The **N** option should be selected if you were unable to key-enter all of your customer data during a previous work session. When you are ready to finish entering the customer data, you may select the *Build Customer Data* option, choose the **N** option, and key-enter the remaining customer data. Strike the **Y** key to erase all previous data and proceed.

The Accounts Receivable File Maintenance input form is used as the source document from which the customer number and name fields are keyed. In order to key-enter the customer number and names, complete the following steps:

1. Key-enter a customer number from one to three digits in length. The cursor will then move to the first position of the corresponding name field.

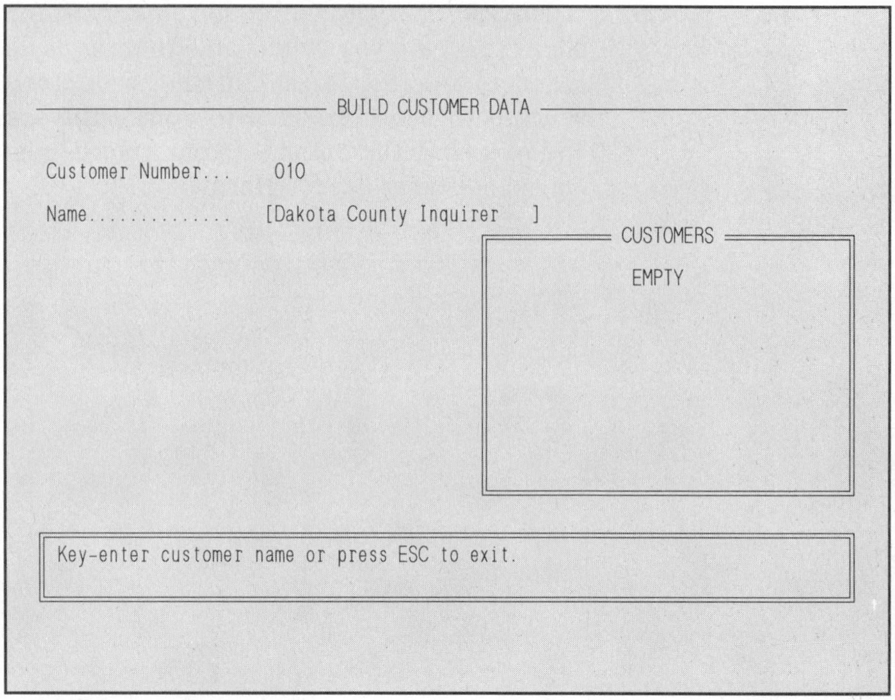

```
┌──────────────────────────────────────────────────────────────────────┐
│                                                                        │
│         ┌──────────────────── BUILD CUSTOMER DATA ──────────────────┐  │
│                                                                        │
│         Customer Number...    010                                      │
│                                                                        │
│         Name.............    [Dakota County Inquirer    ]              │
│                                            ┌════════ CUSTOMERS ═══════┐ │
│                                            │         EMPTY            │ │
│                                            │                          │ │
│                                            │                          │ │
│                                            │                          │ │
│                                            │                          │ │
│                                            │                          │ │
│                                            └──────────────────────────┘ │
│                                                                        │
│                                                                        │
│         ┌──────────────────────────────────────────────────────────┐  │
│         │ Key-enter customer name or press ESC to exit.             │  │
│         │                                                           │  │
│         └──────────────────────────────────────────────────────────┘  │
│                                                                        │
└──────────────────────────────────────────────────────────────────────┘
```

Figure 7.5   Build Customer Data Screen

2. Key-enter the customer name which corresponds to the customer number just key-entered.

   Note: After the customer name is key-entered, the customer number and name will appear in the Customers window indicating that it has been created.

3. Continue key-entering customer numbers and names until all fields have been entered.

If you detect an error or wish to delete a previously entered customer, simply key-enter the customer number of the customer to be changed or deleted. The computer will check to see if the customer number already exists. If the customer number already exists, the computer will display the customer name and number and assume that you wish to either change the customer name or delete the customer. In this case, a decision prompt will ask you to strike **C** if you want to change the customer name, **R** to record the name as it appears on the screen, or **D** to delete this customer. If the customer already exists and you wish to change the customer name, strike **C** for change, key-enter the correct customer name, and then strike **R** to record the customer data. If the customer already exists and you wish to delete it, strike **D**, and the customer will be deleted. You may press Esc to exit and not make any changes. Note that a customer cannot be deleted if the account has any activity. Even though a customer's balance is zero, the account cannot be deleted if it has transaction data. For example, if an invoice has been paid and the balance is zero, the associated customer cannot be deleted until the file is purged or period-end closing is performed.

**Customer List
Option B**

When you select Option B, *Customer List*, from the Accounts Receivable Main Menu, you will be able to print or display a list of customers. When this option is chosen, the usual decision prompt will appear which permits you to display or print the customer list or to exit this option. Select the option of your choice. Figure 7.6 illustrates a displayed customer list for Hardware Plus.

```
RUN DATE: 10/01/--                    HARDWARE PLUS                    CUSTOMER LIST
CUSTOMER    CUSTOMER
NUMBER      NAME
--------------------
010         Dakota County Inquirer
020         Janice Meyer
030         Superior New & Used Autos
040         Sounds Around, Inc.
050         Linda's Exercise Center
060         Greenthumb Florists
070         Harmon Furniture Co.
080         Galactic Insurance
090         Paddock Realty Co.
100         Robert Fox




                            Press SPACE BAR to continue.
```

Figure 7.6   Hardware Plus Customer List

**Set Control
Accounts
Option C**

There are certain account numbers that require special identification and handling by the computer. These account numbers must be established, or set up, through Option C, *Set Control Accounts*, of the Accounts Receivable Main Menu. This setup should be performed immediately after the customers are built and a customer list is displayed or printed. The control accounts may also be changed at any time. When this option is selected, the account titles displayed for which numbers must be set will depend on whether you selected the simplified or expanded Accounts Receivable System during accounting system setup. Once the set control accounts data is key-entered, it is recorded in the computer's memory. Figure 7.7 shows the completed Set Control Accounts data entry screen for Hardware Plus using the simplified Accounts Receivable System.

The data recorded on the General Ledger File Maintenance input form or the Chart of Accounts report may be used as a source document from which the control accounts are keyed. A window may be opened by pressing the F1 key, which will enable you to view your chart of accounts in case you wish to verify an account number. To set the control accounts or to change any control account number, complete the following steps:

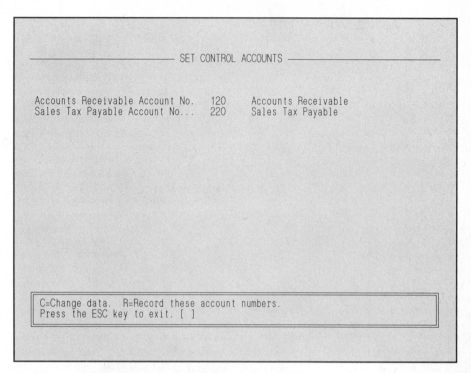

┌──┐
│ ──────────────────── SET CONTROL ACCOUNTS ──────────────────── │
│   │
│ Accounts Receivable Account No.   120   Accounts Receivable │
│ Sales Tax Payable Account No...   220   Sales Tax Payable   │
│   │
│ ┌──┐ │
│ │ C=Change data.   R=Record these account numbers.   │ │
│ │ Press the ESC key to exit. [ ]   │ │
│ └──┘ │
└──┘

Figure 7.7   Set Control Accounts Data Entry Screen

1. Key-enter the appropriate account number for each of the control accounts displayed.
2. After all control account numbers have been key-entered, visually check the accuracy of your keying. If you find an error, move the cursor to the error and make the correction. When finished, move the cursor to the last field of the data entry screen and press ENTER/RETURN to indicate that you want the computer to accept your data.
3. At this time, the computer will match the account numbers just key-entered to the chart of accounts to verify that they exist. If an account number cannot be found, an error message will be displayed and you will be permitted to make a correction. If all the account numbers are found, the computer will display them along with their assigned titles. In addition, a decision prompt will appear at the bottom of the screen telling you to strike **C** to change the data, **R** to record the account numbers, or Esc to ignore the data and return to the Accounts Receivable Main Menu.

Enter/Correct Opening Balances Option D

After the customer data has been built and the control accounts have been set, the opening balance data for each customer with a balance must be key-entered. An Accounts Receivable input form should be completed and used as the source document from which these opening balances are key-entered. When Option D is selected, the Enter/Correct Opening Balances data entry screen shown in Figure 7.8 will appear. This data entry screen is used to enter and make corrections to the opening balances. In this figure, the first opening balance has been key-entered to illustrate how the data appears.

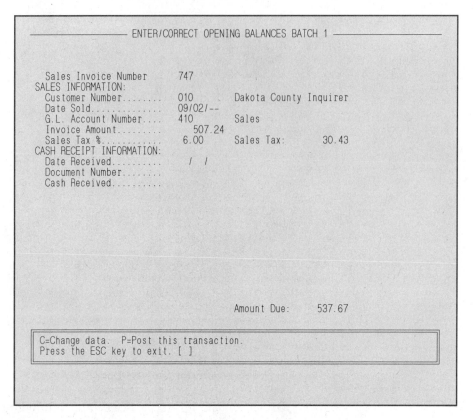

Figure 7.8   Enter/Correct Opening Balances Data Entry Screen

The Enter/Correct Opening Balances data entry screen can also be used to make corrections to opening balances which were previously keyed in error. Three windows may be displayed. The first window option that appears permits you to view invoices previously entered into the system (Function 3 key). The second and third window options that appear permit you to view the chart of accounts (Function 1 key) and the customers (Function 2 key) stored in the computer's memory. You will find these windows helpful in verifying previously keyed invoices, general ledger account numbers, and customer numbers during this data entry activity. Complete the following steps to establish opening balances or to make corrections to opening balances:

1. Key-enter the sales invoice number.

   Note: At this time, the computer will check to see if the sales invoice number key-entered already exists. If the sales invoice number does exist, all the opening balance data will be displayed and you will be permitted to make corrections (proceed to No. 8). If no opening balance data exists for the designated sales invoice number, the computer will assume you wish to set up an opening balance for that invoice.

2. Key-enter the customer number.
3. Key-enter the date of the opening balance in the MMDDYY format (without the slashes).
4. Key-enter the general ledger account number from the Accounts

Receivable input form. Most often this will be the account number for Sales or some other revenue account.

5. Key-enter the opening balance in the *Invoice Amount* field.
6. Key-enter the sales tax percent in decimal format (where 5 1/2 percent is recorded as 5.50).
7. Move the cursor to the last data field and press ENTER/RETURN.
8. A decision prompt will appear asking if you wish to make a change, post the transaction, delete the transaction, or ignore the displayed data. Strike **C** to make changes or corrections. Strike **P** to post and record the opening balance data as displayed. Strike **D** to delete this transaction. Press Esc to ignore the data and display a blank Enter/Correct Opening Balances data entry screen.

*Note: At this time the computer will check the data you have entered to verify its accuracy. If errors are detected, you will be given a chance to make corrections. If the customer number does not exist, a decision prompt message will appear asking if you wish to set up this customer. If you respond **Yes**, the Build Customer Data screen will appear and you will be permitted to set up the customer. After the customer has been set up and recorded in the computer's memory, the Enter/Correct Opening Balances data entry screen will again appear and you will be permitted to continue.*

9. Continue this procedure until all opening balances or corrections have been key-entered. When finished, press the Esc key to exit this data entry screen and return to the Accounts Receivable Main Menu.

Opening Balances Report Option E

When you select Option E from the Accounts Receivable Main Menu, you will be able to print or display the Opening Balances report. This report consists of the customer numbers, customer names, sales invoice numbers and dates, the general ledger account numbers (usually the sales account), the customers' opening balances, the sales tax amounts, the total of the individual customer opening balances, and the total of the sales tax for these opening balances.

When this option is selected, the usual decision prompt message will appear in which you will be permitted to display or print the Opening Balances report or to exit this option. Select the option desired. Figure 7.9 illustrates a displayed Opening Balances report for Hardware Plus.

It is recommended that the Opening Balances report be displayed or printed after the opening balances are set up and after making any corrections. Examining this report and comparing the computer total with the total of the Invoice Amount column on the Accounts Receivable input form will help verify that all data has been recorded properly and provide an audit trail (if printed) for future reference.

Save Data to Disk

As with all the work you complete while using this automated accounting system, be sure to save your data to disk as a work in progress file prior to computer shutdown. If you fail to run this option prior to ending the automated accounting session or before loading another file from disk, all data keyed and processed during your computer session will be lost.

```
RUN DATE: 10/01/--                 HARDWARE PLUS                   A.R. OPENING BALANCES
CUSTOMER                        INVOICE              G.L.        INVOICE         SALES
NO. NAME                        NO.     DATE      ACCOUNT         AMOUNT          TAX
------------------------------------------------------------------------------------------
010 Dakota County Inquirer      747   09/02/--      410           507.24        30.43
020 Janice Meyer                748   09/05/--      410           305.50        18.33
030 Superior New & Used Autos   749   09/08/--      410          1114.50        66.87
040 Sounds Around, Inc.         750   09/12/--      410           275.50        16.53
070 Harmon Furniture Co.        751   09/18/--      410          1734.46       104.07
080 Galactic Insurance          752   09/26/--      410           722.00        43.32
100 Robert Fox                  753   09/27/--      410          1885.80       113.15
                                                               ----------    ---------
    TOTALS                                                       6545.00       392.70
                                                               ==========    =========




                        Press SPACE BAR to continue.
```

Figure 7.9   Opening Balances Report

ACCOUNTS RECEIVABLE SETUP (SAMPLE PROBLEM)

In this problem, you will see how a computerized accounts receivable system is set up for a merchandising business. The general ledger accounts and account opening balances have already been established for you and stored on disk as Problem 7-S (**AA7-S**). Also, the customer data for Hardware Plus has been recorded for you on the Accounts Receivable File Maintenance input form (Form AR-1) in Figure 7.10. Each customer has been assigned a number from one to three digits in length. The customer name is limited to 25 characters in length. The opening balances for Hardware Plus have been recorded for you on the Accounts Receivable input form (Form AR-2) in Figure 7.11.

Instructions

Step 1   Bring up the System Selection Menu according to the instructions for your microcomputer.

Step 2   From the System Selection Menu, select Option C (*Load Data from Disk*). When the Load Data from Disk menu appears, select Option A, *Load Opening Balances from the Program Disk*.

Step 3   When the directory of Opening Balances contained on the disk appears, select Problem 7-S by key-entering the file name: **AA7-S**.

	CUSTOMER NUMBER	CUSTOMER NAME	
1	010	Dakota County Inquirer	1
2	020	Janice Meyer	2
3	030	Superior New & Used Autos	3
4	040	Sounds Around, Inc.	4
5	050	Linda's Exercise Center	5
6	060	Greenthumb Florists	6
7	070	Harmon Furniture Co.	7
8	080	Galactic Insurance	8
9	090	Paddock Realty Co.	9
10	100	Robert Fox	10
11			11
12			12
13			13
14			14
15			15
16			16
17			17
18			18
19			19
20			20
21			21
22			22
23			23
24			24
25			25

RUN DATE 10 01 -- (MM DD YY)

ACCOUNTS RECEIVABLE
FILE MAINTENANCE
Input Form

Problem No. 7-S

FORM AR-1

Figure 7.10   Accounts Receivable File Maintenance Input Form (Problem 7-S)

Step 4   Select Option D, *Company Information*, from the System Selection Menu. Set the run date to **October 1** of the current year. Make sure the company name is **Hardware Plus**, the *Problem Number* field contains **Problem 7-S**, and the type of business is set to **P**. When the data is correct, strike **R** to record this information and return to the System Selection Menu.

Step 5   Select Option H, *Accounts Receivable System*, from the System Selection Menu.

Step 6   After the Accounts Receivable System has been loaded into computer memory, select Option A, *Build Customer Data*, from the Accounts Receivable Main Menu.

Step 7   Key-enter the data from the Accounts Receivable File Maintenance input form (Figure 7.10) on the Build Customer Data screen.

RUN DATE 10 /01 /--				ACCOUNTS RECEIVABLE Input Form			Problem No. 7-S		
MM DD YY							FORM AR-2		
BATCH NO. 1									

	1	2	3	4	5	6	7	8	9	
	SALES INVOICE NO.	SALES					CASH RECEIPTS			
		CUST. NO.	DATE MO.DAY YR.	GEN. LEDGER ACCT. NO.	INVOICE AMOUNT	SALES TAX %	DATE MO.DAY YR.	DOC. NO.	CASH RECEIVED	
1	747	010	09 02 --	410	507 24	6				1
2	748	020	09 05 --	410	305 50	6				2
3	749	030	09 08 --	410	1114 50	6				3
4	750	040	09 12 --	410	275 50	6				4
5	751	070	09 18 --	410	1734 46	6				5
6	752	080	09 26 --	410	722 00	6				6
7	753	100	09 27 --	410	1885 80	6				7
8										8
9										9
10										10
11										11
12										12
13										13
14										14
15										15
16										16
17										17
18										18
19										19
20										20
21										21
22										22
23										23
24										24
25										25

BATCH TOTALS   6545 00

Figure 7.11   Accounts Receivable Input Form (Problem 7-S)

Step   8   If you must exit before all entries have been key-entered, the remaining entries may be key-entered at a later time by completing the following steps:

1. Select Option A, *Build Customer Data*, from the Accounts Receivable Main Menu.
2. Answer **N** to the decision prompt asking whether you wish to erase accounts receivable files.
3. Key-enter the remaining customers.

Step   9   Select Option B, *Customer List*, from the Accounts Receivable Main Menu.

Step 10   Display or print a customer list.

Step 11   Compare your customer list with the correct one shown in Figure 7.12. If your customer list contains errors, return to the *Build Customer*

Data option, strike **N** so the customer list will not be erased, and key-enter the missing or correct data.

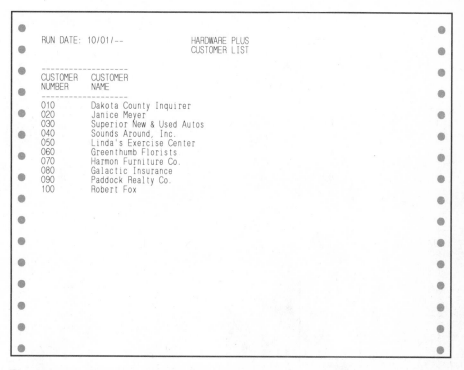

```
RUN DATE: 10/01/--                    HARDWARE PLUS
                                      CUSTOMER LIST

------------------------
CUSTOMER   CUSTOMER
NUMBER     NAME
------------------------
010        Dakota County Inquirer
020        Janice Meyer
030        Superior New & Used Autos
040        Sounds Around, Inc.
050        Linda's Exercise Center
060        Greenthumb Florists
070        Harmon Furniture Co.
080        Galactic Insurance
090        Paddock Realty Co.
100        Robert Fox
```

Figure 7.12   Customer List (Problem 7-S)

Step 12   Select Option C, *Set Control Accounts*, from the Accounts Receivable Main Menu, and key-enter the following control accounts:

Accounts Receivable Account No. 120
Sales Tax Payable Account No. 220

Step 13   If you make an error, strike **C** to change the data and make the correction. When the data is correct, strike **R** to record the Accounts Receivable and Sales Tax Payable account numbers.

Step 14   Select Option D, *Enter/Correct Opening Balances*, from the Accounts Receivable Main Menu.

Step 15   Key-enter and post the opening balances from the Accounts Receivable input form shown in Figure 7.11. After each entry is key-entered, examine it for accuracy. If there are any errors, strike **C** to change the data and make the corrections. If the data is correct, strike **P** to post the accounts receivable customer opening balance.

Step 16   After all customer opening balances have been key-entered and posted, press Esc to exit and return to the Accounts Receivable Main Menu.

Step 17   Select Option E, *Opening Balances Report*, from the Accounts Receivable Main Menu.

Step 18   Display or print the Opening Balances report.

Step 19   Compare your Opening Balances report with the correct one for Hardware Plus shown in Figure 7.13. The computer total for the Invoice

Amount column should be the same as the total for the Invoice Amount column on the Accounts Receivable input form. If your Opening Balances report is correct, proceed to Step 21.

```
  RUN DATE: 10/01/--                    HARDWARE PLUS
                          ACCOUNTS RECEIVABLE OPENING BALANCES

  ------------------------------------------------------------------------
  CUSTOMER                       INVOICE        G.L.    INVOICE    SALES
  NO. NAME                       NO.   DATE   ACCOUNT    AMOUNT     TAX
  ------------------------------------------------------------------------
  010 Dakota County Inquirer     747  09/02/--   410     507.24    30.43
  020 Janice Meyer               748  09/05/--   410     305.50    18.33
  030 Superior New & Used Autos  749  09/08/--   410    1114.50    66.87
  040 Sounds Around, Inc.        750  09/12/--   410     275.50    16.53
  070 Harmon Furniture Co.       751  09/18/--   410    1734.46   104.07
  080 Galactic Insurance         752  09/26/--   410     722.00    43.32
  100 Robert Fox                 753  09/27/--   410    1885.80   113.15
                                                       --------- ---------
      TOTALS                                            6545.00   392.70
                                                       ========= =========
```

Figure 7.13   Opening Balances Report (Problem 7-S)

Step 20   If your Opening Balances report is out of balance, or if you have made an error, select Option D, *Enter/Correct Opening Balances*, from the Accounts Receivable Main Menu. Make the necessary corrections to the opening balances by key-entering the correct data for each part of the opening entry that is in error. When all corrections have been made, press Esc to return to the Accounts Receivable Main Menu. Display or print a new Opening Balances report.

Step 21   Press Esc to exit from the Accounts Receivable Main Menu and return to the System Selection Menu.

Step 22   From the System Selection Menu, select Option E, *Save Data to Disk*, and save your data as a work in progress file (recommend file name **AA7-S**).

Step 23   Press Esc to end your automated accounting session. Then complete the student exercise and transaction problem which follow.

Name _____

Class _____ Date _____

CHAPTER 7
STUDENT EXERCISE

I. Matching   For each of the following definitions, write the letter of the term which best fits that definition in the space provided.

a. Accounts receivable ledger data

b. Accounts receivable input form

c. Customer data

d. Accounts receivable file maintenance input form

e. Accounts receivable data file

1. _____ Consists of a record for each sales invoice. (Obj. 5)

2. _____ Used to set up and maintain the customer records. (Obj. 2)

3. _____ Consists of a separate record for each customer with whom the company does business. (Obj. 2)

4. _____ Used to record the opening balance data for each customer and to record accounts receivable transactions. (Obj. 5)

5. _____ Contains all the data required by the computer to process accounts receivable transactions. (Obj. 2)

II. Short Answer   1. Identify and describe the steps involved in accounts receivable setup. (Obj. 9)

_____

_____

_____

_____

_____

2. Describe the differences between a manual and a computerized accounts receivable system. (Obj. 1)

_____

_____

_____

_____

3. Why must the *Save Data to Disk* option be the last option selected prior to ending the automated accounting system? (Obj. 7)

_____

_____

_____

_____

4. What is the purpose of the customer list? (Obj. 3)

_____

_____

_____

5. What is the purpose of the Opening Balances report? (Obj. 6)

_____

_____

_____

ACCOUNTS RECEIVABLE SETUP
TRANSACTION PROBLEM 7-1

Riding Lawn Mowers, Inc., is a small specialty business which sells riding lawn mowers to landscaping companies. The business is organized as a partnership. The general ledger accounts and account opening balances have already been established for you and stored on disk as Problem 7-1 (**AA7-1**). Your task is to set up the accounts receivable system for Riding Lawn Mowers, Inc.

As of April 1 of the current year, Riding Lawn Mowers, Inc., lists the following customers and the opening balances (sales on account) for those customers to whom the company has sold merchandise. (Objs. 2-9)

Cust. No. & Name	Sales Inv. No.	Date	Gen. Led. Acct. No.	Invoice Amount	Sales Tax %
010 Valley Landscape Co.	525	03/21/--	410	1567.50	6
020 Lakeville Landscape	532	03/25/--	410	4013.75	6
030 North Hill Lawn Service	558	03/28/--	410	475.00	6
040 Egan Lawn Maintenance	561	03/29/--	410	2280.00	6

Instructions

Step   *1*   Remove the blank input forms and the Chapter 7 Audit Test from the end of this chapter. Complete the questions on the audit test as you work through the following steps.

Step   *2*   Using the data in the previous table, record the customer numbers and names on the Accounts Receivable File Maintenance input form (Form AR-1).

Step   *3*   Using the data in the previous table, record as Batch No. 1 the customer opening balances (sales on account) on the Accounts Receivable input form (Form AR-2). Be sure to take a calculator total for the Invoice Amount column and write it in the space at the bottom of the form.

Step   *4*   Bring up the System Selection Menu.

Step   *5*   From the System Selection Menu, select Option C (*Load Data from Disk*). When the Load Data from Disk menu appears, select Option A, *Load Opening Balances from the Program Disk*.

Step   *6*   When the directory of Opening Balances contained on the disk appears, select Problem 7-1 by key-entering the file name: **AA7-1**.

Step   *7*   Select Option D, *Company Information*, from the System Selection Menu. Set the run date to **April 1** of the current year. Make sure the *Company Name* field contains **Riding Lawn Mowers, Inc.**; the *Problem Number* field contains **Problem 7-1**; and the type of business is set to **P**. If not, you may have loaded the incorrect problem. If you have loaded the incorrect problem, repeat Steps 5 and 6 above.

Step **8**   Select Option H, *Accounts Receivable*.

Step **9**   After the Accounts Receivable System has finished loading into computer memory, select Option A, *Build Customer Data*, from the Accounts Receivable Main Menu.

Step **10**   Key-enter the data from the Accounts Receivable File Maintenance input form prepared in Step 2.

Step **11**   Select Option B, *Customer List*, and print or display a customer list. If there are errors on your customer list, return to the *Build Customer Data* option, strike **N**, and key-enter the missing or incorrect data.

Step **12**   Select Option C, *Set Control Accounts*, and key-enter and record the following control accounts:

Accounts Receivable Account No. 120
Sales Tax Payable Account No. 220

Step **13**   Select Option D, *Enter/Correct Opening Balances*. Key-enter and post the opening balances from the Accounts Receivable input form prepared in Step 3.

Step **14**   Select Option E, *Opening Balances Report*, and print or display an Accounts Receivable Opening Balances report. Examine this report and compare the computer total with the total for the Invoice Amount column on the Accounts Receivable input form. If there are errors on your Opening Balances report, select Option D, *Enter/Correct Opening Balances*, and make the necessary corrections.

Step **15**   Press Esc to exit from the Accounts Receivable Main Menu and return to the System Selection Menu.

Step **16**   From the System Selection Menu, select Option E, *Save Data to Disk*, and save your data as a work in progress file (recommend file name **AA7-1**).

Step **17**   Press Esc to end your automated accounting session.

Step **18**   Hand in the completed student exercise sheets, input forms, the audit test, and any printouts to your instructor.

You have now completed the computer exercise for Chapter 7.

Name _____

Class _____ Date _____

	ACCOUNTS RECEIVABLE FILE MAINTENANCE Input Form	Problem No. _____ FORM AR-1

RUN DATE ____ / ____ / ____
                MM   DD   YY

	1	2	
	CUSTOMER NUMBER	CUSTOMER NAME	
1			1
2			2
3			3
4			4
5			5
6			6
7			7
8			8
9			9
10			10
11			11
12			12
13			13
14			14
15			15
16			16
17			17
18			18
19			19
20			20
21			21
22			22
23			23
24			24
25			25

RUN DATE ___/___/___
         MM   DD   YY

BATCH NO. [   ]

ACCOUNTS RECEIVABLE
Input Form

Problem No. _____

[FORM AR-2]

	1	2	3			4	5	6	7			8	9	
	SALES INVOICE NO.	SALES							CASH RECEIPTS					
	SALES INVOICE NO.	CUST. NO.	DATE			GEN. LEDGER ACCT. NO.	INVOICE AMOUNT	SALES TAX %	DATE			DOC. NO.	CASH RECEIVED	
			MO.	DAY	YR.				MO.	DAY	YR.			
1														1
2														2
3														3
4														4
5														5
6														6
7														7
8														8
9														9
10														10
11														11
12														12
13														13
14														14
15														15
16														16
17														17
18														18
19														19
20														20
21														21
22														22
23														23
24														24
25														25

BATCH TOTALS [   ]   [   ]

Name _____

Class _____ Date _____

CHAPTER 7
AUDIT TEST

1. What is the run date printed on the customer list?

   _____

2. What is the customer number assigned to Lakeville Landscape?

   _____

3. What is the name of Customer No. 040?

   _____

4. What is the run date printed on the Accounts Receivable Opening
   Balances report?

   _____

5. What is the invoice number for the merchandise sold to Valley
   Landscape Co.?

   _____

6. On what date was Invoice No. 558 to North Hill Lawn Service
   issued?

   _____

7. What is the amount of Invoice No. 532 to Lakeville Landscape?

   _____

8. What is the sales tax amount for Invoice No. 561?

   _____

9. What is the total of all invoice amounts for the opening balances?

   _____

10. What is the total of the sales tax for the opening balances?

   _____

8 ACCOUNTS RECEIVABLE TRANSACTIONS AND REPORTS

LEARNING OBJECTIVES

Upon completion of this chapter, you will be able to:

1. Perform customer file maintenance.
2. Display or print a customer list.
3. Set the run date and batch number.
4. Enter/correct sales and cash receipts transactions.
5. Display or print a Sales on Account report.
6. Display or print a Cash Receipts report.
7. Display or print a general ledger posting summary.
8. Display or print a schedule of accounts receivable.
9. Print customer statements.
10. Save data to disk and perform the system shutdown procedure.
11. Identify the components and procedures required to generate Accounts Receivable reports.

INTRODUCTION

In Chapter 7, you learned how to set up customers and their opening balances in the accounts receivable data file. This chapter will cover the accounts receivable accounting cycle used in an automated accounting system. You will soon see how transaction data is used to update the computer's files and, in turn, generate the Accounts Receivable reports required to keep track of a company's sales and cash receipts. The procedure used in *Automated Accounting for the Microcomputer* to perform accounts receivable processing is illustrated in Figure 8.1.

Customer data changes constantly during the operation of a business. Customers with whom the company does business must be added, customer names must be changed, and inactive customers must be deleted from the data file. Therefore, the computer's customer data must be updated to show these changes. This process of adding, changing, or deleting customer records is called **customer file maintenance.**

Transactions involving sales of merchandise on account, returns and allowances, and cash receipts on account are called **accounts receivable transactions**. Returns and allowances will be discussed in Chapter 9. Accounts receivable transactions involving the sale of merchandise or services for which the customer will pay in the future are called **sales on account**. Each sale on account must be assigned a transaction number. In this text, a **sales invoice number** is used by the computer to identify each sale on account. These transactions are then key-entered from an input form into the computer. Each group of transactions, or all transactions for a specific period of time, is assigned a batch number. When the transactions are key-entered, they are stored by batch number in the accounts receivable data file.

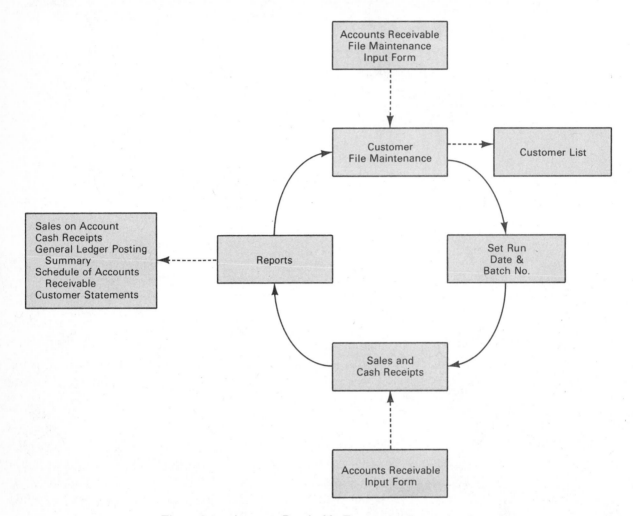

Figure 8.1   Accounts Receivable Transaction Processing Procedure

As sales occur, they are recorded on an Accounts Receivable input form (Form AR-2) and key-entered into the computer. Each sale creates an accounts receivable open item. An **accounts receivable open item** is a sale for which the customer has not yet paid. As cash receipts occur, they are also recorded on an Accounts Receivable input form and key-entered into the computer. A **cash receipt** is an accounts receivable transaction that indicates payment on account has been received. Each cash receipt is applied to the corresponding accounts receivable open item by sales invoice number. The open item is reduced by the amount of the cash receipt. At the end of the month, monthly statements of account are printed showing all accounts receivable transactions and the balance of each customer's account. Because the accounts receivable data file contains all of the unpaid invoices, the sum of the open items in the accounts receivable data file should equal the balance of the accounts receivable controlling account in the general ledger.

As described earlier, the Accounts Receivable input form is used to record both sales on account and cash receipts. In both cases, processing is based on the batch number which was assigned at the time the transaction was key-entered into the computer. Thus, all Sales on

Account and Cash Receipt reports are generated for the specific batch of transactions desired. Each batch of accounts receivable transactions remains stored in the accounts receivable data file. Therefore, if an error is detected after a report for a specific batch has been printed, the error can be corrected and the report can be reprinted. The accounts receivable data file has a maximum capacity of 50 transactions. If this limit is exceeded, the paid transactions (those with a balance due of zero) in all previous batches stored in the file will be purged (erased). This process frees up additional space for the current batch of transactions. Since only the paid transactions are purged, no important data is lost.

ACCOUNTS RECEIVABLE INTEGRATION

As accounts receivable transactions are entered or corrected in the Accounts Receivable System, the journal entries resulting from those transactions are automatically integrated into the General Ledger System by the computer. In order to integrate these entries, the computer must know the control account numbers you have assigned to the general ledger accounts involved. In Chapter 7, you learned how to provide these control accounts during accounts receivable setup. The account numbers for Accounts Receivable and Sales Tax Payable are entered using the *Set Control Accounts* option (Option C) of the Accounts Receivable Main Menu. In addition, the account numbers for Sales Discount and Sales Returns and Allowances must be set if the expanded Accounts Receivable System is being used. By supplying these control account numbers during the setup procedure, only the account number to be credited for the transaction needs to be entered at the time an accounts receivable transaction is key-entered.

When a new sales transaction is entered, the computer will: (1) debit Accounts Receivable and the customer's account, (2) credit the account number which is included as part of the transaction on the input form, and (3) credit Sales Tax Payable (if a sales tax percentage is key-entered). When cash is received, the computer will: (1) debit Cash and (2) credit Accounts Receivable and the customer's account. If a transaction is later found to be in error and is then corrected, the computer will make the necessary correcting journal entries.

COMPLETING THE INPUT FORMS

Accounts receivable data is recorded on two different input forms: the Accounts Receivable File Maintenance input form (Form AR-1) and the Accounts Receivable input form (Form AR-2). You have already worked with each of these forms in Chapter 7 to build the customer data and to establish opening balances in the accounts receivable data file. In this chapter, you will learn how the Accounts Receivable File Maintenance and Accounts Receivable input forms are used to record the data required by a company to keep track of customer account balances, sales, and cash receipts.

Accounts Receivable File Maintenance Input Form (Form AR-1)

As discussed earlier, customer data must be kept current by adding new customers, making corrections to existing customer accounts, and deleting customers with whom the company no longer does business. The customers established for Hardware Plus in Chapter 7 are listed in Figure 8.2.

010	Dakota County Inquirer
020	Janice Meyer
030	Superior New & Used Autos
040	Sounds Around, Inc.
050	Linda's Exercise Center
060	Greenthumb Florists
070	Harmon Furniture Co.
080	Galactic Insurance
090	Paddock Realty Co.
100	Robert Fox

Figure 8.2   Hardware Plus Customer List

Let's suppose that during the course of the month, Customer No. 110, Marsha's Auto Repair, needs to be added; the customer name for Linda's Exercise Center needs to be changed to Linda's Fitness Center; and Customer No. 090, Paddock Realty Co., has become inactive and should be deleted. In order to record these changes, the Accounts Receivable File Maintenance input form shown in Figure 8.3 must be completed. Notice that this form is the same one you used to build the customer data during accounts receivable setup.

The first entry is an addition of a new customer, and the second entry is a name change (the customer name is being changed to Linda's Fitness Center). Note that in either case, you simply record the customer number and the customer name. The third entry is a deletion. Customer No. 090, Paddock Realty Co., is being deleted. To delete a customer, merely record the number of the customer to be deleted in the Customer Number column and a **D** (for delete) in the Customer Name column. Only customers which have no account activity and a zero balance can be deleted. Customer No. 090 has been inactive and has no existing balance in the accounts receivable data file. Therefore, the computer will allow this account to be deleted.

Accounts Receivable Input Form (Form AR-2)

In a computerized accounts receivable system, sales on account and cash receipts must be analyzed, recorded on an Accounts Receivable input form, and key-entered into the computer by batch number. As you have already seen, these accounts receivable transactions are stored by batch number as they are entered. The transactions remain in this file until its maximum capacity is reached. At that time, the computer will automatically purge the paid invoices from all previous batches.

In the Accounts Receivable System, sales and cash receipts are recorded on the Accounts Receivable input form (Form AR-2). This form can be used to record both types of accounts receivable transactions. Figure 8.4 illustrates a partially completed Accounts Receivable input form.

In Figure 8.4, the accounts receivable transactions to be key-entered for Hardware Plus occurred during the month of March, as indicated by the run date located in the upper left corner of the form. The batch number, located beneath the date, contains a one- or two-digit number which identifies a specific group of accounts receivable transactions. Remember that Batch No. 1 is reserved for the opening balances you entered in Chapter 7 during accounts receivable setup. In this exam-

	ACCOUNTS RECEIVABLE FILE MAINTENANCE Input Form		

RUN DATE _03, 15 , - -_
MM   DD   YY

Problem No. _Sample_

FORM AR-1

	1	2	
	CUSTOMER NUMBER	CUSTOMER NAME	
1	110	Marsha's Auto Repair	1
2	050	Linda's Fitness Center	2
3	090	D	3
4			4
5			5
6			6
7			7
8			8
9			9
10			10
11			11
12			12
13			13
14			14
15			15
16			16
17			17
18			18
19			19
20			20
21			21
22			22
23			23
24			24
25			25

Figure 8.3   Accounts Receivable File Maintenance Input Form

ple, the accounts receivable transactions are identified as Batch No. 5. Succeeding batch numbers (6, 7, etc.) should be assigned to subsequent monthly groupings of transactions. The use of batch numbers is helpful in finding and isolating errors by providing a convenient method of tracing an error back to its source.

As you learned in Chapter 7, the Accounts Receivable input form consists of two major sections: (1) the Sales section and (2) the Cash Receipts section. When using this form in an ongoing system to process accounts receivable transactions, sales data is recorded in the Sales section, and cash receipts from customers are recorded in the Cash Receipts section.

Each line on the Accounts Receivable input form represents one accounts receivable transaction. Recorded in the Sales Invoice Number column is a one- to four-digit number used by the computer to identify each accounts receivable transaction. The sales invoice number *must*

RUN DATE 03/15/--	ACCOUNTS RECEIVABLE	Problem No. *Sample*
MM DD YY	Input Form	FORM AR-2
BATCH NO. 5		

	1	2	3		4	5	6	7		8	9	
	SALES INVOICE NO.	CUST. NO.	DATE MO. DAY YR.		GEN. LEDGER ACCT. NO.	INVOICE AMOUNT	SALES TAX %	DATE MO. DAY YR.		DOC. NO.	CASH RECEIVED	
1	447	020	03 01 --		410	297 20	6					1
2	447							03 08 --		2306	315 03	2
3												3
4												4
5												5
6												6
7												7
8												8
9												9
10												10
11												11
12												12
13												13
14												14
15												15
16												16
17												17
18												18
19												19
20												20
21												21
22												22
23												23
24												24
25												25
	BATCH TOTALS					297 20					315 03	

Figure 8.4   Accounts Receivable Input Form

be supplied for each accounts receivable transaction, whether it is a sale or a cash receipt.

In the Sales section of the form, the Customer Number column represents the number of the customer to whom the sale was made. The Sales Date column contains the date of the invoice in the MM/DD/YY format. The General Ledger Account Number column contains the account number used by the computer to perform the integration with the General Ledger System. The account number entered in this column will be credited. For example, if equipment is sold, the equipment account number is recorded in the General Ledger Account Number column. If merchandise is sold, a revenue account is recorded. Since most businesses have several revenue accounts, the computer must be informed which revenue account a sale on account affects. The next column, Invoice Amount, contains the gross amount of the invoice before any sales tax is calculated. The Sales Tax Percentage column contains a sales tax percentage recorded in decimal format (for example, 5 1/2 percent is recorded as 5.50, and 6 percent is recorded as 6).

In the Cash Receipts section of the form, the Cash Receipts Date column contains spaces for the date of the cash receipt in the MM/DD/YY format. The Document Number column may be used to provide additional information about the transaction (such as the cash receipt number or customer check number) that may be useful in providing an audit trail. The Cash Received column contains the amount of cash received for an invoice. This amount represents the total amount received to date which is to be applied against a particular invoice. Finally, the total of the amounts in the Invoice Amount and Cash Received columns should be determined using a calculator and written in the spaces provided at the bottom of the columns.

Two different types of accounts receivable transactions are illustrated on the Accounts Receivable input form in Figure 8.4. The first transaction is an example of a sale of merchandise on account.

March 1, 19--
Sold merchandise on account to Janice Meyer, $297.20, plus 6 percent sales tax (Sales Invoice No. 447).

The entry to record this transaction is shown on line 1 of the form. The sales invoice number, 447, is recorded in the Sales Invoice Number column. Janice Meyer's customer number, 020, is recorded in the Customer Number column. The month, day, and year of the sale are recorded in the Sales Date column. The sales account number, 410, is entered in the General Ledger Account Number column since this transaction is to be a credit to Sales. The total amount of the invoice, $297.20, is entered in the Invoice Amount column. The transaction is subject to a 6 percent sales tax, so a 6 is entered in the Sales Tax Percentage column.

The second transaction is an example of a cash receipt on account.

March 8, 19--
Received cash on account from Janice Meyer, $315.03, covering Sales Invoice No. 447 (Customer Check No. 2306).

The entry to record this transaction is shown on line 2 of the form. Sales Invoice No. 447 is an open accounts receivable item for which payment is now being received. The only items that need to be recorded for this transaction are the sales invoice number (447), the date of the cash receipt, the document number (the check number of Janice Meyer's check), and the amount of cash received ($315.03). The information in the rest of the columns (Sales section of the form) is not required because it was already recorded with the sale of merchandise on account on March 1 (see line 1).

ACCOUNTS RECEIVABLE OPERATIONAL PROCEDURES

Once the Accounts Receivable File Maintenance input form and the Accounts Receivable input form are completed, the data contained on them must be key-entered into the computer. Various reports may then be printed or displayed in order to complete the processing of accounts receivable transactions. The following sections explain how Options F through N of the Accounts Receivable Main Menu (illustrated in Figure 8.5) are used to accomplish this task.

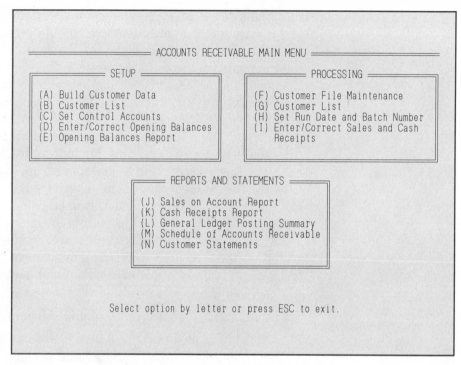

Figure 8.5   Accounts Receivable Main Menu

The options on the Accounts Receivable Main Menu should be completed in the sequence in which they appear to complete accounts receivable processing (Option F, then Option G, and so on). As you learned in Chapter 7, the Accounts Receivable Main Menu is divided into three sections: the first section, Setup, contains Options A through E; the second section, Processing, contains Options F through I; and the third section, Reports and Statements, contains Options J through N.

Customer File Maintenance Option F

The *Customer File Maintenance* option permits you to make additions, changes, and deletions to the existing customer data. When this option is selected, the Customer File Maintenance data entry screen shown in Figure 8.6 will appear.

In order to add, change, or delete customers, complete the following steps:

1. Key-enter a customer number. The computer will check to see if that customer number already exists in its memory. If not, the computer will assume that you wish to add a new customer account (proceed to No. 2). If the customer number already exists, the computer will assume that you wish to delete the customer or change its name. In either case, a decision prompt will appear asking you to strike **C** if you wish to change the customer name, **R** if you wish to record the name as it appears on the screen, or **D** if you wish to delete the customer. Remember that a customer cannot be deleted unless that customer account has no activity.

2. If you are adding a new customer account, key-enter the name of the customer. A decision prompt will appear asking you to strike **C** to correct the customer name if entered incorrectly, **R** to record the

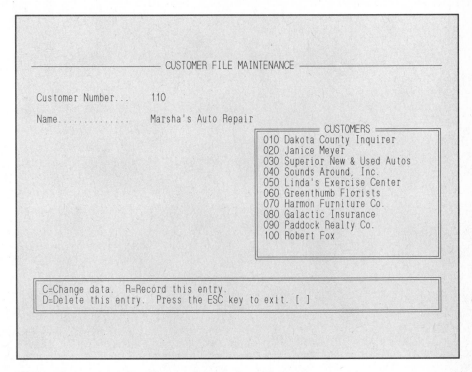

```
─────────────────────── CUSTOMER FILE MAINTENANCE ───────────────────────

  Customer Number...   110

  Name.............    Marsha's Auto Repair
                                                    ┌──────── CUSTOMERS ────────┐
                                                    │ 010 Dakota County Inquirer │
                                                    │ 020 Janice Meyer           │
                                                    │ 030 Superior New & Used Autos │
                                                    │ 040 Sounds Around, Inc.    │
                                                    │ 050 Linda's Exercise Center │
                                                    │ 060 Greenthumb Florists    │
                                                    │ 070 Harmon Furniture Co.   │
                                                    │ 080 Galactic Insurance     │
                                                    │ 090 Paddock Realty Co.     │
                                                    │ 100 Robert Fox             │
                                                    └────────────────────────────┘

  ┌────────────────────────────────────────────────────────────┐
  │ C=Change data.   R=Record this entry.                       │
  │ D=Delete this entry.  Press the ESC key to exit. [ ]        │
  └────────────────────────────────────────────────────────────┘
```

Figure 8.6   Customer File Maintenance Data Entry Screen

customer number and name as keyed, or **D** to delete the entry. Strike **R** to record the customer when the data is correct.

3. If the customer account already exists and you wish to change the customer name, strike **C** for change, key-enter the correct customer name, and strike **R** to record the data.

4. If the customer account already exists and you wish to delete it, strike **D**, and the account will be deleted.

5. Repeat this procedure until all additions, changes, and deletions have been key-entered from the Accounts Receivable File Maintenance input form. After all data has been key-entered, press the Esc key to exit this menu and return to the Accounts Receivable Main Menu.

Customer List Option G

The **customer list** is a report which shows the data stored in the computer's memory. The customer list may be displayed or printed at any time and used to verify customer file maintenance data that has been entered into the Accounts Receivable System. Whenever an addition, change, or deletion has been made, an updated customer list should be generated. This *Customer List* option is identical to the one you used in Chapter 7 during accounts receivable setup. When this option is chosen, a decision prompt will appear that will permit you to display or print the customer list or to exit this option. Select the option desired. Figure 8.7 illustrates a displayed customer list for Hardware Plus.

Set Run Date and Batch Number Option H

The purpose of this option is to provide the computer with the run date to be used on reports and the batch number that will identify each group of accounts receivable transactions. The run date which is key-entered should correspond to the run date recorded on the upper left

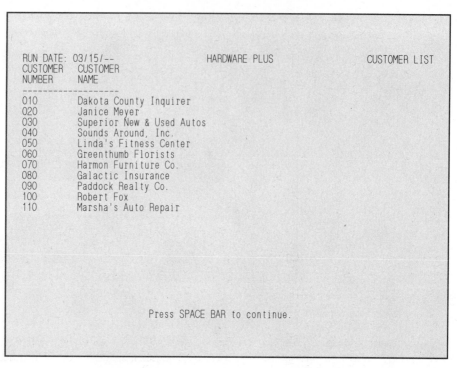

Figure 8.7   Hardware Plus Customer List

corner of the Accounts Receivable input form. This date must contain the month and year the sales and cash receipts occurred. The day should be the day of the month the transactions are key-entered. The batch number key-entered should correspond to the batch number located on the upper left corner of the Accounts Receivable input form. Remember that Batch No. 1 is reserved to identify the opening balances you entered in Chapter 7 during accounts receivable setup. Succeeding batch numbers should be assigned to subsequent groups of accounts receivable transactions as discussed earlier. The batch number will prove helpful in locating errors and providing an audit trail by which you will be able to trace a transaction to its source. The Set Run Date and Batch Number data entry screen is shown in Figure 8.8.

In order to key-enter the run date and batch number, complete the following steps:

1. Check the run date and batch number displayed. If both data fields are correct as displayed, exit this menu and return to the Accounts Receivable Main Menu by pressing the Esc key.
2. Position the cursor in the data field you wish to change and key-enter the correct data. Key-enter the date in the MMDDYY format without the slashes.
3. Verify the accuracy of the run date and batch number, then strike **R** to record your changes and return to the Accounts Receivable Main Menu.

Enter/Correct Sales and Cash Receipts Option I

The purpose of the Enter/Correct Sales and Cash Receipts data entry screen is to permit you to: (1) enter new accounts receivable transactions, (2) make corrections to previously entered transactions, (3) enter cash receipts, and (4) delete previously entered transactions. The pro-

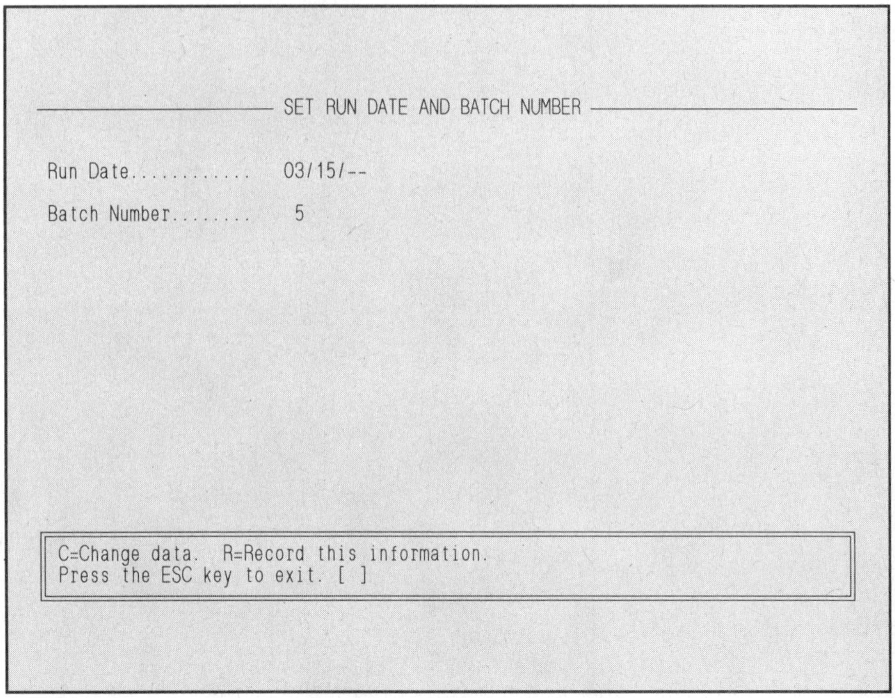

```
┌─────────────────────────────────────────────────────────────────┐
│                                                                   │
│  ────────────────── SET RUN DATE AND BATCH NUMBER ──────────────  │
│                                                                   │
│   Run Date...........    03/15/--                                 │
│                                                                   │
│   Batch Number........    5                                       │
│                                                                   │
│                                                                   │
│                                                                   │
│                                                                   │
│                                                                   │
│                                                                   │
│   ┌─────────────────────────────────────────────────────────┐    │
│   │ C=Change data.  R=Record this information.              │    │
│   │ Press the ESC key to exit. [ ]                          │    │
│   └─────────────────────────────────────────────────────────┘    │
│                                                                   │
└─────────────────────────────────────────────────────────────────┘
```

Figure 8.8   Set Run Date and Batch Number Data Entry Screen

cedure for key-entering this data from the Accounts Receivable input form is identical to the procedure introduced in Chapter 7 for key-entering the opening balances during accounts receivable setup. Windows may be opened using the function keys to enable you to reference the chart of accounts (Function 1 key), customer list (Function 2 key), or active invoices (Function 3 key) in case you need to verify a particular account, customer number, or invoice.

If the last option selected was not the *Set Run Date and Batch Number* option, a window display will appear that allows you to verify the current settings of the run date and batch number. If these data fields are correct, press the Space Bar to continue. If these data fields are incorrect, press Esc to exit back to the Accounts Receivable Main Menu, select the *Set Run Date and Batch Number* option, and key-enter the correct data.

The Enter/Correct Sales & Cash Receipts data entry screen (with a sales and cash receipt transaction already keyed) is shown in Figure 8.9.

Complete the following steps when key-entering accounts receivable transactions or making corrections:

1. Key-enter the sales invoice number. At this time, the computer will check to see if the sales invoice number key-entered already exists. If it does exist, and cash has not previously been received, the cursor will position itself in the *Date Received* field ready for you to enter cash receipt data. If the sales invoice number exists, and cash has previously been entered, all transaction data will be displayed and a decision prompt will be displayed. Strike **C** to change the data, **D** to delete the transaction, or press Esc to exit, leaving the data unchanged. If no transaction data exists, the com-

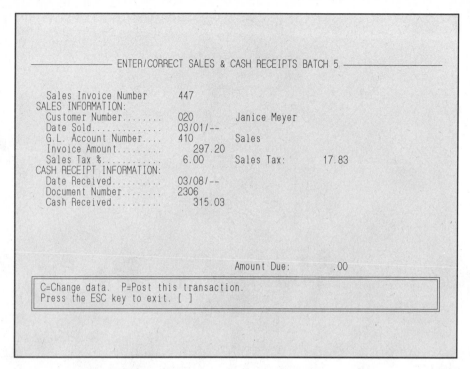

```
┌──────────── ENTER/CORRECT SALES & CASH RECEIPTS BATCH 5 ────────────┐

     Sales Invoice Number      447
  SALES INFORMATION:
     Customer Number.......    020        Janice Meyer
     Date Sold.............    03/01/--
     G.L. Account Number...    410        Sales
     Invoice Amount........    297.20
     Sales Tax %...........    6.00       Sales Tax:      17.83
  CASH RECEIPT INFORMATION:
     Date Received.........    03/08/--
     Document Number.......    2306
     Cash Received.........    315.03



                                          Amount Due:        .00

  ┌──────────────────────────────────────────────────────────────┐
  │ C=Change data.   P=Post this transaction.                     │
  │ Press the ESC key to exit. [ ]                                 │
  └──────────────────────────────────────────────────────────────┘
```

Figure 8.9   Enter/Correct Sales and Cash Receipts Data Entry Screen

puter will assume you wish to enter a new accounts receivable transaction for the sales invoice number, and empty data fields will be displayed. If data fields should appear on the screen for *Discount Percentage* and *Credit Memo Amount* (fields which do not appear on your input document), leave these fields blank. This means that you have mistakenly selected the expanded Accounts Receivable System. The expanded system will be explained further in Chapter 9.

2. Key-enter the customer number.
3. Key-enter the date of the sales transaction.
4. Key-enter the general ledger account number (account to be credited).
5. Key-enter the amount of the invoice.
6. Key-enter the sales tax percentage in decimal format (where 5 1/2 percent is recorded as 5.50).
7. Key-enter, if shown, the date of the cash receipt.
8. Key-enter, if shown, the document number.
9. Key-enter, if shown, the total amount of cash received.
10. A decision prompt will appear asking if you wish to make a change, post the transaction, delete the transaction, or ignore the displayed data (do nothing). Strike **C** to make changes or corrections, **D** to delete the transaction, **P** to post and record the transaction data as displayed, or press Esc to exit and disregard the data on the screen.

Note: At this time the computer will check the data you have entered to verify its accuracy. If errors are detected, you will be given a chance to make corrections. If the customer number does not exist, a decision prompt message will appear asking if you *wish to add this customer. If you respond **Yes**, the Customer File Maintenance data entry screen will appear and you will be permitted to add the customer. After the customer has been added and recorded in the computer's memory, the Enter/Correct Sales and Cash Receipts data entry screen will again appear and you will be permitted to continue.*

11. Continue this procedure until all transactions or corrections have been key-entered. When finished, press the Esc key to exit this data entry screen and return to the Accounts Receivable Main Menu.

When key-entering accounts receivable transactions, not all errors are discovered as the transactions are being entered on the data entry screen. It is easy to correct these errors even though they are not discovered until later. Following are two examples of typical errors and the procedure for correcting each.

Error 1: A data field in a transaction from a previous batch is in error.

To correct this error, set the batch number to the batch which contains the error. Key-enter the sales invoice number. Follow the procedure for making corrections explained previously. Corrections may be made to a transaction even though cash has been received for payment in full. After the correction has been made, all the Accounts Receivable reports for that batch can be reprinted.

Error 2: A transaction has been key-entered with an incorrect sales invoice number.

To correct this problem, set the batch number to the batch which contains the error. Rekey the incorrect sales invoice number. The computer will display the transaction in error. When the decision prompt appears, strike **D** to delete the entire transaction. Finally, key-enter the transaction with the correct sales invoice number.

Sales on Account Report Option J

The **Sales on Account report** lists all transactions, by batch, for which cash is to be received. This report should be printed or displayed after accounts receivable transactions are key-entered into the computer and after making any corrections. Examining this report and comparing the computer totals with the calculator totals at the bottom of the Accounts Receivable input form will help verify that all data has been recorded properly and provide an audit trail (if printed) for future reference. When this option is selected, a decision prompt will appear which permits you to print, display, or exit the Sales on Account Report. Select the option of your choice. Figure 8.10 illustrates a displayed Sales on Account report for Hardware Plus. Note that only the transactions from Batch No. 5 are included on the report.

Cash Receipts Report Option K

Cash receipts are receipts of cash for sales on account or open accounts receivable items. The **Cash Receipts report** lists all transactions in which cash has been received and applied to open items in the accounts receivable data file. This report should be run after the cash receipts transactions are key-entered and after any corrections have been made. This will help verify that all data has been recorded properly

```
RUN DATE: 03/15/--          HARDWARE PLUS            SALES ON ACCOUNT BATCH #5
CUSTOMER                    INVOICE              G.L.    INVOICE     SALES
NO. NAME                    NO.    DATE       ACCOUNT    AMOUNT      TAX
----------------------------------------------------------------------------
020 Janice Meyer            447  03/01/--      410       297.20      17.83
080 Galactic Insurance      448  03/02/--      410       826.00      49.56
050 Linda's Fitness Center  449  03/03/--      410       100.50       6.03
040 Sounds Around, Inc.     450  03/04/--      410        48.00       2.88
030 Superior New & Used Autos 451 03/05/--     410      2123.20     127.39
110 Marsha's Auto Repair    452  03/09/--      410        72.00       4.32
070 Harmon Furniture Co.    453  03/10/--      410       106.86       6.41
010 Dakota County Inquirer  454  03/12/--      410       270.00      16.20
050 Linda's Fitness Center  455  03/15/--      410       104.50       6.27
                                                        --------    --------
    TOTALS                                              3948.26     236.89
                                                        ========    ========




                        Press SPACE BAR to continue.
```

Figure 8.10   Sales on Account Report

and provide an audit trail (if printed) for future reference. The procedure for displaying, printing, or exiting the Cash Receipts report is similar to that of the Sales on Account report. Figure 8.11 illustrates a displayed Cash Receipts report for Hardware Plus. Note that only transactions from Batch No. 5 are included on the report.

```
RUN DATE: 03/15/--          HARDWARE PLUS            CASH RECEIPTS BATCH #5
CUSTOMER                    INVOICE          DOC.
NO. NAME                    NO.    DATE      NO.    AMOUNT TYPE
----------------------------------------------------------------------------
060 Greenthumb Florists     442              1585   2660.07 Receipt
100 Robert Fox              443               917   1033.50 Receipt
020 Janice Meyer            447              2306    315.03 Receipt
080 Galactic Insurance      448.             1145    875.56 Receipt
030 Superior New & Used Autos 451            1428   2250.59 Receipt

    TOTAL CASH RECEIPTS     7134.74








                        Press SPACE BAR to continue.
```

Figure 8.11   Cash Receipts Report

A Sales on Account report or Cash Receipts report may be displayed or printed by batch number at any time. Both the Sales on Account report and the Cash Receipts report serve two important functions: (1) they are useful in finding and correcting errors, and (2) they become permanent accounting records (if printed). Thus, the reports serve a function similar to that of handwritten journals in a manual accounting system by providing an audit trail whereby transactions may be traced to their original source documents.

General Ledger Posting Summary Option L

The **general ledger posting summary** shows in summary form all journal entries which are automatically generated and posted to the general ledger *only* from the current batch of accounts receivable transactions. At the end of the work session, these journal entries are summarized by account and added to the journal entries file. The general ledger account balances are then updated. When this option is selected, a decision prompt will appear which permits you to display the report, print the report, or exit the *General Ledger Posting Summary* option. If a printer is available, it is recommended that the general ledger posting summary be printed for future reference. Figure 8.12 illustrates a displayed general ledger posting summary for Hardware Plus. Notice that the Accounts Receivable account (Account Number 120) appears twice in order to show the total debits and credits integrated into the General Ledger System during the current computer session. The $4,185.15 Accounts Receivable debit amount represents the total amount of sales during the current computer session; the $7,134.75 Accounts Receivable credit amount represents the total amount of cash receipts during the current computer session (see Figure 8.12).

```
RUN DATE: 03/15/--           HARDWARE PLUS          G.L. POSTING SUMMARY BATCH #5
ACCOUNT ACCOUNT
NUMBER  TITLE                              DEBIT     CREDIT
-----------------------------------------------------------------
110     Cash                             7134.75
120     Accounts Receivable              4185.15
120     Accounts Receivable                         7134.75
220     Sales Tax Payable                            236.89
410     Sales                                       3948.26
                                        ---------  ---------
        TOTALS                          11319.90   11319.90
                                        =========  =========




                        Press SPACE BAR to continue.
```

Figure 8.12   General Ledger Posting Summary

Schedule of Accounts Receivable Option M

The **schedule of accounts receivable** lists all outstanding or open sales invoices by customer, the total amount due from each customer, and the total amount due from all customers. When the *Schedule of Accounts Receivable* option is selected, the decision prompt which permits you to display, print, or exit the Schedule of Accounts Receivable will appear. A displayed schedule of accounts receivable for Hardware Plus is illustrated in Figure 8.13.

```
RUN DATE: 03/15/--        HARDWARE PLUS          SCHEDULE OF ACCOUNTS RECEIVABLE
CUSTOMER                  INVOICE
NO. NAME                  NO.   DATE      AMOUNT
-------------------------------------------------------------------------------
010 Dakota County Inquirer   454  03/12/--    286.20
                             CUSTOMER TOTAL    286.20

040 Sounds Around, Inc.      438  02/18/--   1219.00
040 Sounds Around, Inc.      450  03/04/--     50.88
    CUSTOMER TOTAL                            1269.88

050 Linda's Fitness Center   449  03/03/--    106.53
050 Linda's Fitness Center   455  03/15/--    110.77
    CUSTOMER TOTAL                             217.30

070 Harmon Furniture Co.     440  02/21/--   1661.78
070 Harmon Furniture Co.     453  03/10/--    113.27
    CUSTOMER TOTAL                            1775.05

110 Marsha's Auto Repair     452  03/09/--     76.32
    CUSTOMER TOTAL                              76.32

                                            -----------
    FINAL TOTAL                                3624.75
                                            ===========

            Press SPACE BAR to continue.
```

Figure 8.13   Schedule of Accounts Receivable

Customer Statements Option N

When this option is selected, the computer will list a statement for each customer. A **customer statement** is a report which shows the customer number and name, invoice number, date, and amount of each outstanding sales invoice or open accounts receivable item for that customer. A running balance after each invoice and the total amount due from each customer is also shown. When this option is selected, the usual decision prompt will appear which permits you to display, print, or exit the *Customer Statements* option. If the option to print statements is chosen, the computer will check to see if preprinted customer statement forms are required (as specified in accounting system setup). If preprinted customer statement forms are required, the computer will prompt you to insert the forms before continuing. If not, the computer will draw an outline of a customer statement as it prints the data on plain paper. Examples of customer statements on both a preprinted statement form and a computer-drawn statement are illustrated in Figure 8.14.

Save Data to Disk

After all accounts receivable transactions have been processed, be sure to save your data to disk as a work in progress file after returning to the System Selection Menu and prior to computer shutdown. This

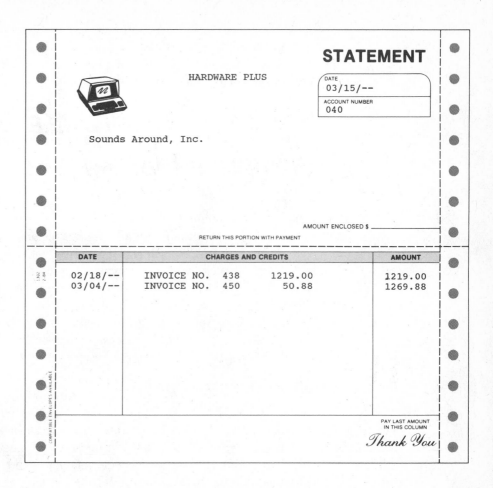

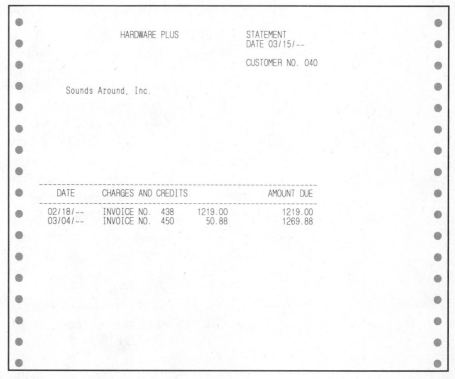

Figure 8.14   Customer Statement

option must be the last option selected prior to ending the automated accounting session or before loading another file from disk into your computer's memory. If you fail to run this option, all data keyed and processed during this session will be lost.

ACCOUNTS RECEIVABLE TRANSACTIONS AND REPORTS (SAMPLE PROBLEM)

This sample problem illustrates the principles and procedures required to process accounts receivable transactions using an automated accounting system. The chart of accounts, control accounts, customers, and opening balances for Hardware Plus as discussed and prepared in the previous chapters will be the basis of this sample problem. The data for Hardware Plus has been stored on disk under the file name **AA8-S**. To complete this sample problem, you will be shown how to process accounts receivable transactions for the first half of March.

Instructions

Step 1 The following accounts receivable transactions for Hardware Plus occurred during the first half of March of the current year. Additions, changes, and deletions to the customer data have been recorded for you on the Accounts Receivable File Maintenance input form in Figure 8.15. The transactions have been analyzed and recorded for you as Batch No. 5 on the Accounts Receivable input form in Figure 8.16. Compare these transactions with the completed input forms.

March 01   Sold merchandise on account to Janice Meyer, $297.20, plus 6 percent sales tax (Sales Invoice No. 447).

02   Sold merchandise on account to Galactic Insurance, $826.00, plus 6 percent sales tax (Sales Invoice No. 448).

03   Sold merchandise on account to Linda's Fitness Center, $100.50, plus 6 percent sales tax (Sales Invoice No. 449).

While handling this transaction, Hardware Plus learned that the name of Linda's Exercise Center had been changed to Linda's Fitness Center. The current customer list shows the old name, Linda's Exercise Center. The change in the account name is recorded on the Accounts Receivable File Maintenance input form in Figure 8.15.

03   Received cash on account from Greenthumb Florists, $2,660.07, covering Sales Invoice No. 442 (Customer Check No. 1585).

04   Sold merchandise on account to Sounds Around, Inc., $48.00, plus 6 percent sales tax (Sales Invoice No. 450).

05   Sold merchandise on account to Superior New & Used Autos, $2,123.20, plus 6 percent sales tax (Sales Invoice No. 451).

08   Received cash on account from Janice Meyer, $315.03, covering Sales Invoice No. 447 (Customer Check No. 2306).